AMIRAM EZOV

CROSSING

SUEZ, 1973

Senior Editors & Producers: ContentoNow
Translator: Zvi Hazanov
Editor: Barry Rosenfeld
Cover Design: Liliya Lev-Ari
Book Design: Ksana Kravtsova

ISBN: 978-965-550-549-8

International sole distributor: ContentoNow
3 Habarzel Street, Tel Aviv 6971005, Israel
www.ContentoNow.com
netanel@contentonow.com

AMIRAM EZOV

CROSSING
SUEZ, 1973

TABLE OF CONTENTS

INTRODUCTION

Lieutenant-colonel Amram Mitzna, commander of the 79ᵗʰ Battalion of Israel's famed 7ᵗʰ Armored Brigade, remembers well the night of October 15ᵗʰ, 1973. He recalls it as being a dark night, with a persistent sense of tension that seemed to grip your very bowels, never letting up. When it was all over, Mitzna would recall that experience as one of entering into a situation in which you doubted your very chance of surviving.

The moon rose late that night. Each of the members of the battalion was feeling this impending doom, each dealing with it in his own way, as best he could. Company Commander Rafi Matan was also experiencing this sense of fear, but it was combined with another feeling, a feeling that something great was about to happen, a sense of elation. Matan scanned the horizon. Hardly discernable in the late afternoon dusk, in a perfect column stretched out in what seemed like a never ending line, stood a massed army of steel. At 1800 hours the order to attack was given. Destination: westward, to the Suez Canal.

* * *

The next day, at daybreak of October 16ᵗʰ, Colonel Amnon Reshef, commander of the 14ᵗʰ Brigade, looked around, hardly believing his eyes. It was the morning following a horrendous night in which all of his brigade's assaults against the Tirtur-Lexicon roads junction were thrown back, wave upon wave, in what was to become known to the world as the battle of the Chinese Farm. Not far from him, ammunition dumps were being blown up, as hundreds of scattered Egyptian trucks and artillery pieces stood abandoned. Through the thick fog could be seen the twisted steel remains of scores of blackened smoking tanks, tossed about at various angles, as if crying out in agony. It had been a duel to the death, fought at close quarters, at a distance of less than 200 meters, and sometimes only one meter, or even less. The remains of both Egyptian and Israeli tanks stood turret to turret amidst the lingering smell of combat—a mixture of odors assaulting the senses, of spent gunpowder mixed with dust, and the widespread pervasive smell of death. A great many bodies could be seen strewn about, those of Reshef's troops as well as those of the enemy. And the junction was yet to be cleared; Tirtur Road, leading to the canal, was yet to be cleared; the special military bridge, over which the IDF was planning to cross the Suez to the west, still lay by the road, shattered and useless, like a spent monster.

An atmosphere of crisis permeated at all levels, starting from the Chief of Staff, down through the Southern Command command at Dvelah tactical HQ, down to the soldiers of the 14th Brigade, a feeling that persisted into the following days. It all seemed so precarious, to be hanging by a thread.

Thirty-six hours later, on the afternoon of the 17th, although a foothold had been gained on the west bank of the canal, a war council was convened on a dune, where the "Kishuf" strongpoint had formerly stood. The Minister of Defense, Chief of Staff and all three division commanders, attended.

Major General Sharon, with his forehead wrapped in a white bandage, approached the tactical HQ at a fast pace, accompanied by journalist Uri Dan and others. Front Commander Haim Bar Lev, with a cigar in his mouth, watched him. Sharon was met with general silence. No one breathed a word. Then, speaking extremely deliberately and in a low voice, Bar Lev began: "Arik, there's a gulf between what you promised and what you delivered." Sharon was immediately consumed with anger: "At that moment I felt dead tired, after all our bloody battles and losses…I looked around, seeing them all smartly dressed, neat and tidy. I felt there was just one thing I must do: slap Bar Lev's face"*

In *The Guns of August*, Barbara Tuchman reports about a night ride of Field Marshal Von Schlieffen, late 19th century Prussian Chief of Staff, with some of his staff members. By dawn, they reached a riverbank. When one officer, pointing at the sunrise glittering in the calm water, admired the beautiful sight, the Prussian strategist removed his monocle, stating: "It's just an insignificant obstacle".

Since time immemorial, rivers and watercourses were always regarded by military thinkers as significant tactical obstacles, the handling of which involves considerable preparations and trainings.

At the end of the Six-Day War, the IDF, for the first time, faced two water obstacles, namely the wide, deep-water Suez Canal, west of Sinai, and the narrow and shallow Jordan River, east of Israel. Due to the absence of crossing machinery and bridging vehicles suitable for wide water-obstacles, the IDF had grown to regard the west bank of the Suez as the unreachable Promised Land, and the canal itself, as a quite significant, even critical obstacle.

The borderline in the western Sinai stretched from Port Said to Ras Sudar, 210 kilometers long. The canal, from Port

---

* See, Sharon, *Warrior*, p.326.

Said to the city of Suez, was 160 kilometers long, and 180 meters wide on average. Another 31-kilometer long barrier line stretched along the Mediterranean coastline, all the way to where the Traklin fortification stood, at the northern-most point of the front.

The thought of the inevitable crossing of that obstacle seriously preoccupied IDF commanders between the Six-Day War and Yom Kippur War. Major General Avraham "Bren" Adan, one of the designers of the IDF's military buildup in those years, confessed that the crossing "had haunted the IDF like a stormy cloud, and was conceived to be the 'purgatory' we must pass on our way to the 'paradise' of a decisive battle.*"

In order to get through this purgatory, while proceeding to paradise, to use Adan's poetic vocabulary, one first had to reach that purgatory. The challenges facing the IDF in order to reach the canal on October 15th bore no resemblance to those perceived in the war plans and training carried out during the six years preceding the crossing. By October 15th, ten days following the outbreak of the battle in the Sinai, it had already become clear that this was not going to be the "seventh day" of the Six-Day War. By the tenth day of fighting, the IDF and the Egyptian Army were locked in combat, like two exhausted wrestlers, probing for any weak spot that had yet to be exploited by either side.

The IDF went on the crossing campaign after performing preliminary maneuvers testing its plans and assets under what one might call laboratory conditions, as compared to the actual

---

* See Adan, *On Both Banks of the Suez* (ff. "Adan, *On both Banks*"), p.180 [in Hebrew].

difficulties it faced from October 15th onward. In the words of a
senior former Engineering Corps officer, "if we had fed the data
available to us on October 15th to a computer, asking it whether
the crossing would be successful, the computer would've blown
itself up."

Nothing in the field—the actual schedule, order of battle, or
performance, was according to the initial plan. For about two
and a half days of incessant fighting, everybody involved in this
campaign, from most senior commanders down to privates,
kept questioning, wondering and doubting the moves to be
made. Yet, all the while, our forces kept pouring westward, only
westward, toward the west bank of the Suez Canal.

By the late hours of the night of the 15th and 16th of October,
the 247th Paratroopers Brigade of the 143rd Division had already
secured a foothold on the west bank of the canal. By dawn of
October 18th, Maj.-Gen. Avraham Adan's 162nd Division had
crossed the Suez westward, over the pontoon bridge, and was
on its way southward, to the city of Suez. This was the end of
the crossing campaign, and the beginning of the IDF's decisive
campaign on Egyptian soil. It was, probably, the most difficult
campaign the IDF had ever experienced, unprecedentedly
ferocious and grinding for both troops and commanders, and,
like any difficult campaign, in which some battles were lost, it
provoked many questions, reservations, and disputes, some of
which kept sounding for many a day, till this very day.

Four decades after the Yom Kippur War, the units engaged
in that campaign are still fighting for their place in history. The
wounds of some of the combatants are still bleeding, and many
of them, either physically or mentally, are still there, between
the dunes and the asphalt and sandy roads.

Many a book has been written about the Yom Kippur War,

some of which deal with the Israeli Crossing as well. But, it will take many more to grasp what happened in those awful days of October 1973 on the Southern Command, before, during and after the Crossing. That is the purpose of this book: to close, if only slightly, the gap between what is already known and what is yet to be learned.

PART 1:

LET MY PEOPLE CROSS

1. ALL THAT COULD BE DONE.

October 11th, IDF High Command HQ, GHQ Compound, Tel Aviv, late in the night:

Late in the night, on October 1st 1973, IDF's Chief of Staff, David Elazar, entered the office of Israeli Air Force Commander, Major General Benny Peled, in the GHQ Compound, following a request of the latter. Peled had some unpleasant news. As Peled explained it, within a few days, the IAF would hit its "lowest threshold", remaining with about 220 aircraft, just about enough for one offensive operation over a small sector of the Suez Canal. After October 14th, as he estimated it, the IAF would only have a complement of aircraft sufficient to defend the "heartland" of Israel. The conclusion to be drawn was clear: the longer the IDF delays taking the initiative, the worse it would be on the ground, and the less the IAF would be capable of supporting ground forces. This was something Peled didn't have to spell out to Elazar. "The IAF can only be restored under ceasefire conditions, and that will take two years", Peled said. Elazar tried to fathom the meaning of this: could the IDF still take the initiative, and turn the tide of the war?

During their conversation, General Peled received an urgent call: Major General Yitzhak Hofi reported on the IDF's ongoing counterattack on Syrian forces at the Northern Front. Its objectives lay deep in Syrian territory, near the southern foot of Mount Hermon, about ten kilometers west of the 1967 armistice line. Five days after being taken by surprise, when the war was initiated by Egypt and Syria, the IDF managed to stabilize one front, the Syrian one: the Syrian Army was forced from all the positions it had occupied at the beginning of the war, and defeated on land, at sea and in the air, yet had not collapsed. The IDF had gained a foothold about ten kilometers within Syria proper, preparing to get on with its offensive, but didn't expect it to achieve much.

While the battle raged on all fronts, a ceasefire, conceived by USSR leader Leonid Brezhnev and US Secretary of State Henry Kissinger, was being negotiated at the UN Security Council, so Elazar had to consider whether he had advanced the IDF to the best possible armistice lines. On the northern front, indeed, everything possible had been achieved considering the circumstances under which the war had begun. But, on the Egyptian front, it was a different kind of ball game. The Egyptian Army had successfully maintained its gains from earlier battles, while the IDF had failed to score even one success that could be traded off for political gain if and when a ceasefire were to be negotiated. The IDF was thus faced with the inevitability of the need for taking the initiative since what they had was a war without one decisive military advantage.

2. BAD BLOOD AMONG THE HIGH COMMAND.

Four days earlier, on the morning of October 7th, twenty hours after having crossed the Suez Canal, the Egyptian Chief of Staff, General Shazly, stated his crossing campaign "was crowned with victory."* Though it was a somewhat early celebration, his achievements were indisputable: most of the Bar Lev Line had already been occupied by Egyptian forces, between three and five kilometers deep; thousands of Egyptian troops and armored vehicles had already crossed the Suez eastward, and the Israeli 252nd Division, commanded by Major General "Albert" Mandler was almost totally destroyed, losing about 200 armored vehicles.

The next day, October 8th, while the two hastily mustered reservist divisions were already engaged at the front, each side had already followed their preconceived routine: the Egyptians fortifying their bridgeheads, while the IDF initiated a counter attack aimed to "sweep the Egyptians out of their positions." The counter attack failed, at the terrible cost of two shattered battalions of the 162nd Division under Maj.-Gen. Avraham "Bren" Adan, as well as the confidence of Israeli strategists.

The failed counterattack triggered a distrust of Southern Command and IDF Command in general. The IDF had no textbook solution to the new situation created by the Egyptians. Neither did it know what to do next, whether to carry on the offensive, or to prepare for a defensive campaign,

---

*   Shazly, *The Crossing of the Suez*, [in Hebrew],   [ff. Shazly, *Crossing*]
      Maarachot, 1987, p.187.

settling for the objectives already achieved. The crisis on the front worsened the already tense relations between Southern Command commanders. In the evening of October 8th, Maj.-Gen. Adan arrived exhausted to a Southern Command High Command conference in Dvelah Command Post. "It was my third sleepless night in a row," he would write. "I was tired, and felt as if I was being put through unjustifiable tests. I was terribly furious at the straying from the initial plan (that is, failing to approach the canal), and the hours of helplessness when we were just treading water, under the Egyptian artillery pounding."* Part of that straying was a premature crossing command. Yet the crossing of the Suez, thus taking the war to enemy territory, was the IDF's prewar strategy. Even after the Arab armies had taken the IDF by surprise, seizing Israeli-occupied territory during the first two days of the war, the IDF's Chief of General Staff attempted to create, as soon as possible, circumstances favorable for taking the war to enemy territory, and his generals, too, thought and acted along this line.

On the night of the 8th of October, following the High Command conference at Dvelah HQ, even the GHQ started to get wind of the bitter outcomes of the first days of fighting. At 04:30 AM, at dawn on the 9th of October, Lt.-Gen. "Dado" Elazar, when back from that Sinai HQ post, reconvened his flanks' commanders for an emergency conference. "Well," Dado said, "on the Egyptian front, we're doing very badly. Bren's counterattack in the Sinai failed, with heavy losses. He left at least 50 tanks behind. I was told we had 200 dead, and people are afraid to admit we had more. We have over 500

---

*   Adan, On both Banks, p.126.

injured. It's critical. We started the war poorly, and failed to decide it with the counterattack. Yesterday I thought we must counterattack, since it might get us out of this mess. Well, it was a partial success on the Golan Heights, but in the South, we had a day of attrition. The going is very tough on us, so we must consider whether the opposing side suffers as much as we do, and whether it will snap now. Right now, it doesn't seem to be happening. They had a bad day yesterday, yet there is no chance of them snapping before we do."

It felt like the apocalypse in the war room. Defense Minister Moshe Dayan, as told by the Deputy Chief of General Staff, referred to the situation as a new Masada and compared it to the Red Army's position in 1941. In his autobiography, *Milestones,* Dayan wrote: "If the expression 'mad as hell' ever had any meaning, it described how I was feeling then. After all, we had a three-division strong force on the Southern Command, with air support (when the war broke out), and even this day of fighting was wasted."*

"Moreover," Dayan wrote, "many of our convictions were proved untrue, for example, that our Armored Corps could prevent them from bridging the canal. None of us could have imagined their sea of anti-tank missiles. Well, one must relearn the facts of life. The Arabs had a lot of troops, and there were no magic tricks to be used against them, just a decisive campaign. If they had succeeded on the Golan Heights, they could have rolled into Israel proper. We had to avoid an attrition of forces and ineffectual moves. I would have liked to have established a defense line, but they could have moved more divisions

---

*   Dayan, *Milestones* [In Hebrew], p.607.

across the canal, so we would have gained nothing. I wanted to tell them (the High Command) what to do, but I was also a Cabinet member, and at that time the Cabinet was ignorant regarding the condition of the Bar Lev Line fortifications and the numbers of casualties."

Lt.-Gen. Elazar presented to the attendants his conclusions regarding the October 8th operations, concluding that another counterattack on the Egyptian forces east of the Suez was out of the question at the time, since it would have been too costly. He said that the battle would have to be decided otherwise: if the Egyptians did what the IDF expected them to, namely, deploy their 21st and 4th Armored Divisions east of the Suez, in an attempt to reach the Mitla and Gidi Central Sinai Passes, considered to be vital, the decisive battle would be fought east of the Suez, in which Israel's superior armored force would overpower the Egyptian one, allowing for the crossing of the Suez westward. But, it was an assumption that the Egyptians might prove or disprove. Until then, the Chief of General Staff ordered the Southern Command to prepare for a defensive battle.

The switch from an offensive to a defensive philosophy, on October 9th, generated conflicts between the Southern Command commanders. Maj.-Gen. Ariel Sharon, the 143rd Division commander, had his own interpretation of the order to defend his sector, namely the center of the front, by leading an attack, focusing on the main route to Alexandria, code named Talisman, wearing down his armored vehicles in futile assaults on perimeters codenamed Hamutal and Machshir, about 12 kilometers from the canal. The Egyptians, to the amazement of the IDF Southern Command commanders, wouldn't relinquish them. From October 8th on, Egyptian forces partially blocked the Artillery Road running parallel to the canal. If they could have controlled it completely, they would have succeeded in cutting off all of the routes reaching the canal, threatening the IDF's maneuverability throughout the entire Sinai Peninsula.

As mentioned above, from October 10th onward, both belligerents prepared for a defensive battle. The Egyptians launched some sporadic attacks, making some gains here and there. Yet they never got beyond their twelve-kilometer front, nor did they ever completely secure the Artillery Road.

October 12th, GHQ Compound, Tel Aviv:
The seventh day of the Yom Kippur War was spent in an extended General Staff meeting. It started at 07:00 AM, with a meeting of the Chief of General Staff with close staff members: his deputy, Maj.-Gen. Israel Tal; Chief of Military Intelligence, Eli Zeira; and IAF Commander, Benny Peled, and went on all day long, with varying attendees. Some meetings were attended by members of the top brass in small rooms in the GHQ Building's 3rd floor; others, by the entire General Staff. Some were War Cabinet meetings, attended by Major Generals Tal, Zeira, Zeevi, Aharon Yariv and Benny Peled, alongside Defense Minister Moshe Dayan, and Government Ministers Yigal Alon and Israel Galili. Meanwhile, Southern Command Commander Lt.-Gen. (Res.) Haim Bar-Lev was summoned to GHQ Compound to provide his input. On October 12th, three days after the IDF had gone defensive on the Southern Command, it ran into a stalemate favorable to the Egyptians. The General Staff Forum members felt this way, as well, and the pessimistic appreciation of IAF capabilities, shared by IAF Commander Peled with Elazar the night before, was just one of those expressed during the meetings. No one had figured out as

of then the minimum plan of Sadat and his general, Shazly, of crossing the canal, securing strongholds no further than twelve kilometers east of the canal, to be used as leverage for achieving major political gains.

The main subject discussed in the meetings was whether or not Israeli forces should cross the Suez Canal as part of a decisive campaign, or keep waiting for the Egyptian armored division, still deployed west of the Suez, to cross eastward, thus opening a breach allowing Israeli forces to seize the exposed territory west of the Suez.

Elazar sadly concluded from the meetings that "we must end the war by October 14th. The option of having no ceasefire on the 14th of October is bad for us, and it's getting worse day by day. We have no reserves, and those we do have cannot change the balance of power," he said. "Even the US-supplied aircraft and tanks cannot turn the balance in the short run. The enemy can continually muster forces, turning the balance to its favor. So how can we force them into a ceasefire? By a ground forces' maneuver combined with American pressure. Come what may, we must have a ceasefire by October 15th. Ideally, we should be able to say then, 'all forces will resume their prewar positions, on the Syrian as well as the Egyptian front'," the Chief of Staff concluded.

In a private meeting, he explained this to Defense Minister Dayan in this way: "Moshe, let me diagnose our problem. It is not a military one. We have some chance—not a one hundred percent chance, yet some chance, of crossing the Suez, gaining a foothold on the other bank, and turning the tide at the canal tomorrow morning. We would be better positioned then, and the Egyptian forces will take a blow. I assume it won't be a fatal blow shattering the Egyptian Army and forcing Egypt into a ceasefire. I reckon the Egyptians would take the blow without suing for a ceasefire. So we should consider whether or not to carry out the operation in this light: whether we would have a better chance of getting a ceasefire with or without it."

Thus, the objectives set by Elazar were securing a defense line on the Syrian front and launching an offensive on the Egyptian front on the night between the 13th and the 14th of October. He expressed his doubts as to whether the crossing of the canal and aerial bombings could pressure the enemy into a ceasefire resulting in ending the war.

At 09:30 AM, the meeting was joined by Southern Command Commander Lt. Gen. Haim Bar Lev. Accompanied by former IAF commander Maj.-Gen. (res.) Moti Hod. Bar Lev brought with him maps presenting the Southern Command's crude plans for crossing the Suez. The atmosphere as well as the attitude in the GHQ post had changed. "Considering all undesirable choices," He explained, "I suggest crossing the canal, and there, knocking out the core of the Egyptian armored forces and securing a perimeter. Then, if they break down, we can go south to Suez or drive on west. If they don't, it would go as the Chief of Staff said, that is, the IDF will have a foothold on the west bank of the Suez, the Egyptian forces' condition on the east bank getting worse with time, and they may even surrender."

Examining the options, Bar Lev recommended, on behalf of the Southern Command, crossing the canal at its center, near Déversoir, at the Matzmed fortification, which was on the banks of the canal and which had been seized by the Egyptians on October 9th. Its southern flank was covered by the Great Bitter Lake, and, once a breach between two Egyptian armies was accomplished there, the breakthrough all the way to the water seemed easy. Once across the canal, Israeli forces could advance a couple of kilometers westward, deploying into an open field maneuver. The two Israeli divisions, with a total number of 400 tanks, would be facing 500 enemy tanks, a balance of power guaranteeing the advantage to the Israeli forces.

Later that day, the Defense Minister submitted the plan for the War Cabinet for approval. The meeting was also attended by Prime Minister Golda Meir, Government Minister Galili and the Chief of Mossad. The Chief of General Staff re-presented to the attendees the major points of his suggestion for the next phase of the war, focusing on the crossing of the canal. Yet before making a final decision, Elazar asked Military Intelligence and the Southern Command commanders for additional information.

Not all General Staff members accepted the necessity of the Crossing operation. Deputy Chief of General Staff, Maj.-Gen. Tal, objected, arguing that this move, in his words, "is a most risky gambit, and we should better prepare for a battle in which our forces could make the most of their advantage, namely, a tank battle with Egyptian armored divisions."

Before the Yom Kippur War, the Chief of Staff and his deputy used to be close friends, yet during the first days of the fighting their relationship grew increasingly colder. Tal felt as if Elazar was expressing an increasing disregard for him, getting impatient whenever Tal spoke his mind. They had many differences. According to Tal, "On October 12th, Bar Lev suggested we should cross the Suez Canal either that night or the next day, on October 13th. I disapproved of crossing at both of the proposed times, since at the moment we had no more than 600 useable tanks. I also argued we were not trained in crossing water-obstacles while fighting, and there were Egyptian armored forces on the other bank. Then, the IAF Commander reported that within a few days our air force would be reduced to the critical minimum of 200 attack aircrafts, just enough to safeguard national airspace. Hence my hesitation, between opposing the crossing, and avoiding a critical situation where the IAF could provide no air support after October 14th. I argued that it was an enormous bet, and that if we lost, it would have left Tel Aviv exposed. As I said, our forces were too exhausted to stand up to Egyptian armored troops, and if the Egyptian Army stood its ground, all those who were so keen on crossing would cry disaster."

Maj.-Gen. Tal also disapproved of the planned launching point and the objectives of the Crossing, advocating a crossing on the flanks, either to the north, near Port Said, or the south, on the western Gulf of Suez.

3. ZVIKA, YOU'VE GOT AN URGENT PHONE CALL!

Before Tal could explain his reservations, the Chief of Staff, presented his suggestions, and the ministers commented on the military's plans and assessments. Then something happened which turned everything upside down, delaying the initiation of the crossing. The Prime Minister's secretary entered the conference room, and addressing Chief of Mossad Maj-Gen (res.) Zvi Zamir, said: "Zvika, you have an urgent phone-call!"

He left the room. His aide-de-camp was on the phone, reporting to him that according to a report from a reliable source, Egyptian commando battalions were planning a landing at the Sinai Passes. According to the Egyptian tactical doctrine which the IDF knew about, it meant Phase II of the

Egyptian offensive was about to begin, to be followed by a massive delivery of Egyptian armored troops from the west to the east bank of the canal. Such a maneuver, though forcing the IDF to defend itself, would offer the IDF opportunities on the west bank of the Suez. This was the very move Elazar and all of the Israeli High Command members had been anticipating. "I told him," Zamir recalls, "to get it to me right away, since the Mossad's office was nearby. So they stopped the conference, putting it on hold. That fellow brought me a report, according to which, on Saturday night, the Egyptians would drop their commandos on our second line of defense. Yet the report was fragmented. I got back to the conference room, ten meters away from where I received the report, presenting it to the participants, telling them its source was a reliable one. Later on, I got back to my assessment, referring to the dispute between Sadat and his generals. I argued that Sadat probably prevailed, so I assumed, that Egyptian commandos will land, and the Egyptian armored forces would cross earlier than planned, following their doctrine. I told the audience that the Egyptians are getting to their second offensive, after their infantry divisions had done their job, in an attempt to secure the Passes. We knew their objective was just getting to our second line, going no further."[*]

"They all," Zamir explained, "accepted my assessment." Dado regarding the report as a sure sign of an approaching offensive, while the Military Intelligence representative said nothing. So it was decided not to cross the canal at that stage, but to prepare to stop the attack instead. So we got

---

[*]   An interview with Maj.-Gen. (res.) Zvi Zamir.

ready to stop the attack, and we all know how it turned out. That information was priceless. Just imagine if we had been crossing the canal while they were dropping commandos at the Passes! I considered it my duty to say 'look, that's the deal,' and they approved of it. Until Brig.-Gen. Aryeh Shalev, Chief of the Military Intelligence Analysis Department, phoned me, reporting that the Egyptian armored troops had crossed the canal, I was not able to sleep, fearing that the reassessment had been based on my misinterpretation."

The Egyptian offensive which spread over the entire front line, planned to begin on October 14th, as anticipated by the Chief of Mossad, based on the fragmented telegram, ended the difficult dilemma over the Crossing.

By the dawn of October 14th, the Egyptians attacked with their armored troops only, finding the Israeli divisions prepared and vengeful. The Egyptian High Command had made this move without setting any final strategic objectives, despite an intense dispute within the Egyptian leadership. It was supported by President Anwar Sadat and War Minister Ismail Ali, and opposed by his Chief of Staff, General Shazly. Sadat, who still considered himself victorious at this stage, failed to mention this battle in his memoirs. He had essentially three motives for launching the attack: to counter the international pressure on Egypt to sue for a ceasefire; to assuage the Syrians' demand to ease the pressure on them on the Golan Heights; and to fulfill his desire to expand Egyptian territorial gains to include the Passes, about sixty kilometers east of the canal, or to the hills, all the way to Tasa.

For the Egyptians, this attempt was a resounding failure. As General Shazly wrote, "By 1100 hours, five hours since its initiation, it was already clear our offensive had been hopelessly smashed."* At the end of the day, the Egyptians lost about 200 tanks, compared to twenty lost by the IDF's Southern Command. The Egyptian 21st Division, the core armored force of the Second Army, was severely beaten and forced back. In the northern sector, an Egyptian T-62 tank elite division was soundly beaten, its remnants retreating to their initial lines, scoring no achievements. The daring attempt of Egyptian Fourth Division elements to advance through Wadi Mab'uq, in the Israeli 252nd Division's sector, proved costly and futile. Yet the Egyptians lost more than assets. General Shazly arrived at 1600 hours to the Second Army HQ, asking to meet its commander, Maj.-Gen. Maamun. He found him in bed, suffering a breakdown. He was hospitalized, and did not recover until after the ceasefire.

Waiting for the Egyptian attack proved the right thing to do: the blow suffered by Egyptian armored troops east of the Suez left the west bank relatively exposed. Eventually, Minister Bar Lev remarked, "the Egyptians are being themselves again, while we are ourselves again," expressing the satisfaction of the entire Southern Command. But, what mattered most for the Southern Command commander was that Defense Minister Dayan, despite having his misgivings, left the Front HQ intending to recommend to the Government to initiate the Crossing on the next day.

Bar Lev instantly summoned his division commanders to discuss the next move. Maps had been prepared in advance for them in the main war room. On October 14th at 2240 hours, the Southern Command commanders met at the Dvela Command Post, to prepare for the Crossing. Meanwhile,

---

*   Shazly, *Crossing*, p.181.

hundreds of kilometers away, the Israeli government met to discuss the approval of the maneuver.

4. SURRENDER AND DESTRUCTION.

The IDF's Southern Command HQ, dug into Um Hashibah Ridge in the central western Sinai, was the very model of a command compound's location and architecture: the 150-meter high ridge commanded the surrounding hills, allowing, on a clear day, a view of the canal's watercourse, about 100 kilometers away. Yet it was far enough from any immediate threat. It was connected, directly, but through a most crooked road, twenty-five kilometers long, to the logistics center of the Refidim air base. Yet it was designed to serve as a tactical GHQ, not just for the hundreds of officers and men of a rear HQ. Despite the size of its Main War Room, the excessive amount of officers and visitors impaired the decision-making process, which required tranquility. So occasionally, some senior officers retreated to a corner or a small room, for confidential talks intended for their ears only.

The gigantic bunker, only the massively reinforced top of which projected above ground level, was dug ten meters under the ground, and was absolutely bomb-proof. All its corridors led to a main conference hall where, at the head of a long table, and in a magnificent leather armchair, sat the Southern Command commander. To one side of the chair sat a black phone, manned by an operations' secretary. On the other side there was another, ivory-white colored phone, manned by another secretary. The middle of the desk was occupied by a row of phones connected to the Front's division operations rooms. The desk served as the regular workspace for senior staff officers.

The rise of Southern Command Commander Shmuel "Gorodish" Gonen, was meteoric even by the standards of the 1970s' youthful IDF. He was a man of average build who wore thick horn-rimmed glasses, through which one could see his piercing, sometimes menacing expression. He had made a name for himself during the Six-Day War, commanding the 7th Armored Brigade. In 1972, his exploits were described this way: "This brigade had the lion's share of the heavy, bloody fighting…Gorodish and his men broke the neck of the Egyptian Army, winning undying glory." In the summer of 1969, he was assigned as a reservist to the position of division commander on the Golan Heights, with the rank of Brigadier-General. At thirty-nine years of age, when he was assigned as the Chief of Military Training, and as the 143rd Division commander, he was the IDF's youngest major-general. In July 1973, he was assigned to the Southern Command, the IDF's most important one, replacing Ariel Sharon. In an interesting twist of fate, the latter assumed command of the 143rd Division. But the early days of the Yom Kippur War were unfavorable for Gonen, and even less so for his command. On October 10th, he was surprised when he became a subordinate to Lt.-Gen Haim Bar Lev, who was assigned to the Southern Command as a so-called Chief of Staff's Special Advisor, but practically, the Front's Commander. Gonen struggled with his surprise shift in status, threatening to resign, but was eventually convinced to cooperate. On his part, Bar Lev kept their relationship businesslike.

Occasionally, mostly in the evening, division commanders were summoned for operational commands or briefings. Meanwhile, the command was assumed, in turn, by Bar Lev, Gonen, Gonen's deputy Uri Ben Ari, and the Southern Command's chief of staff, Brig.-Gen. Asher Levy.

The walls of the main War Room were covered with large operational maps filled with arrows and tactical rectangular signs, standing for the individual forces and their occasionally shifting boundaries. Operations, sergeants and officers carefully recorded movements of enemy forces in red, and of Israeli forces in blue. Loudspeakers connected to the Front's brigades' and sectors' communication networks were fitted along the walls, turning the already dense air, in times of emergency, even denser. The main War Room was surrounded by dedicated operation rooms, such as that of Military Intelligence, Operations Department, Air Force, etc., and next to it was the front commander's private room, where he could retire to rest.

On the night of October 14th, when the senior officers were convened to receive the commands for the Crossing, codenamed Stout Hearts, the Operation Room was already in place, effective working procedures. Definitely, the arrival of Bar Lev four days earlier, had taken its effect, turning the tense and chaotic atmosphere into a more businesslike one. The room was crowded: Maj.-Gen. Gonen reviewed the senior officers present. There was Ariel Sharon, the 143rd Division commander, who had been advocating a crossing from the very first day of the war. Seated next to him, was Maj.-Gen. Avraham "Bren" Adan, who argued the best tactic would be to initiate an offensive. Opposite him, was Maj.-Gen. Kalman Magen, 252nd Division Commander since the previous day, following the death of Maj.-Gen. Avraham "Albert" Mandler. He was awarded a Major General's rank in a private ceremony at Tasa HQ. Since rank insignia were unavailable, Major General Ezer Weizmann gave Magen his insignia. Next to Magen, sat his successor as Leopard Force Commander, Northern Sector commander, Brig.-Gen. Sasson. Only the Chief of General Staff was missing the briefing, being on his way to a Government meeting which was also discussing the crossing.

On the wall facing the attendees, amidst the battle charts, was hung the operational command for the crossing of the Suez, titled Operation Stout Heart, written in large conspicuous letters. Under "purpose," it was written that Israeli forces are to cross the canal near Deversoir, securing a perimeter deep in the west bank, from the Cultivated Strip's canal in the north to the city of Suez in the south. Under "tactic," Southern Command ordered the crossing to be carried out by two divisions, successively, assigning the actual crossing and the securing of a bridgehead to 143rd Division under Maj.-Gen. Sharon, while the exploiting of success was assigned to 162nd Division under Adan. Two reduced divisions, namely Leopard Force under Brig.-Gen. Sasson and the 252nd Division under Kalman Magen, were to remain on the east bank, to stop a possible enemy advance, serving as the anvil for the hammer pounding from the west.

The territory to be secured stretched from the Fresh Water Canal, south of Ismailia to Jebel Ubeid and the city of Suez, was one-hundred kilometers long, and about thirty kilometers wide in its northern portion, and about fifty kilometers wide in the southern portion.

The terrain of the west bank of the Suez Canal was totally different from that of the east bank. A fresh water canal ran from Ismailia to Suez, along a territory called the Cultivated Strip. The ground, dump-irrigated by water drawn in canals from the Nile, was divided between farmed plots, wild vegetation and muddy soil. It was considered a very difficult terrain for armored combat. West of it, about eight kilometers west of the canal, was an open ground, from the Faid Base and its airport all the way to the city of Suez. South of Faid Camps, was Gnifa Ridge, highly essential for commanding the ground south of it. It was broken by wide ravines, and negotiable to a limited extent. Yet the ravines formed relatively convenient north-south routes. West of it, lay a desert territory with a plain on its north, hills in its center and steep mountains in its southern portion. The desert rear was bounded in the south by the Suez-Cairo Road, and steep cliffy ridges, the most prominent of which was Jebel Ataqah, an inaccessible mountain commanding the entire territory north of it. The plains, called Aida Plains, were crossed by the north-south road running from Ismailia to Cairo and from Deversoir to Cairo, codenamed Sakranut, and the east-west roads codenamed Havit, (running parallel to the canal Road), and Vadaut. The perimeter's southern tip was the city of Suez, now mostly deserted due to the blocking of the canal and the War of Attrition. From it, another road ran to Cairo, codenamed Serge.

The seizure of the territory was also to serve for negotiating a land-swap with territory seized by the Egyptians on the east bank of the canal at the beginning of the war, as part of post-war negotiations.

Southern Command assessed the timeframe of the operation, from the launching of the force until the final objective, namely the city of Suez is taken, to be forty-eight hours. The 162nd Division was to cross the Suez Canal, after the bridges were built and a bridgehead was secured, ten hours after H-Hour, which was set at October 15th, 19:00 hours.

Thus, the taking of the launching point of the Crossing on the east bank of the canal was assigned to 143rd Division, under Sharon. To this purpose, the Division had to secure a four-kilometer corridor leading to the water, clearing Akavish and

Tirtur routes, securing Chinese Farm, codenamed Amir, and at least a four-kilometer long perimeter between Shik Route and Matzmed Fort's perimeter. It was also assigned with delivering two bridges: one was the raft bridge, one part of which was carried from Refidim and its other part, from Baluza, northern Sinai; and the Roller Bridge, from a position codenamed Yukon, on Akavish route. "And," as Gonen explained, "you are also to carry a paratroopers' brigade, in the dead of night, on board rubber boats, on their way to secure the west bank of the canal."

Certainly, Southern Command had great expectations from Sharon's division. But considering the timeframe, just one night, its tasks—included controlling the routes, as well as securing the corridor, and carrying out the Crossing—it stands to reason to assume these assignments were beyond its capacity in the first place. As Sharon stated in a lecture after the war, "One must also bear in mind that Southern Command followed an improper procedure: instead of easing the division commanders' burden, allowing them to focus on fighting, it assigned them with jobs which were clearly its own. This is why my division carried out the main strategic maneuvers on the Southern Command." Yet it is also noteworthy that Sharon never complained of this overburden during the conference in Dvelah.

In military doctrine, securing a bridgehead means "the taking of territory which may undermine the entire enemy defense, allowing main effort forces to be poured through the breach to carry on the offensive." The core of the plan was that right after Sharon's division secures the bridgehead, 162nd Division, under "Bren", was to cross the canal, dashing westward and southward, destroying the remaining Egyptian forces and encircling the Egyptian 3rd Army near the city of Suez.

The divisions assigned with the crossing were reinforced and restored to their full strength for the task. The 143rd and 162nd Divisions had 240 tanks and 200 tanks, respectively. In total, Southern Command allocated 440 tanks for the initial stages of crossing and breaching, thus enjoying a certain numerical superiority in the planned theater.

The crossing maneuver was expected to cut off the rear of the two Egyptian armies entrenched on the east bank, severing their supply routes, and allowing for the development of further maneuvers, either southwards or northwards on the west bank of the canal, codenamed Goshen perimeter. Yet the initial objective of the crossing, as Maj.-Gen. Gonen's briefing carefully stressed, was to destroy Egyptian forces. "I wish to remind you of it, because sometimes it is overlooked in the heat of the battle," he said. It was so important for Southern Command to drive it home, that Operation Officer, Lt.-Col. Shay Tamari read out the "purpose" section one more time, explaining: "Southern Command will check any further Egyptian advance in Sinai, while forcing the Egyptian forces on the east bank into surrender," he was interrupted by Lt.-Gen Bar Lev who exclaimed: "Read it again, it doesn't say surrender. Luckily, there is no press here. It says surrender and destruction!"

Gonen's and Bar-Lev's statements were to make clear, if anyone didn't get it, that the planned crossing had additional purposes besides the forcing of a ceasefire, the major one being generating an impression of victory by overpowering the core of the Egyptian Army on the west bank, and restoring the prewar balance of power. This task was assigned to Bren's 162nd Division. Later on, it was to be joined by the 252nd Division under Major General Magen and relieve the 143rd Division under Sharon, allowing the latter to advance southwards, joining the 162nd Division's thrust.

In hindsight, Gonen admitted that the planned Crossing involved "a great yet calculated risk, like walking on a razor-edge." The risky part was launching two divisions by the same route. "We ran that risk because we had no other way of carrying out any game-changing operation throwing the enemy off balance. However, the risk was to be taken on one condition, that the routes were secured. It was calculated because it was decided to carry out the offensive gradually, with one division only. "If we got one division crossing, while the other one is waiting up, and something goes wrong, at least there is one reserve division to do it again." Since there was to be only one planned launching zone, and gradual crossing, the corridor to it, in the first place, was a "risky bottleneck, the securing of which decided the fate of the entire campaign."

By midnight of October 14th, Southern Command Commander Lt.-Gen. Haim Bar Lev concluded the meeting, stating: " It feels like the IDF is being itself once again, while the Egyptians are being themselves again, as one gathers, both from what they say as well as from how they fight. It makes a difference, since so far, they have been fighting rather well. So today, things have changed, and I cannot say whether it is the result of the deployment of their glorious armored divisions, or for any other reason.

"Secondly, we are engaged in an extremely complex operation, unlike anything we've been training to do, for three reasons:
   a. All our training was under the assumption that we held control of the east bank of the canal, and none of the war games included the securing of a bridgehead on both banks of the canal. Currently, we control neither bank.

b. We must carry out the crossing during or after an engagement.

c. Most of the forces assigned to the Crossing were never trained in it.

The question is whether to carry it out under these or other risky circumstances. Definitely, we should do it now, since now it's possible."

Addressing Kalman Magen and Yitzhak Sasson, commanders of the 252nd Division and Tiger Force, respectively, Bar Lev made clear that checking the Egyptians on the east bank, too, should significantly contribute to frustrating Egyptian offensives and pressuring the Egyptian forces on the west bank, who were to face encirclement.

Bar Lev and Sharon had the following discussion about the planned securing of a bridgehead:

Bar Lev: We must secure the territory up to at least four kilometers north of the northernmost bridge, throughout the campaign. If we can push any further, we must, in order to have no troubles with their missiles and all those tricks. So securing this, Arik, is under your responsibility throughout the campaign.

Sharon: Is under what?

Bar Lev: Your responsibility. Moreover, it will remain your responsibility even when you make it to the Cairo Hilton. So before you get there, we may relieve you of it.

Sharon: This should be assigned to the Front's Command.

Bar Lev: If so, one should also assign the actual seizure of territory to Sasson.

Sharon: In that case, I'd rather keep it.

Bar Lev: Keep it then.

Sharon: If Sasson cannot do it, I will.

Bar Lev: So you take at least four-kilometers north of the bridge and guard it. Maybe on that afternoon we'll tell you to forget it.

That bargaining affected the future operations: Sharon, the 143rd Division's commander, was keen on maneuvers and mobile combat, while his superior, Bar Lev, assigned him with tasks disagreeable to him, such as guarding a bridgehead. In Defense Minister Dayan's poetic words, Sharon was a charging steed struggling to break free of its bridle, while his rider, Bar Lev, reined him in harshly. And so it was from the very first day of the war, to its very end.

When the briefing ended, Maj.-Gen. Adan spoke up, with words of warning mixed with encouragement: "The troops must be told where we stand. I repeat, a crossing is a very complex operation, but we will prove it can be improvised, and yet done right, provided that all is carried out exactly by the plan presented here. Otherwise, if units start overtaking each other, it will get messy. If people start forgetting about all kinds of details we agreed on, we may get into trouble. So I wish all of us good luck, and we'll meet, God willing, on the other side."

The briefing was over on October 15th, at 0100 hours, with Bar Lev urging the Front's commanders to rest, before the hard day's work awaiting them.

Governmental Compound, Jerusalem, October 15th, midnight: At almost the very same time, at 2100, several hundred kilometers away from Dvelah, the Israeli Government met to discuss the next maneuver of the IDF. The meeting opened with a statement by Dayan: "I suggest we should cross the Suez. It was unanimously recommended by all commanders."*

Dayan had just come from his visit to the Southern Command HQ Post, and from a meeting with the Chief of General Staff, and had been impressed by a day of fighting in which Southern Command had smashed an Egyptian offensive throughout the front line. Dayan reported that the Front's Command was in high spirits, and noted the urgings of the Americans to push on, in support of his advocating of the crossing, and by the improbability of the Egyptians calling for a ceasefire, and by the stalemate on the Syrian front. Due to all of this, Dayan said that he was "wholeheartedly for letting my people cross." Yet Minister Alon had his reservations. He argued for an attempt to crush the Egyptian forces east of the canal, rather than crossing it. He felt the enemy was being underestimated, and therefore, as he said, "I cannot vote either for or against it. I'd rather go to the Sinai tomorrow, and see how it's going there."

At 0300 hours, the Government approved the resolution of Minister Galili: "We authorize the IDF's crossing of the canal in the following days, as suggested by the Defense Minister and the Chief of General Staff, in order to destroy the core of Egyptian forces. The time of execution is to be approved by the Defense Minister and the Chief of General Staff. The

---

*   Aryeh Bar-On, *Moshe Dayan in the Yom Kippur War* [ff. Bar On, *Moshe Dayan*], p.181. On that occasion, Dayan also said that even Maj.-Gen. Tal, who objected to the crossing on October 12, did not suggest otherwise. At that meeting, Minister Varhaftig had some reservations, while Minister Alon said he could not vote before examining the situation at first hand, so he went to the Sinai. Four Government ministers were absent, namely Even and Sapir, who were abroad, Bar Lev, who was a frontline officer, and Gvati, who was sick.

Government notes the Prime Minister's statement that the operation has a military purpose. Any suggestion of our forces remaining further west of the canal should be discussed and approved by the Government."

Due to the Government's resolution, the General Staff phrased the intended next phase of the war in a directive codenamed "Ashur 12": "The IDF should launch an offensive on the Egyptian front, crossing the canal, and destroying the Egyptian forces on both banks. It will keep attacking and destroying the Syrian Army, and staying on the defense in the Central Front. All this is to be carried out starting from October 15th at 1900 hours.

"During the operational briefing held on the morning of October 15th, Lt.-Gen. Elazar said the time was ripe for launching an offensive which is to bring about a decisive change of our positions, the balance of power and our situation in the Sinai in general."

PART 2:

IT'S TIME TO STRIKE!

1: "WE CAN ASSIGN HAIM."

Dvelah, Southern Command War Room, October 15th:

On October 15th, at 0835 hours, Chief of General Staff, Lt.-Gen. David "Dado" Elazar, who was in the GHQ Compound, called Lt.-Gen (res.) Haim Bar-Lev, who was in Dvelah bunker. Elazar, who missed the meeting the night before since he had attended the Government meeting, wanted detailed information about the Southern Command's preparations for the Crossing. Bar Lev, as usual, reported in his slow and authoritative tone that the preparations hadn't been completed yet, but that he, Bar Lev, was in favor of the Crossing. He repeated to the Chief of General Staff what he had said the night before, when the Operation Stout Hearts plan was presented. The successes of October 14th must be exploited, Bar Lev argued. The Egyptians' confidence was shaken, and it's time to strike.

If there was any top brass member from whom David "Dado" Elazar wanted to hear such a conclusion, it was Bar Lev. They first met in a socialist-Zionist summer camp in Zagreb, when Bar Lev was 13, and Elazar, born in Sarajevo, Bosnia, was 11. Since then, they had been following in each other's footsteps, that is, "Dado" was following Bar Lev's. He was Dado's instructor at the 1946 Haganah Platoon Commanders' School in Ramat Yochanan. After the War of Independence, they joined the team led by Yitzchak Rabin, the Chief of the IDF's Battalion Commanders Course. They also followed each other to the Armored Corps: Bar Lev was made an armored brigade commander during the 1956 Suez campaign, while Elazar was reassigned to the Armored Corps two years later. When Bar Lev resigned the command of the IDF's Armored Corps in 1959, he made Elazar his successor, preferring him to Israel Tal. Their family members made friends, too. It was Bar Lev to whom "Dado" confessed his hesitations during the anticipation of the 1967 offensive on the Golan Heights. In late 1969 Bar Lev, as Chief of General Staff made "Dado" the Chief of The Operations Department. Consequently, no eyebrow was raised at the report that Bar Lev chose to make Dado his successor, as the ninth Chief of Staff in the history of the IDF. They had been lifelong companions, and, when in the right mood, conversed in Serbo-Croatian.

On the morning of October 9th, the day after the Southern Command Command's disastrous day, Defense Minister Dayan met with Lt.-Gen. Elazar, asking him "whether he was happy" with the performance of Frontline Commander Shmuel "Gorodish" Gonen. Elazar said Gonen's performance still fell short of a Front Line Commander's standards, since he ran the campaign as a division commander.* Southern Command started showing a deficiency of command.

"What we need there is a creative mind to help us out of this mess," Dayan remarked.

---

*   Carmit Gai, *Bar Lev* [in Hebrew], Am Oved Publishers, 1998, p.251

"Well, we can assign Haim Bar Lev," Dado said.

On that very day, Bar Lev was made the Chief of Staff's Advisor on the Southern Command, without resigning his government office of Minister of Industry and Commerce.

At 0930 hours, about forty-five minutes after the meeting of the Chief of General Staff with Bar Lev, Deputy Prime Minister Yigal Alon arrived at the Dvela War Room. Despite his reduced status, ever since his opponent, Moshe Dayan had been given the Ministry of Defense, Alon was still an important member of Golda Meir's cabinet, and had her ear.

At the Government meeting convened the previous night, October 14th, Alon expressed his misgivings about the benefits of the proposed crossing, despite being told that all of the IDF's top brass, including the Deputy Chief of General Staff, who had first objected it, were now advocating it. At the end of the meeting, Alon admitted to not being familiar enough with military affairs to be impressed by the demonstrated confidence of Lt.-Gen. Elazar. Therefore, as he said, "I will neither support nor oppose it, but go to the Sinai, to learn the facts at first hand." He remained in the War Room until 1315 hours, attending the main operational briefings of that day. What he had heard and saw there made him believe the maneuver was feasible.

That very morning, while the Southern Command Command was preoccupied with the planning of the crossing, a dramatic event took place at the northernmost end of the Southern Command, away from the campaign's planned theater. A battle was being fought over Budapest Fort, the northern tip of the Bar Lev Line, situated on a long strand opposite Port Fuad, on the Mediterranean Coast. It was surrounded with marshes, and had just one narrow approach route. It was the only Israeli fort on the Bar Lev Line not to have succumbed when the entire line collapsed, from October 6th to October 9th. It became a thorn in the side of the Egyptians, threatening Port Fuad and Port Said, while covering the IDF's northern, Mediterranean flank and securing the road leading to the North Sinai bases. It was first attacked on October 6th, and by the 10th of October, it was cut off, by a persistent Egyptian ambushing commando force. On October 10th the siege was breached, and that day, the fort was occupied by a Nahal company, relieving the Jerusalem Brigade reservists, under Captain Moti Ashkenazi, (later the leader of the post-war protest), in addition to a regular artillery battery stationed there in the beginning of the war. Since its siege had been lifted, it seemed the Egyptians gave up their attempts to take the fort. Yet now, something seemed to happen: at 0500, the Baluza war room, of the Command's northern sector's division, codenamed Tiger Force, reported that Budapest Fort was sustaining Egyptian artillery fire and infantry assaults since 0400 hours.

This hour marked the initiation of one of the bloodiest battles fought on the northern part of the canal. Brig.-Gen. Yitzchak Sasson, commanding a reduced division called Tiger Force, had been assigned with this sector only two days earlier. Earlier in the War, he served as the Front Command's chief of staff, but, on October 13, Maj-Gen. Albert Mandler, the 252nd Division commander, was killed, and replaced by Brig.-Gen. Kalman Magen, Northern Sector Commander. He was succeeded, in the Northern Sector, by Brig.-Gen. Sasson.

The Egyptian assault that morning was launched with a combined infantry, armored and artillery force, aimed at seizing the Fort with a battalion-strong infantry and commando force, advancing on foot and on-board amphibious APCs.

An armored column advancing at the Fort over the strand, east of Port Fuad, supported the enemy infantry. The shelling commenced at 0330 hours. Through the morning mist, the defenders detected several figures approaching the Fort from the surrounding marshes. At 0500 hours, they saw Topaz amphibious APCs carrying infantry force intending to assault the Fort. The assault, initiated a few minutes later, was checked mostly by the Fort's tanks and Nahal company. The estimated enemy losses were about 60 men, mostly killed between the APC's positions and the Fort's westernmost outposts.

Meanwhile, the retreating Egyptians shifted the fighting to the Fort's approach route, the man-made trail, running between the Port Fouad strand and Lake Bardawil. The road, built by a Technion team, headed by Prof. Dan Zaslavski, cooperating with the IDF, was designed to serve as an approach route for the Fort through the marshes.

During the head-on assault on Fort Budapest, a 150-men strong Egyptian elite commando unit, equipped with anti-tank missiles, advanced unnoticed through the marshes, cutting off the road. Early in the morning, when the artillery barrage on the fort intensified, a mechanized infantry battalion of the IDF's 204th Brigade was ordered to check the road. The force, two-platoon strong, suffered an ambush by Egyptian commandos deployed south of the road. Taken by surprise, the force unsuccessfully attempted to break through, and sustained many casualties. Being called to the scene, the Battalion Commander, Col. Zvi "Rami" Ram, realized reinforcement was required. Then, Brig.-Gen. Sasson deployed a mechanized infantry force of the 11th Armored Division commanded by Col. Arahon Pedaleh, which shared the Northern Sector with the 204th Brigade. That company-strong force, too, proved useless:

the road remained cut off and most commanders, including the Company Commander, were injured. Corp. Moshe Levi, who commanded an incapacitated halftrack, had his forearm blown off by an RPG rocket. Dismounting his halftrack, Levi advanced at the nearest enemy position with a hand grenade in his right hand, pulling the safety with his teeth.

"When people say they were bedazzled, it's usually taken for a joke," he recalls. "Well, not in my case. I was literally bedazzled, realizing I am about to faint."

He threw the grenade, which exploded in the air, killing the enemy force in that position. But, being too close to the position, Levy suffered a shrapnel injury from his own grenade. Nonetheless, he declined any medical aid, sending the medevac team to the injured halftrack's crew. Meanwhile, the vehicle took a direct hit, caught fire and blew up. For his act, Moshe Levy was awarded the Bravery Decoration.

Another part of the force hesitated to assault through the exposed terrain lying between the Israeli and the entrenched Egyptian force, so the battle plan was disrupted. At this stage, an APC-mounted paratroopers' company, of the 564th Paras Battalion, under Lt.-Col. Yossi Yaffe, was thrown into battle, and the Egyptian force gave way, leaving behind about seventy dead.

The costly battle, resulting in eighteen dead and sixty injured, was harshly criticized by Southern Command Command both during the war as well as during the post-war analyses. Eventually, this battle was considered unnecessary, since the fort could have handle the Egyptian assaults unassisted. On the other hand, if the route to it was that vital, some wondered, to merit battles which cost tens of dead and injured men, why hadn't it been properly secured in the first place?

When it was all over, the Southern Command Commander, Lt.-Gen. Bar Lev, questioned Brig.-Gen. Sasson as to what actually happened at the Battle of Fort Budapest.

As Sasson explained it: "The men heard small arms firing, so they advanced. A company of Rami, the 204th Brigade's commander, assaulted the ambushing force. We took a terrible shelling. Finally, I threw in Yossi Yaffe's paratroopers."

Bar Lev: How can you prevent such a mess from happening again?

Sasson: By deploying a platoon-and-a-half strong force on that road. As simple as that.

2. CROSS AT ANY COST!

Tasa, 143rd Division War Room, October 15 1973:

During peacetime, the West Sinai Tasa perimeter served as the frontline division's main base. It consisted of two camps, each with its own war room: one was a Brigade's war room, codenamed Yalta, and the other a regimental one, codenamed Ceylon, at 4 kilometers distance from each other. Since October 6, the 14th Brigade, under Col. Amnon Reshef had used the Brigade's war room, while the 143rd Division, under Maj.-Gen. Sharon, occupied the regimental one. During emergencies, the small underground bunker was too small for all five of the men crowding into the Main War Room. Though the air was stifling, the atmosphere was one of elation.

At 1220 hours, members of the Southern Command's top brass, as well as the Defense Minister and the Chief of General Staff, arrived at Maj.-Gen. Ariel Sharon's operation room bunker, in the Tasa Compound. All of these illustrious gentlemen came for an operations approval procedure.

For their host, 143rd Division Commander Maj.-Gen. Sharon, this day was long awaited, aspired, pleaded and prepared for. He had ardently worked for that day since the evening of October 7th, when he was first summoned for a council meeting in Dvela, arriving after a great delay, and happened to meet the Chief of General Staff by the entrance to the bunker, telling him the canal must be crossed as soon as possible. This was the only way to throw the Egyptians off balance, Sharon argued. Yet so far, it was the IDF who have been thrown off balance.

During the conference in Dvela, held on October 8th at midnight, Sharon addressed a group of exhausted commanders who had just been defeated by Egyptian forces. Surprising them, Sharon said: "We must leave no Arab soldier on this side of the Suez. Once it is possible, we must cross over to the west bank. We have a roller bridge, and I can cross in the Northern Sector, at the Mifreket perimeter. Such a maneuver could fold the Egyptian lines in on both sides of the canal." From then onward, he relentlessly pressed for a crossing, his pressure being effective far beyond that of his obvious influence as a division commander. One must bear in mind that for three years, until July 1973, Sharon, as the Commander of Southern Command, prepared the Command for war, making war plans, building military roads and carefully supervising every detail in territory that he knew as well as the back of his hand. Being the front line commander, Sharon doubted the necessity of a fortified line along the canal, conceived by, and named after, Bar Lev.*

---

*   Originally, it was Nasser who gave it its name.

Now, Bar Lev had in effect been made the Southern Command Commander, and therefore, Sharon's superior. The 143rd Division commander fundamentally disagreed with the military doctrine that had evolved out of the Bar Lev Line. Sharon believed the Egyptian Army must be met in open spaces, not on a fortified line which is bound to be breached anyway. From January 1972 to July 1973, Sharon reduced the number of Bar Lev Line Fortifications from thirty-three to just sixteen, while constructing the second Strong Points Line, which was not part of any defensive line, but rather a rear base for the frontline armored units.

The decisive campaign of crossing the canal, taking the war to the other side, suited Sharon's philosophy and aggressive strategy.

There were no strategic disagreements between his colleagues: this had been the IDF's doctrine since the Six-Day War, practiced in IDF war games. It was only the timing and method that was being disputed.

Sharon didn't just present his plans, but worked toward their fulfillment. On the evening of October 9th, a portion of the 87th Reconnaissance Battalion of his division got nearly to the canal, so Sharon asked for permission to cross it. The Chief of General Staff, then adhering to a defensive doctrine, went ballistic. "No crossing! I repeat, no crossing! It's insane!" announced Dado, ordering the immediate withdrawal of that force to return to the defensive line. Commenting on this, Sharon told his staff members, "So this is what the Chief of the General Staff thinks....what the hell is on their minds?! It's absolutely outrageous!"

Sharon's conflicts with his Southern Command superiors were on both personal as well as professional grounds. As usual, he appreciated his subordinates more than he did his superiors, especially since, not long before then, he used to command the entire theater. His disputes with his superiors stemmed from their conflicting ideas of conducting the war, and were intensified by mutual distrust, on his superiors' parts, of his motives and battlefield performance, and on his part, of the motives of the orders received from them. Eventually, these differences boiled down to personal animosity, mutual as well.

In May 1973, Southern Command Commander Major General Ariel Sharon, then forty-five years old and in his prime, was summoned to Defense Minister Dayan's office, where Dayan made it clear to him his military career was over and that he was to be demobilized in January 1974.

Sharon, who considered himself to be a potential future Chief of General Staff, was frustrated, and attempted in vain to reverse the verdict. Sharon suspected it to be a personal vendetta on the part of the Chief of Staff and Labor Party leaders, for his short flirtation with opposition leader, Menachem Begin, four years earlier.

Having no other choice, Sharon began a second career as a politician. Since he had to undergo a cooling-off period, Sharon resorted to an early retirement, in July 1973. For him, leaving the army was like leaving a home, a career, and a life's work, so he took out his rage on those whom he suspected to have schemed for his dismissal. On the occasion of his retirement party, he astonished the guests with a speech criticizing the Chief of Staff and senior members of the Ministry of Defense, stressing that he was leaving the army against his will, and then left his retirement party refusing to participate.

He had only one request from Dayan: to be assigned a senior position as a combat reserve officer. Dayan granted his wish immediately, making Sharon commander of the 143rd Division of the combat reserves, one of the three wartime combat divisions of the Southern Command.

Sharon spent the following months forming a new political alignment. His differences with Herut leader Menachem Begin resolved, they began together, on September 10th, 1973, the alliance of parties called the Likud, challenging, for the first time, the Labor Party's predominance. Despite being a political newcomer, Sharon became one of the leading candidates in the upcoming election campaign.

On the morning of October 5th, he was called to arms once again, and since October 6 at 1400 hours had been leading his division southward. On the very next day, October 7th, he led his division as commander during the first battles of the Front's Central Sector, an assignment he had received that very day. The sector stretched between Maj-.Gen. Adan's 162nd Division's Northern Sector, and Maj. Gen. Mandler's 252nd Division's Southern Sector.

Sharon led the three armored brigades of his division, the 14th, 421st and 600th, in the fierce defensive battles during the first week of fighting. During all that time, he stood out for his aggressive approach and high level of initiative, proposing an immediate offensive aimed at rescuing the troops of the Bar Lev Line Forts, as early as October 7th. On October 9th he entered into an attack, unauthorized by the front commander, on the center of the Egyptian line. As mentioned above, one evening he attempted to exploit the achievements of a reconnaissance battalion that had reached the canal, urging that the fighting immediately be taken to the west bank. On October 14th, his division smashed the Egyptian offensive in its sector, preparing the ground for next day's decisive maneuver.

Sharon's tactical HQ consisted of officers united by their years-long personal companionship with their chief, and their deep mutual trust and appreciation for him. The HQ included the control center for the Division's Intelligence, Signal, Artillery, and Medical Corps, mounted on six or seven APCs, packed with maps and radios, huddled around the division commander's APC. Sharon's deputy, Col. Yaakov "Jacky" Even, had risen up through the Armored Corps. Yehoshua Sagi, his Intelligence Officer, was the staff officer most closely associated with Sharon. When not in the field, the tactical HQ converged at the Tasa outpost.

The Tasa Command Bunker, known as "The Submarine," consisting of small rooms with narrow corridors running between them, bred its own traditions. Maj.-Gen. Adan, who happened to get there on some evenings, reports "two experiences I have long forgotten about," one being taking a shower, the other being a surprising address to "Arik" by one of his staff officers, suggesting it was about time to eat some really good cheese. Sharon knew how to have a good time.

And he also had his own style of generalship. In the words of his Operations Officer, Lt.-Col. (res.) Aharon Tal, "Sharon was a general who gave his officers a lot of free hand, only after making sure they understood what he was up to. He didn't always follow procedures, occasionally cutting a deal with the officers, tête-á-tête, without involving his staff. He conducted the fighting with a 1:50000 map with no tactical marks, making an air of fully controlling the situation, commanding the campaign calmly, and impressing you he could read the battle as no one else could."

Sharon used to roam the field wearing his red Paratrooper's beret or sticking it under his epaulette. What his subordinates felt for him was something between total commitment and adoration.

Yet this was not the case for Sharon's relationship with his superiors. Their mutual misunderstanding was a part and parcel of the hierarchy formed when Sharon was placed as a subordinate to the younger Major General Shmuel Gonen, who had succeeded Sharon as Southern Command commander, shortly before the war. The failed October 8th counteroffensive was the cause of their mutual distrust, with Sharon accusing Gonen of poor judgment along with a series of tactical errors. The frustration of Sharon's initiatives on October 9th only served to fuel their distrust with further mutual suspicion and bitterness.

On top of his reservations with regard to the wisdom of the politicians and his superiors' ability to lead, Sharon developed strong resentment regarding the Chief of General Staff's attitude towards him. Sharon and Elazar had a lot of scores to settle, Sharon considering Elazar as the one responsible for the end of his military career. On top of the career-related vendetta, Sharon had also developed a political sensitivity, suspecting that the decisions concerning him were being made on spurious grounds, due to his membership in the Likud party.

"Throughout this war," one of his senior staff members remarked, "one felt there was some clique making its own decisions, assigning tasks to its members in the field, and there were second-class officers, like us." By contrast, Southern Command Commander Haim Bar Lev noted that "one of my division commanders is somewhat of a politician," responding to Sharon's pressuring for crossing the canal in the very beginning of the war, despite Bar Lev and the Chief of General Staff's objection. By this, Bar Lev sarcastically implied that Sharon was trying to achieve personal political gain out of the crossing, disregarding its possible cost.

As mentioned above, Shmuel Gonen had assumed command of Southern Command three months earlier, struggling to contain his predecessor's heavy pressuring and frequently complaining about him to the Chief of General Staff, to the extent of asking to relieve him from his division's command, on October 9th. The Chief of General Staff consulted Defense Minister Moshe Dayan about the issue, and Dayan said: "I looked at Arik the other day, thinking he must be wondering what's in it for him? How will this whole thing make him look? He certainly doesn't want to sit on his hands, in a defensive position. Not him, he is not like Mandler, Magen and Gonen. People might ask: Where is the great Arik, who came to the Sinai to set things right?!' So he wants an 'OK, go ahead!' If it works, fine. But if it doesn't, the nation will lose 200 tanks! He would have made a Rommel-style thrust, wholeheartedly believing this was the best way to do it. He has a problem called 'Ariel Sharon.' He cannot accept himself being regarded like other commanders. But this is not to say he does nothing useful."

Dayan was aware of Sharon's preoccupation with how his part in the war would go down in history. Yet he confessed, to the Chief of General Staff, he preferred Sharon's spirit of initiative to the hesitation of other division commanders.

Dayan's solution to the conflicts between Gonen and Sharon was, as mentioned above, making Lt.-Gen. (res.) Bar Lev the effective Southern Command Commander. When summoned to a briefing by the deputy Chief of General Staff,

Maj.-Gen. Israel Tal, on the morning of October 10th, Tal told him, "Whatever you told about the Arik-Gorodish affair, is absolutely true, and Gorodish is in the right. Arik is just waging his own war." Armed with this information, Bar Lev embarked on his mission.

3. WE FAILED TO NOTICE THAT.

On the morning of October 15th, the most urgent challenge seemed to be reducing the antagonism between Southern Command commanders. Sharon, facing a multitude of senior officers in the Tasa Operations Bunker, was holding a long pointer. In front of him was the operational map codenamed Sirius covered with directional arrows; his red beret was tucked under his epaulet; behind him stood the section of the Operation Stout Hearts plan labeled "objectives". Sharon's operational plan was being scrutinized by the high command.

As Sharon explained it later, "My division's task was to secure a bridgehead west of the canal. We were to cross the canal, breaching and securing a four-kilometer wide corridor, and handle the entire bridge-building business, as well as the towing of amphibious tank carriers." Sharon's division was also given the assignment of securing the routes. After the war, Sharon would claim, "Since no one was assigned with supervising the transportation, we undertook this job as well."

Sharon trusted his division to be capable of carrying out the numerous tasks it had assumed. Thanks to the arduous work of maintenance personnel, its current consignment of tanks was back to 230, nearly the prewar number. He had at his command, three complete armored divisions. Yet he couldn't ignore the mission before them and the possible cost.

Sharon had conceived of a four-phase battle plan for his division:

1. A Deceptive attack: the 600th Brigade, under Col. Tuviyah Raviv, was to attack the Egyptian perimeter east of the canal, codenamed Missouri, making the Egyptians believe the division's main effort was against "Missouri," thus diverting them from the point of the crossing.

2. Pushing the Egyptians north of the planned point of crossing. This was to be done by an armored brigade augmented with infantry. The idea was that this force would advance northward, on the north-south route along the east bank of the canal, infiltrating the rear of the Egyptian forces. This task was assigned to the 14th Brigade under Amnon Reshef.

3. Covered by these two maneuvers, the 247th Paratroopers Brigade, under Col. Danny Matt, was to reach, unnoticed, with assault rubber boats, the perimeter of what used to be Matzmed Fort, currently Deversoir, cross the canal, and secure a bridgehead on its west bank.

4. While Matt's troops were crossing, the crossing equipment, covered by an armored brigade, was to be delivered to the canal. Then, over a bridge built across the Canal, an armored brigade was to cross westward, to reinforce the bridgehead.

Seemingly, the plan was simple yet genius. Still, it raised several eyebrows, including those of the Chief of General Staff, due to its all too optimistic schedule: the actual H-Hour was set at 1800h; the bridges were to be completed by the morning of October 16th; and the force planned to cross the canal—162nd Division, was to move south right afterwards. As mentioned above, the entire campaign was planned to be over within forty-eight hours, once the city of Suez was encircled.

The 247th Paratroopers Brigade planned to cross the canal, by boats, at 2030 hours, and bridges were to be completed by the morning after. Then, Adan's division was to cross the canal, storming through the area west of the canal. Sharon explained, or explained away, this very unreal schedule by necessity. "I had no choice," he said, "It was absolutely clear we had to gain a foothold west of the canal that night, since, if the Egyptians saw through our trick, they might have deployed forces to the crossing area, and the cost of it for us would have been very or too high." He expected no substantial obstacles on his way to the canal.

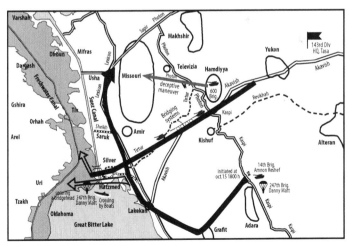

Planned Crossing of the Suez by 143rd Division

Just like his audience, Sharon, too, realized that the success of the maneuver depended on the clearing of two routes allowing the delivering of forces to the launching point of the crossing at Deversoir. The routes were codenamed Akavish and Tirtur. Akavish was an asphalt road, about thirty kilometers long, running from Tasa southwestwards, all the way to Fort Lakekan. About twelve kilometers east of the canal, Tirtur route branched from it, running parallel to it. The latter was a dirt road built by Israeli Engineering Corps in 1970, designed to deliver water-crossing equipment when the time comes.

The route seemed short and easy, yet it was rife with obstacles: at the launching point of the crossing north of Deversoir, near the perimeter codenamed Amir, with the ruins of the so-called Chinese Farm's main buildings in its center, dried irrigation ditches ran a few kilometers south of Tirtur Road. These ditches could have seriously impeded an armored force's advancement, channeling it to a few routes which could be easily blocked. Some of the routes near Deversoir were boggy; a minefield was located along the bank of the Great Bitter Lake, originally placed by Israeli Engineering Corps when the Bar Lev Line was built. Thus, the potential advancement routes to the canal in the Crossing area were through the Nahalah and Tirtur routes only. The plain north of Matzmed compound was easy to travel, yet the canaled area in the east and the partly boggy area in the west restricted the advancement of Armored Corps and vehicles containing them to a narrow strip along the canal road or the north-south route codenamed Lexicon, running parallel to the canal, a couple of kilometers from it. Intelligence Officers considered the maneuverable area to start only west of Lakekan-Akavish junction. Only north of the Chinese Farm buildings, codenamed Amir, was an area negotiable both eastwards and westwards.

By the time the Divisional Intelligence Officer, Col. Yehoshua Sagi, introduced the audience to the intelligence concerning Operation Stout Hearts, the division had already been fighting for nine days, in its own sector, gathering much tactical intelligence. "We had an opportunity to get well acquainted with the field, deploying many observers and launching many reconnaissance patrols. We had a clear idea where the field is more crossable," Sagi told the attendees. Sharon added, "we know this place," pointing at the crossing area east of the canal, on the map, "the area near the Chinese Farm is occupied by the Egyptian 16th Infantry Division, reinforced by remnants of an armored division reassigned as an infantry force....I know that place as well as the back of my hand. I am well aware that it's crisscrossed by canals, so we should have no surprises".

Some of those attending remembered Sharon saying the night before, when presenting his plan of attack to the Southern Command Command: "By nightfall, the 14th Brigade should advance on the road running along the Great Bitter Lake's shore. We are constantly observing this route. There is no living soul there (referring to the Chinese Farm perimeter). That force could drive on, getting there without firing a shot. It's deserted." Eventually, the force launching the attack was in for a very nasty surprise.

The actual crossing was to take place at the gap in the Egyptian lines, set for as early as October 9th, by the 87th Reconnaissance Battalion, between the southernmost elements of the 2nd Army, south of the 16th Division lines, codenamed Missouri in the Israeli operational map, and the northernmost elements of the 3rd Army, north of Botzer Fort, opposite the Great Bitter Lake. It was this breach, about twenty-five kilometers wide, which allowed for the forming of the corridor to the Crossing location. The most critical part of it was a seemingly enemy-free area, stretching from where Fort Lakekan used to be, to Shik Road. In its center, was the Fort Matzmed perimeter, which was planned to serve as the assembly point for the crossing.

As Maj.-Gen. Gonen would explain after the war, the Crossing was planned near Deversoir because the IAF aerial photographs of the area had shown "less Egyptian infantrymen than anywhere else." The trenches detected in the aerial photographs looked like abandoned prewar irrigation ditches, "and failed to be interpreted as enemy positions," in Gonen's words.

Thus, what the Southern Command commanders saw was an area with nearly no Egyptian forces, which made it, considering all the alternatives, the most appropriate Crossing point. But, what the Southern Command commanders failed to notice or maybe could not have noticed was that on the morning of October 15th, while Sharon was presenting his planned Crossing in the Tasa HQ outpost, Egyptian infantry, tanks and AT elements were entrenching themselves at the Lexicon-Tirtur Junction, two kilometers east of the Matzmed assembly perimeter, blocking its approaches.

Col. Yehoshua Sagi, the Divisional Intelligence Officer, argued, post factum, that he had no detailed intelligence on the fortifications in the junction, namely, of enemy infantry and tank positions. The Front's Intelligence Officer, Lt.-Col. Gedalia. Col. Amnon Reshef, Commander of the 14th Brigade, operating in the area, explicitly admitted afterward, to having no information on any enemy forces at the junction. His Intelligence Officer would later claim that "the Tirtur-Lexicon Junction area was clear in the interpreted aerial photos. It is possible that, though during the last aerial photography sortie there had been no tanks there, they were moved there during the night, and there was no way of knowing that."

Consequently, the Lexicon-Tirtur Junction was not regarded as being of any particular challenge.

Since October 14th, most of the Egyptian force was deployed on the east bank of the canal. Of the 2000 tanks that the Egyptians had when the war broke, 1300 had crossed the canal eastward. At the end of the October 14th fighting, when about 200 tanks were destroyed, the Egyptians possessed about 1400 tanks on the east bank. The theater of the crossing, including the entire area north of Tirtur all the way to Ismailia, was defended by two infantry and armored Egyptian divisions. North of Tirtur Road, within the operational sector of the 143rd Division, the Egyptians had deployed 220 tanks, 330 artillery pieces, and numerous infantry and AT units.

The Egyptian High Command assigned, for the defense of Cairo, two tank brigades, four paratroopers' brigades, Armored Corps Academy units and a Republican Guard brigade.

Thus, in the key area south of the planned breach area in the west bank, and south of it, the Egyptians deployed rather small forces, estimated at 120 tanks and being several infantry brigades strong, although in all Egyptian war-games, it was the Deversoir area which was prone to breaching and crossing attempts. They also supposed they would have no problem containing the westward thrust with a coordinated response of the two armies east of the canal. They also didn't take seriously a scenario of Israeli forces infiltrating west of the canal, since they believed that they had sufficient forces to deal with such a nuisance. Egyptian Chief of Staff, Colonel General Shazly, had suggested that in such a case, trained forces should be redeployed from the east bank to the west one, to isolate and neutralize the infiltrating force.

Neither did the Egyptian High Command suspect the Israeli forces assembling in the Second Army's sector to be a preparation for a crossing, but assumed its purpose was to wipe the Egyptian forces from the east bank, similar to the October 8th offensive. This is what Sharon's deceptive attack relied on (see map on opposite page).

Sharon was well aware that a breakthrough was not enough, and at the end of the day, the success of the crossing campaign depended on delivering the crossing equipment to the launching point. He had to deliver rafts from Refidim, tens of kilometers away from the canal, over the main east-west road, as well as from Baluza, in the north Sinai, meet the roller-bridge carriers at the Yukon perimeter, on Akavish Road, and coordinate the transportation of amphibious tank carriers and boats from Refidim. In addition, he had to arrange approach routes for the division's logistics elements, and coordinate the use of the east-west road with another of its users, namely the 162nd Brigade.

As a result, control of the transportation routes became a critical issue. Sharon argued, as he stressed following the war in a critical tone, that the supervision of the roads was to have been the responsibility of the Front Line Command, or maybe the entire IDF. It should have involved great efforts, mostly of administration and organization. As it happened, he argued, it wasn't even organized at the Southern Command level: "No one was assigned with controlling the routes, or assumed control of them, so we just did it. And the roads were very narrow and few in number."

On top of its logistics problems, the Division had also to overcome its inexperience in the towing of the crossing equipment. The few teams of 7th Brigade that had been trained to tow the Roller Bridges had been redeployed to the Northern Front on the eve of the war.

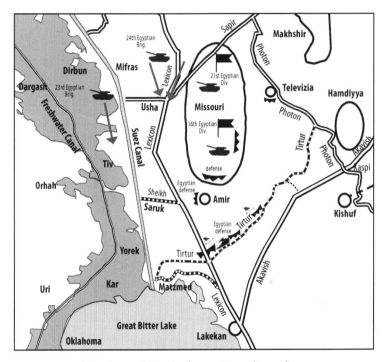

Egyptian positions in the crossing military theater on the night between the 15th and 16th of October

So special roller-bridge towing teams had to be trained, and the 24-hour time period available for this was too short, considering the terrain and circumstances. To somehow compensate for this incompetence, Sharon assigned the entire 421st Armored Brigade with the task of delivering the machinery to the canal.

The concerned faces of the attendees of the meeting at the Tasa War Room, during Sharon's presentation of that part of his briefing, betrayed their doubts about the timing and means of delivering the various crossing equipment items to their assembly points, and then, to the canal, since the entire campaign's success depended on bridging the canal. After the war, as a senior Israeli Engineering Corps officer told it, "We joked that if we fed the data on October 15th to a computer, asking it whether the crossing could be successful, the computer would've blown up." The centerpiece of the crossing was the launching of the roller bridge that had secretly been under construction at the Yukon perimeter, near Tasa, since October 6th.

4. LASKOV HAS AN IDEA.

Born in 1903 in Omsk, Russia, Col. David Laskov immigrated to Palestine in 1923, graduating from the Technion's Faculty of Architecture. When the 1948 War of Independence ended, his career as an IDF Engineering Corps officer started, and in 1957 he had already made Deputy Engineering Corps Commander, being promoted to Colonel as a special reward. Since then onward, he dedicated himself to developing special unusual weapon systems, as part of a unit initially named the "Laskov Squad," and then renamed "Yiftah." For this service he had been awarded three Israel Security Prizes, two of which he had received before the Yom Kippur War. When the war broke out, he was the IDF's longest-serving officer. Despite spending most of his service in the Engineering Corps, he and his men were, to a great extent mavericks, as far as their projects were concerned. Actually, they only answered to those ordering the devices, rather than to their military superiors, and had a variety of funding sources. The Engineering Corps Command was not always informed about what Laskov's workshops were working on. Formed as early as 1957, Yiftah Unit, during the 1970s, was responsible for designing, among other things, the Or Yekarot System, designed to set the Suez Canal on fire in case of an Egyptian crossing attempt, and the Zeev Rocket, which was used, during the War of Attrition, to kill the Egyptian Chief of Staff. But most of its numerous designs were kept secret. As Col. (ret.) Fredo Raz, a Yiftah man, would later confess, "We were classified top secret, and had no reason to share our business with the rest of the Engineering Corps." One day, in late 1971, Laskov, Fredo Raz and his deputy had a meeting in Laskov's Haifa residence, on their way to their office in Tel Aviv. While on the road, Laskov shared with the other two an idea he had on designing a bridge for crossing the Suez Canal. When they got to the office, Laskov sketched the bridge with a chalk on a blackboard, writing down four requirements the bridge must meet:

1. It must be constructed beyond the range of enemy artillery, that is, 40km. In other words, the bridge must be towable for long distances.
2. It must be launched into the water with no soldier exposed to the enemy, which means, while all the towing crewmen are inside tanks.
3. It must be launched into water with no need to level the canal's embankment.
4. It must be transportable on roads other than the main roads used by the advancing forces.

Thus, the Roller Bridge was conceived. Now, a proper patronage and funds were needed, which was anything but easy to find, since the concept, as well as its realization, had to compete for their place in the IDF's tactical doctrine and priorities list.

After the 1967 Six-Day War, when it occupied Sinai, the IDF faced obstacles unforeseen by its original doctrine, of immediately taking the war to enemy territory. These obstacles were the Suez Canal and its lakes, that is, water obstacles to be crossed before the war could be taken to enemy territory. In the words of Major General Adan, then the IDF's Armored Corps commander, "The idea of us having to cross the canal was in the back of every IDF officer's mind, as part and parcel of the philosophy of taking the war to enemy territory. It practically haunted Southern Command, as a Purgatory we must go through on our way to the Paradise of the decisive battle."

The borderline in Western Sinai stretched from Port Said to Ras Sudr, 210 kilometers long. The canal stretched along 160 kilometers of it, from Port Said to the city of Suez, and was between 150 and 180 meters wide. It had served as one of Egypt's main trade routes, until, as a result of the Six-Day War, IDF troops occupied its east bank.

In 1967, four years before Laskov conceived of the Roller Bridge, the IDF started creating its crossing tactics, including the technical means, from scratch. Shortly before the Six-Day War ended, the IDF Engineering Corps sent a delegation to Europe. Its members first met a Dutch Engineering Corps, offering them the Unifloat bridge, consisting of pontoons with versatile connection systems. The metal pontoons were 5.5 meters long, 5.2 wide and 2.1 meters high, attached together Lego-like. England, for instance, used them for constructing piers and canal rafts. As a result of the tour, the IDF bought Unifloat pontoons and accessories in an amount sufficient for constructing four bridges and six rafts. Each raft was to be 2 meters long, 11 meters wide and to weigh about 60 tons, cruise at a maximum 60 kilometers per hour, and capable of carrying one tank. Yet Unifloat rafts were not the only European crossing technology considered by the IDF.

As Brig.-Gen (ret.) Avi Zohar, a member of the acquisition delegation recalled, it examined the fording technologies arsenal of the British and German armies. As he told it, "In Germany, we saw a state-of-the-art amphibious vehicle, invented by French Engineering Corps Col. Gillois in the 1960s: boats capable of carrying a tank, which can be assembled to make a bridge. I thought it suited us, yet the IDF's Engineering Corps commander wanted the crossing to be carried out with rudimentary means, warning me not to breathe a word about it, or he would get me off this case." So the Giliois carrier, later called Alligator, had to wait a few years before being launched in the canals and ponds of Israel.

In 1969, the IDF's Chief of Doctrine Development, Col. Moshe "Musa" Peled, staged a bridging demonstration for the IDF top brass. Only then did the Israeli High Command realize that the crossing involved extremely difficult technical, tactical and administrative challenges of which the IDF was completely unaware. The demonstration consisted of a boat-mounted infantry force fording a water obstacle. Then, the senior officers were amazed to see a column of crane vehicles unloading Unifloat pontoons and connectors on the shore. The Engineering Corps men struggled for hours to assemble the pontoons into a raft, fitting it with engines and delivering tanks to the other bank in several rounds. The audience considered this technique desperately time-consuming and ill-suited for the tactical doctrine they had been brought up on.

The fording of a wide canal would have taken 108 trucks delivering about 100 pontoons along with the necessary tools and equipment. To deliver the bridge components, gigantic, eighty-ton trailers were constructed, and the pontoons' transportation and assembling into a bridge took a lot of training. According to IDF Engineering Corps experts, the construction of such a bridge over the Suez Canal, with no enemy interference, would have taken at least twelve hours. The main challenge of a Unifloat raft would be its capability to carry a tank, and of a Unifloat bridge, its capability to allow a safe and uninterrupted crossing of armored vehicles. Though the bridge stood up to the challenge, those watching its construction considered it ill-suited to the doctrine of an armored blitz attack.

To operate the bridging technology, the IDF formed, on October 1st, 1967, the 605th Bridging Battalion, stationed near Haifa, next to the IAF's Technical Corps base, in an abandoned British Army barracks. Its training ground was about 200 meters of the Kishon Harbor coastline, opposite the docks. Its founder and first commander was Avi Zohar, then a major. In the words of one of his men, "Zohar used to dream of bridges and water obstacles to be crossed,"* and Major General Ariel Sharon, then IDF's Chief of Doctrine Department, considered him an authority in this field.

Zohar rallied a group of young officers who initially could contribute little more than their ardor. They worked like beginners, learning by trial and error, constantly building up and developing new systems. "Alligator man," Col. (ret.) Amikam Doron, would later tell how they conceived the Gillois training procedure: "We were a team of 10, including Leshem Edelstein, Arnon Golan and myself. The first Gillois models we got came

---

*   Col. Amikam Doron, *Serving the Crossing.*
**   In an interview with Col. Amikam Doron, 1972.

with German manuals, so we had to translate them, conceiving a rudimentary tactic. We had to learn it on the job."**

The development of new systems entailed professional differences as well as ego-driven conflicts. This development was shared by all military and industrial organizations related to crossing water-obstacles, and there were many other bodies competing over resources, conflicting development concepts, and manpower.

Despite the intensive engagement of the IDF in constructing and developing fording technologies, by early 1972 it only had two Unifloat-type pontoon bridges, the advantages and flaws of which had been well known by then. By all means, this build-up was too slow to offer the IDF a significant means for carrying out the crossing at a desirable speed.

Then they recalled that old sophisticated scrap they saw thrown out somewhere in the woods of Europe. It was turned down by its potential European users due to the too high vulnerability of its floats. So eventually, it ended up with its parts scattered all over the forests of Europe, like giant corpses. Yet it was a self-propelled amphibious vehicle, with a flexible MO, and, unlike rafts, less dependent on delivery by roads, requiring a relatively short adjustment to buoyancy, and, an advantage just as important, being relatively inexpensive.*

Outwardly, the Gillois resembled an enormous wheeled truck. Three Gillois carriers attached together in the water formed a long carrier capable of carrying a tank from one bank to another. Compared to other amphibious vehicles, the Gillois

---

* For further details on the Alligators, see Ronen Bergman, *Real Time* [in Hebrew], Yediot Aharonot Press, 2003, pp.203 ff.

had rather modest features and performance: eleven meters in length; three meters wide when traveling on roads; 60.3m high; 60 km maximum road speed; 15km/h maximum off-road speed; 10 km/h maximum loaded swimming speed. So its advantages were amphibiousness and self-propulsion; its downsides, low survivability under fire, especially while in water. Seemingly, the Gillois carriers suited the IDF perfectly: its launching involved no complex logistics, nor any preparation or construction on a specific launching zone. Yet, due to their difficult maintenance and vulnerability, Engineering Corps Commander in those days objected to their purchase, thus condemning this asset to a three-year oblivion on the part of the IDF. Yet this objection had its reasons. Here, we must get ahead of ourselves, mentioning that on October 17th, 1973, a day after being launched into the canal, eight of seventeen Gillois carriers, renamed Alligators, were sunk due to either direct hits or shrapnel.

In January 1971, the Gillois carriers were discussed once again. One reason for that was a pressure by various Engineering Corps commanders. Yet Avi Zohar had to overcome many obstacles, some of them were his colleagues' objection. As he recalls, "When I left the army to study in the Technion, our team was visited by David 'Dado' Elazar, then Chief of the Operations Department. We played it out for them, saying that without an amphibious carrier, the crossing might fail. Dado fell for it, and Logistics was forced into it."* So, in April 1971, secretly and under camouflage, sixty-two dismantled Gillois scraps were unloaded in Haifa Port. They were restored by Merkavim, a civilian bus factory. Now, the Gillois was renamed "Timsah," Hebrew for alligator. The first

---

* An interview with Brig.-Gen.(res.) Avi Zohar.

"Alligators" were handed over to the IDF by the summer of 1972, and by October 1973 the IDF had twenty such vehicles.

Between January 1st, 1971 and October 6th, 1973, the IDF had carried out nineteen divisional and inter-divisional maneuvers where wide water-obstacle crossing played a major part. The most massive one, Oz, was held from February to March 1972. It was a divisional maneuver of an unprecedented extent, aimed, among other things, at testing the IDF's crossing tactics and technologies. Ariel Sharon, then Southern Command Commander, had the brilliant idea, of using the Rwaifa dam across the El-Arish watercourse, east of Abu 'Ageila, to create a seventy-meter wide pond simulating the Suez Canal. During preparations for the maneuver, the Armored Corps Command hastened the development of crossing means and techniques, forming dedicated crossing units. The command of the exercise was assigned to Sharon, with Brig.-Gen. Shmuel Gonen as his deputy. The main maneuvering force was the 162nd Division under Major General Adan.

This mega-maneuver tested the IDF's capability of a crossing assault, that is, crossing a water obstacle while maintaining the momentum of assault. Though the demonstrated performance was by far better than in earlier demonstrations, most of the viewers and participants remembered it as a major chaos with schedule disruptions and all kinds of malfunctions. Yet they drew some optimistic conclusions as well, so, at the completion of the maneuver, the Armored Corps commander, General Adan, stressed that despite the problems, "At the end of the day, we had a bridge." Once there was a bridge, a tank battalion with all its elements was deployed across the water obstacle in two hours. Meanwhile, the upgrading of Unifloat pontoons went on. Its floats were filled with polyurethane, a less vulnerable substance, and its engines were steel-armored. It was to serve as a one-way bridge for tanks and other armored vehicles.

But then the concept changed: Major General Israel "Talik" Tal was promoted to Deputy Chief of Staff, in January 1972, and started severely interfering in the crossing vehicles development. Tal did not like what he saw in the Oz maneuver, nor the red tape, meager resources, priorities list, or the progress of preparations. In his words, "The Oz maneuver had its glitches. So, in June 1972, I had a hot dispute regarding whether the crossing vehicles should be transported on wheels or hauled. There were too many fingers in this pie, with the Armored Corps usurping this task from the Engineering Corps. We had clashes with no clear decisions." Too meager resources were distributed between too many technologies. The promotion of Major General Tal to Deputy Chief of Staff was good news for Laskov and the Yiftah squad. Employing his curiosity about technologies, they asked him to join them for coffee at their base, and presented him with a model of the Roller Bridge, while Laskov presented him with the concept. As Col. (ret.) Fredo Raz described it, "Talik was thrilled, suggesting using not rectangular but cylindrical buoys, which could serve both as wheels as well as floats. Talik was fully engaged in this project, both in the engineering, the allocation of resources and the development of tactical use doctrine. It happened about 1972. I recall a meeting in the Development Center, when all the participants were saying that the Roller Bridge won't work. After the meeting, Laskov told us that from that moment on we must work on the bridge even harder than before. Talik secured the funding, so we designed the bridge ourselves, assisted by the Technion. The very first bridge was built in an Israeli Military Industry plant, and we tested its tank-carrying capability at

Palmachim beach, in a canal we had dug especially for that purpose. We documented the MO of the bridge in a nice little film, narrated by Radio and TV show host Ehud Manor, whom I had befriended when he served in the Engineering Corps. For the testing, we were allotted a tank company commanded by Lt. Eli Geva. His company carried out all the launching and crossing tests, and we made many modifications in the bridge. The trouble was that besides Geva's force, no other armored units were trained in crossing. Later on, we had constructed an entire complex in Rwaifah, complete with an embankment, and demonstrated a full launching complete with a few kilometers towing. That took place in late 1972, and the entire army watched this demonstration. Following this war game, I was made a Lieutenant-Colonel."*

The concept was to assemble a bridge out of attachable buoys, towing it to the canal and quickly pushing into the water through a breach in the embankment. This would allow it to unfold within a few minutes, allowing columns of tanks to drive across it.

The front pontoon was to be fitted with an anchoring nose and a dismounting ramp, while the rear pontoon was to serve as a mounting ramp. The rollers were designed to be of dual use: serving as wheels, while the bridge is towed on land, turning into buoys once the bridge is launched. Laskov formally submitted the design to the IDF's Engineering Corps Commander in January of 1972, in a booklet entitled "Roller Bridge," which was enthusiastically and generously embraced.

Yet not all Engineering Corps officers shared Major General

---

* An interview with Col.(res.) Fredo Raz.

Tal's enthusiasm about the rolling bridge vision, which he considered to be his baby. Even some Armored Corps officers disagreed with Tal's technological philosophy. One of them, the Corps Commander, Maj.-Gen. Adan, was underwhelmed, due to the inflexible and cumbersome performance. The Chief of the Development Department detected a major flaw in that bridge: it was enormously heavy and difficult to launch into the water. The objectors also pointed to the terrain being unfavorable to towing, the necessity of towing the bridge to the very shore, its being too unstable to carry unarmored vehicles due to wave motion, its costliness and difficulty to repair.

But, as that officer recalls, "Talik was extremely stubborn, and only yes men could have worked with him. He got obsessed with this concept, and secured its funding, believing the Alligators were unnecessary, since the Roller Bridge was the answer to everything."*

Engineering Corps Col. (res.) Yaakov Yerushalmi reveals the key role Tal played in setting the priority and suppressing dissent: "I attended a meeting with Talik in which it was decided to stop upgrading the Gillois. Due to my opposition, Talik ordered me out of the meeting. He wanted to call off the Alligators program, while I advocated developing other technologies in addition to the Roller Bridge. I objected, arguing the Roller Bridge was ill-suited for towing on sandy terrain. Yet Talik stopped all works on the Alligators and pontoon bridges, shifting all these programs' budgets to the

---

* An interview with Col. (ret.) Ami Radian.
** An interview with Yerushalmi. (cf. Yaari's words in Millstein, *The Lessons of the Collapse*, (ff. *Collapse*),[in Hebrew] 1993, p.137).

Roller Bridge program. Towards late 1973, the development of all technologies other than Roller Bridges was stopped. Talik's decision was irreversible, so all other programs had to eke out budgets on the sly. He wouldn't hear any other opinions."*

Yet it must be noted that the successful demonstrations of the roller bridge won it many advocates among the Armored Corps and the Engineering Corps alike. Adan wrote that during the winter of 1972, a year after the Oz war game, the Rwaifa pond swelled with rainfall, and the advanced versions of the Roller Bridge were tested in it. Though the bridge's performance impressed the viewers, its design wasn't fully developed yet. In the demonstrations, it was not tested for towing along tens of kilometers of challenging terrain, but along a bulldozer-leveled 800 meters only.**

Its potential users, namely Armored Corps officers, criticized the tactical rigidity the Roller Bridge might force on its users. Handling the challenge of such a monster, with its 80 rollers, 400 tons in weight and 200 meters in length, became critical. To be rotated, it had to be towed on a straight and levelled route all the way to a predesigned launching point, with no maneuverability. As one of the Engineering Corps officers, Col. "Georgie" Gur recalled, "Our prewar crossing plan was based on sterile conditions, or an undisturbed towing of the crossing machinery; two divisional assembly zones and two brigades' sectors; we take the initiative after an air and artillery bombardment; our training was conducted in accordance with these presumptions. The Roller Bridge had never been tested in long-distance towing."

Due to the supposedly successful tests, the Deputy Chief of Staff ordered the manufacturing of three full length, 200-meter long Roller Bridges, ordering one bridge to be transported to Refidim, another one to be assembled near Rwaifah Dam for testing, and the third one deployed near Romani, in the Northern Sector, to be on standby for a crossing there.

During 1973, the IDF started experimenting with yet another crossing technology, a model of the Unifloat Assault Bridge nicknamed "Austerity Bridge," since it had been developed with hardly any budget. It was a version of the Unifloat bridge, designed by Engineer Yaakov Yerushalmi. By October 1973, it was ready to use yet never tested. All this arsenal was under intense development yet uncompleted. According to Engineers Col. Menashe "Georgie" Gur, "During the Blue-And-White Alert of May 1973, we had no opportunity to practice an actual fording, so when the war broke out, we were caught with our pants down. During the war, we had the machinery, yet some of it was insufficiently developed. If the war had broken out in December of 1973, for example, we would have been much better prepared."

Thus, the crossing doctrine of the IDF by early October 1973 was the following:
• Armored force secures a perimeter on the east bank;
• While the fording machinery is delivered, paratroopers cross the canal on board rubber boats, securing a foothold on the opposite bank;
• Once the opposite bank is secured, the fording machinery is launched into the water, allowing armored and infantry forces to cross, driving over a rapidly built bridge or a raft;
• The fording division's elements prepare the ground for the main force's crossing by securing, maintaining and expanding the bridgehead.

Yet on October 15th, 1973, something went wrong with this

doctrine: the Egyptians still held a ten to twelve kilometers wide perimeter east of the canal.

In Avi Zohar's words, "The IDF's prewar philosophy was that a crossing could by no means take place under the actual conditions of that war, when the frontline was twelve kilometers east of the canal. Its main consequence was that the fording machinery had to be delivered to the canal from quite a long distance, about thirty kilometers away, near Tasa. This is critical for understanding the crossing campaign. The Roller Bridge was considered by many IDF commanders to be a wonder weapon of Rwaifah demonstrations, when four tanks easily towed it along 200 meters, and the ultimate fording technology. But now, serious doubts were raised about its towing over many kilometers of dunes and sandy roads."

Only two roads, Tirtur and Akavish, were open and prepared to serve as the main routes for the crossing. The question of whether they sufficed was answered during the actual fighting, since logistics roads have to meet other standards than operational ones, and the major point was controlling them.

Just like the rest of the IDF, the Engineering Corps, too, was caught unprepared for the war. All the machinery, namely the Alligators, rafts and the Roller Bridge, weren't at the Crossing's assembly areas. What made matters worse, some of them had yet to be constructed.

Thus, on October 6th, the 17th Alligators Battalion was stationed at its base, near the Sea of Galilee. It wasn't until October 8th that carriers delivered the Alligators from the southern shores of the lake all the way to the Refidim base in the Sinai.

The Unifloat rafts were gathered in two areas, in the Northern Sector, near Romani, and the Central Sector, at Refidim, and they had yet to be constructed. According to the 630th Raft Battalion Deputy Commander, "We arrived at Refidim on the night between the 7th and 8th of October. It was total chaos: even the hardware brought back from the Rwaifah training camp hadn't been repaired yet." The Battalion also suffered from an incomplete command staff, so its actual commander was Lt. Col. Avi Zohar, who was recalled from his academic leave.

It wasn't until October 5th that the Roller Bridge construction started, after it was shipped straight from its factory. The construction took place at Yukon perimeter, southwest of Tasa.

Thus, between October 6th and October 13th, all dedicated Engineering Corps units were either in a state of construction or on alert. This is what Col. Menasheh "Georgie" Gur saw in the field on October 11th:

"I first saw how we were doing when I was deployed in the field as the Engineering Corps Commander's special emissary. I saw how the 630th Battalion was still constructing its rafts on their trailers, in Refidim; the 605th Battalion, with its rafts, was away up north, in Baluzah; another Roller Bridge, too, was in Baluzah. By the way, in the first week of fighting, Col. "Johnny" Tenne, Chief of the Southern Command's Engineering Corps, wanted to blow it up, fearing it being captured by the Egyptians. So we were caught in rather poor shape. I reported what I had seen to Brig.-Gen. Ben-Dov, the IDF's Engineering Corps Commander. The construction of the Roller Bridge had just begun then, and I found it unfit for towing. And there wasn't a single Engineering company trained in towing it."

Considering the pressures from the 143rd Division commander, Maj.-Gen. Sharon for crossing as early as October 9th, the inevitable question was whether the crossing could have taken place earlier than October 14th. That is: when the technical units could actually allow for the combat units to carry out this decisive maneuver. After the war, Col. Zohar answered unequivocally, that the technical preparations were only completed by October 13th.

At any rate, from October 13th onwards, while all command levels intensely discussed the crossing plans, the Engineering Corps units started advancing their machinery towards the assembly area.

5. ONE BIG MESS.

It occurred to nobody that delivering the fording machinery to the assembly point and then to the canal, would involve towing them for tens of kilometers, occasionally under fire. So on the morning of October 15th, the 605th Engineer Battalion, with its dozen Unifloat rafts in Romani, in the Northern sector, was about sixty kilometers away from Tasa. The 630th Unifloat Battalion was still near Refidim, about fifty kilometers from the assembly point, codenamed Yukon, waiting for the tanks to tow it. The gigantic Roller Bridge, the great hope of the crossing campaign, was assembled and ready to be placed, under the makeshift command of Col. Menashe "Georgie" Gur and Yiftah team members, who had designed it, at the Yukon perimeter, twenty-seven kilometers from the canal. Only the 634th Engineer Battalion had managed to bring its Alligators to the Akavish road. Yet the distance of the fording equipment from the launching perimeter and the troublesome issue of its towing was only one part of the problem, the other part being the absence of the one person who was supervising and conducting this entire complex operation. Yet there were some other candidates, at least self-appointed ones. Avi Zohar described the lack of a clear chain of command, as being "one big mish mash." And it was not just Zohar who felt marginalized and underused.

Maj.-Gen. Sharon was aware of the need to form a dedicated divisional crossing support unit. To this purpose, on October 13th, he summoned the crossing campaign's deputy chief engineering officer, Col. "Georgie" Gur, ordering him, on the spot, to assume command over the Crossing operation. This is what happened next, in "Georgie's" words: "I saluted him, yet struggled to put his command into practice. We had neither command halftracks nor communication systems, so I had no idea how to control the troops. I bumped into Brig.-Gen. Avraham "Abrasha" Tamir, Sharon's aide, out at the HQ, asking him how I could carry out the command. So he told me to sit next to Col. 'Jacky' Even in their halftrack. I did, and asked Jacky how I should command and where I should be. He told me, "right next to me." Since Avi Zohar had taken charge of the rafts, I realized the Alligators had been assigned to the most knowledgeable man in the field. So I told Jacky I was the most knowledgeable serviceman in the field of roller bridges. But actually, I had only recently joined the Roller Bridge unit."

Col. Jacky Even, the 143rd Division's Deputy Commander, who had also assumed responsibility for the operational logistics, was aware of the difficulties regarding transportation of the fording equipment. "On the night between the 14th and 15th of October," he recalled, "We were sure the Roller Bridge was an excellent fording technology, even though none of the Division's men had ever tested it."

* * *

Sharon worked hard to convince the senior officers crowded into Tasa HQ that his plan was feasible, stating that he was on schedule and that most of the fording equipment was already in hand. Yet he knew this was wishful thinking, since most of the machinery was stranded somewhere along the roads. As mentioned above, his plan was to deploy all of the bridges and to allow all forces to cross within one night.

The IDF's Chief of Staff commented on this, post factum: "I found the plan workable, though its schedule seemed overly optimistic. It was hard to believe that by 2300 hours two bridges would be deployed, yet I told him (Col. Even), that if we had one bridge by dawn, it's OK by me."

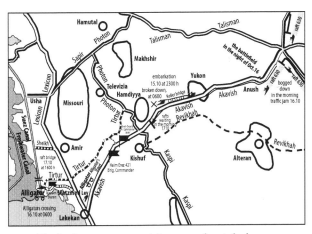

The fording equipment delivery on the night between October 16ᵗʰ and October 17ᵗʰ, 1973

While the 143ʳᵈ Division officers were working on their tactics, a considerable part of the fording equipment was being held up by traffic jams, mostly on the roads to and from Tasa. By October 15th, 1000 hours, in the midst of an operational briefing held by the Deputy Division Commander Col. "Jacky" Even, it was found that none of the transportation units' officers attending the briefing knew the route to the canal. It was also unmarked, and, worst of all, mostly held by the enemy. So it was decided to assign the Southern Command Reconnaissance Team to mark the road with lights. At the end of the meeting, Even, who was in charge of all the logistic aspects of the crossing campaign, voiced his pessimism about the fording equipment's capability and availability. But, at 1500 hours, good tidings were received: the Alligators had cleared the Akavish Road.

6. WE'RE CROSSING TONIGHT!

October 15th, 1973, 162nd Division's War Room:

At 1013 hours, when Sharon's briefing was over, all ranking officers moved on, to the 162nd Division's War Room south of Tasa, where Major General "Bren" Adan presented his own plan. As opposed to the relatively orderly War Room of Tasa, Adan's was located outdoors, in some tent-covered APCs.

Joining the IDF's Armored Corps in 1956, Avraham "Bren" Adan had been a battalion commander during the 1957 Suez campaign, and since then, he had dedicated his career to the Armored Corps. During the 1967 Six-Day War he was already deputy to the division commander, Maj.-Gen. Avraham Yaffe. In 1968 he had headed an inter-divisional team which planned the defense of the Sinai. That year he was made the commander of the Sinai Armored Forces, and was in charge of forming the 162nd Armored Division and the construction of the Bar Lev Line Forts. He also participated in designing all of the crossing plans and of the relevant fording equipment, and commanded the massive pre-war training for the crossing of the canal. Since 1969 he had headed the IDF's Armored Corps, and had commanded the 162nd Armored Division, with a combination of regular troops and reservists serving as its core. By October 1973, Adan was about to leave his command and the army, yet the fires of war greeted him instead of a farewell, so he rejoined his troops.

He had a rather complicated relationship with Southern Command Commander Maj.-Gen. Gonen. When the war broke out, Adan was surprised to find himself as a subordinate to his former subordinate, whom he wasn't especially appreciative of, and whom he appreciated even less after the disastrous IDF counter attack of October 8th. Failing in his mission, "Bren" had placed much of the blame on Gonen's unrealistic, vague and constantly changing commands. He referred to Gonen's generalship, with blunt sarcasm, as "cycling": pushing those under him hard, while acting with deference toward his superiors. Bren wasn't happy with the way Gonen disciplined his subordinates. Disapproving of his meteoric promotion, he warned the Chief of General Staff, David Elazar, that, "such officers are out of place in the IDF." On the eve of Gonen's promotion to Southern Command Commander, "Bren" stated Gonen was "unripe for the job." Yet, Maj.-Gen. Adan was a soldier, so once the decision was made he complied with it, maintaining a businesslike relation with Gonen throughout the war.

Adan gave his October 15th briefing battle scarred, exhausted and depressed by everything he had gone through since October 6th. It was he who bore the major brunt of the October 8th counterattack and the responsibility for its failure. Later on, he would write about his October 8th experience this way:

"We were dead tired, depressed by the blows we'd taken, yet steadfastly resolved to fight on."* Indeed, Adan was sure the planned Crossing maneuver and his division's assigned part in it would turn the tide of war. But, on October 15th, he had only a reduced division, of just two brigades, each with seventy tanks: the 460th, under Col. Gabi Amir, and the 217th, under Col. Natan "Natkeh" Nir. His third brigade, under Col. Arieh Keren, had been usurped, to serve as Southern Command's reserve force. His divisional staff consisted of Armored Corps staff members. "Bren's" deputy, Paratroopers Brig.-Gen. Dov "Dovik" Tamari, preferred battlefield command to handling logistics, so this was left to his chief of staff, Col. Ami Radian.

It was planned that the 162nd Division would join the campaign during the decisive fighting stage, after the bridgehead was already established. Accordingly, the decisive fighting was to achieve the surrender of all Egyptian forces west of the canal, in a perimeter codenamed Goshen, stretching from the breaching point, at Deversoir, to the city of Suez. Adan planned a rapid sickle-like maneuver southwards, through Genifa Hills, all the way to Suez, dealing with the pockets of resistance later. Once his forces had assumed a semicircular line around Suez, the entire Egyptian 3rd Army, with its back against the canal, would be encircled by Bren's Division, on the west bank, and by Kalman Magen's 252nd Division on the east bank. Bren assigned the 460th Armored Corps Academy Division, under Col. Gabi Amir, to be the first to cross the canal westward. Having taken heavy losses from the Egyptian attack of October 6th and the October 8th counterattack, it had

---

* Adan, *On Both Banks*, p.115.

recovered, and was reinforced with restored or newly formed battalions. Amir was an experienced tank commander, with a long list of senior commands in his record: during the Six-Day War, he had commanded a battalion of the 7th Armored Brigade, and after the war, commanded the entire brigade. In 1972, he was made the IDF's Armored Corps Academy Commander, and had led its commanders and cadets to the Sinai. By Bren's plan, Amir's brigade was assigned with crushing the Egyptian defenses on the west bank of the canal, once it was crossed.

Amir's brigade was to be followed westward by the 217th Brigade, under Col. Natan "Natkeh" Nir. That reserve brigade, too, had taken hard blows from the Egyptians on October 8th. Nir even had some physical scars from previous battles. Sustaining a serious injury in the Battle of Um Kataf, during the Six-Day War, he underwent dozens of surgeries and became an iconic figure for the Armored Corps and the entire IDF. In 1971, against all odds, he resumed his combat active service, achieving the rank of brigade commander in 1972. Adan assigned Nir's brigade to push southwards, alongside Amir's, to Genifa and Suez City.

After Adan had fully presented his plan, Southern Command Commander Bar-Lev, stressed that the brigade's top priority assignment was the destruction of Egyptian SAM batteries, which was a precondition to any land forces advancement. No one disagreed.

At 1405 hours, the Chief of General Staff and his companions returned to Dvelah, Southern Command HQ. Amidst all that, they found time to promote Gonen's deputy, Uri Ben Ari, to Brigadier-General. That promotion was highly significant, since Ben Ari had been Elazar's superior toward the end of the 1948 War of Independence, and had to leave the army in the late 1950s under unpleasant circumstances, while being considered for a most senior, actually *the* most senior command. An emergency appointee at the Beersheba HQ of Southern Command, assigned just a few minutes before the fighting broke out, Ben Ari served as the butt for the front commander's tantrums during the first days of fighting. As Ben Ari put it, "Major General Gonen found it very hard to make any unbiased conclusion or estimation, due to the atmosphere of terror in the War Room. So what did I do? I brought order to the War Room."

Assigning Lt.-Gen. Bar Lev as theater commander on October 10th was the right thing at the right time. Many of his contemporary Armored Corps commanders were either his acquaintances or previous subordinates, and his authority kept the War Room functioning in an orderly manner. Now it was time to repay Ben Ari, a Palmach veteran and an experienced tank commander, who had led the 7th Armored Brigade during the Sinai campaign, for an old debt.

While the preparations for the promotion ceremony were under way, the Southern Command commander saw fit to complain to the Chief of General Staff about the conduct and operations of the 143rd Division's Commander Major General Ariel Sharon. He complained about Sharon having his entourage of journalists serving his personal glory, about his disregard for and disobedience of orders, and about his failing to report his division's conduct to Southern Command. To support his complaints, Gonen recalled the October 9th events when Sharon had pushed to cross the canal. This effort seemed to do little more than allow Gonen the opportunity to blow off steam.

After Ben Ari's promotion ceremony, the Chief of General Staff made a phone call to his deputy, Major General Israel Tal, in the GHQ, informing him of the final decision concerning the crossing: it was to be that night, the Chief of Staff remaining in the Sinai to monitor the campaign.

7. MOVE OUT!

14th Brigade HQ, Tasa, October 15th, 1973:

The 14th Brigade's commander, Col. Amnon Reshef, entered the HQ's briefing hall at Tasa HQ, codenamed "Yalta," with his hair disheveled and his glasses coated with dust. Seeing him, the Brigade's battalion commanders stood at attention. Amnon Reshef, 35, had been an Armored Corps serviceman since 1956. He was a tank crewman through and through: persistent, strict, courageous, pedant. He spent the War of Attrition in Sinai, as the 189th Reconnaissance Battalion's commander, and since 1972 had been stationed in the Sinai as the 14th Brigade's commander. On October 6th, his brigade sustained the first Egyptian assault, with all its battalions and companies struggling to survive. But, like a phoenix, the brigade reappeared in the war theater on October 15th, in full force.

Reshef reviewed those sitting opposite him. Most of them were, in a way, regenerations: the 184th Battalion's commander, Col. Almog, replaced Maj. Shaul Shalev, who had been killed on October 9th; 79th Battalion Commander, Col. Amram Mitzna, replaced Col. Moni Nitzani who had been wounded in action on the second day of fighting. Reconnaissance Battalion commander, Maj. Yoav Brome, replaced the killed Col. Benzion Carmeli. Next to them, sat three infantry forces' commanders assigned to the operation: 87th Reconnaissance

Battalion commander, Col. Moshe Spector; Officers Academy Cadets Battalion Commander, Maj. Zamir, and Maj. Shmuel Arad, commander of Shmulik Force Paratroopers unit. Due to the intense schedule and the late grouping of forces, two commanders recently assigned to the Brigade were absent. One of these was the 407th battalion commander, transferred from the 600th Brigade, Captain Yeshayahu Beitel. He replaced Lt.-Col. Oved Maoz whose brother had been killed in action. The other was Maj. Natan Shunari, a reservist paratroopers' force commander. These two officers had managed to join the operating force just before it was launched. The paratroopers' battalion joined the operation quite accidentally, after its commanders had been long looking for action, and had to use their connections with Division Commander Sharon, to be allowed to join the 14th Brigade's forces.

As Reshef would later tell it, "On October 15th, I arrived at the Division HQ to attend to some business, and saw two men walking about. They were Micha Kapusta and Natan Shunari. When I asked what they were doing there, they told me they were looking for some action. Hearing this, I told them, 'You've got it.' I went to Sharon, asking him for the Reconnaissance Battalion, and got it."

Preparing for the operation, the brigade swelled nearly to a reduced division, with four tank battalions, seventy-nine tanks, and first-rate infantry forces.

Reshef presented to his audience the brigade's assignments during the crossing maneuver: advance as secretly as possible northward, seize the launching zone on the east bank in a nighttime attack; clear Akavish, Nahala and Tirtur roads for IDF forces, and support the seizing of the west bank by firing from the east bank. Then, the brigade was to stand by for crossing the canal following the 421st Brigade under Haim Erez, and hand over the securing of the Passages to the 600th Brigade under Tuvia Raviv.

There was very meager intelligence regarding the Egyptian force opposing the brigade at the Lexicon-Tirtur Junction. Intelligence Captain Vardi stressed, during the briefing, he had no detailed information on the size, composition or armament of the opposing force. This Intelligence lacuna was filled in the midst of the battle, when the junction was found out to be a dense Egyptian battalion defense line facing south, towards the brigade's advance. The perimeter included tanks, AT arsenal, bazookas, AT small arms, and mines. The Egyptians considered it a flanking defense. Though the 14th Brigade had prepared for a battle, it wasn't of this kind.

Eventually, the brigade achieved all its objectives: the securing of the launching zone on the east bank, the clearing of Akavish and Tirtur roads for the IDF, advancing eastward, and supporting the forces already across the Suez by firing westward. Its achievement had depended on crushing the Egyptian defended perimeter which no one had any idea about.

On the other hand, the briefed officers were handed out maps of Cairo, and instructed on how to handle the Sager missile, that menace of an anti-tank weapon used by camouflaged Egyptian infantry teams and seriously taking its toll on Israeli forces during the first days of fighting. Now, at least, some way to deal with it had been found.

Thus, on the night of the thrust, the brigade was to spread out in three different directions, carrying out three different missions: securing a bridgehead by thrusting northward; securing the east bank by moving westward, and securing the roads by moving eastward. Even a brief examination of its assignments would have shown this burden to be most heavy, if not unbearable.

At 1600 hours the brigade left its assembly perimeter, codenamed Yukon, moving towards Kaspi road. Fifteen minutes before embarking, at 1745 hours, Reshef addressed the 87th Reconnaissance Battalion men: "What we have to do now is to crush the Egyptian Army. So far, due to circumstances, we have had no opportunity to throw it off balance. We plan to hit their flank and rear. Following us, two armored divisions are to invade Egypt. We believe this wedge we are to drive at the enemy's throat will crush them—maybe not in one day, but it will crush them, throwing them off balance and gradually breaking them. This afternoon, I had a chat with the Chief of General Staff and top brass members, and I inspired them with confidence. I only could have inspired them with such confidence after I had seen you in action. The entire nation is behind you!"

Suddenly, some reservist raised his hand to ask a question: "Brigade-commander, sir, before we go to fight, could you please place the entire nation before us?"

And all the guys yelled "Move out!"

Though this is what the warriors said with their mouths, their gut feeling was different. As Captain Rami Matan, commander of the 79th Battalion's 7th Company would later tell it: "I knew I would not survive the battle which awaited us. It felt hard, like a decisive battle, yet it also felt like elation, since at last, we were on the offensive." As another combatant recalled, "My strongest memory of all that was the constant fear. Just fear, which, fortunately, was not a paralyzing one." Another confessed: "I heard myself talking to myself saying: Look at the sun really good, since this is the last time you will have to see it." In one officer's words, "We knew we were going into a battle we cannot survive."*

8. EREZ IS IN TROUBLE!

Col. Haim Erez, the 421st Armored Brigade commander, was assigned with delivering the fording machinery to the waterfront. Though it wasn't what the brigade had been trained to do, Haim accepted the assignment, and on October 15th in the afternoon, gave an operational briefing to Engineering Corps officers at Tasa HQ. He found them a bunch of confused men who had to muster the fording equipment to the canal from all over the western Sinai. "So what do you think?" Erez asked them. "How should we do it?" His listeners scratched their heads, replying: "Do as you please!" He realized he should better assign the delivery of these dedicated units to his own battalion commanders, whom he trusted. The 421st Armored Brigade started preparing for its part in the crossing campaign as early as October 15th, when the 257th Battalion, under Lt.-Col. Ben Shoshan was assigned with the task of towing the Roller Bridge. On October 15th, the 264th Battalion, under Maj. Giora Lev, was assigned with delivering the Unifloat pontoons and escorting the Alligators Battalion. Only the 599th Battalion, under Maj. Ami Morag, remained free of any assignment, so it was planned that he would cross first once a bridge was completed.

---

* Berti Ohayon, *We're Still There,* [in Hebrew], Kineret Zmorah-Bitan Publishers, 2008. P.124.

Erez's Brigade was a recently formed reservist brigade, and most of its men were doing their first reserve duty in the war. But they were not entirely inexperienced in battle, since most of its combatants had spent their regular service in the War of Attrition. Others had been demobilized as late as August 1973, and had enjoyed a couple of peaceful days. When the war broke out, the brigade was still being formed, so it still lacked a significant portion of its logistic system and its equipment was dispersed. Its commander, Col. Haim Erez, was well acquainted with the Sinai. During the Six-Day War, he had succeeded the 79th battalion commander, Ehud Elad, who had been killed, and had played a key role in the successes of the 7th Armored Brigade. He then served in the Sinai during the War of Attrition, as the 14th Brigade's deputy commander, and later, in 1972, was assigned with forming the 421st Brigade.

On the night between the 14th and 15th of October, the brigade was still stationed in its bivouacs, positioned along Talisman road, in the Central Sector, away from the planned campaign's theater of battle. While plans were being drawn and the forces gathered, the brigade had to drive its forces to the assembly perimeter codenamed Yukon, on Akavish road. On the afternoon of October 15th, Erez revealed to his officers that "We're crossing tonight," sending them to muster all the Engineering Corps machinery and deliver it to the various assembly points. He ordered them to meet again at 1700 hours, when he intended to give them the full details of the plan.

Col. Tuvia Raviv, 600th Brigade commander, was assigned by Sharon for a secondary, deceptive attack. It was to attack westwards, on the Egyptian force positioned on the edge of the perimeter codenamed Missouri. This was in order to divert Egyptian forces from the planned causeway and the main effort against Matzmed perimeter, thus allowing the 14th Brigade's thrust northwards, clearing Akavish and Tirtur roads.

Thirty-nine-year-old, Yugoslavian-born Raviv had served in the Armored Crops since being drafted, in 1952. In the 1956 Sinai campaign, as a company commander, he was seriously wounded, and when he recovered, he served as the aide of the Armored Corps Commander at the time, Haim Bar Lev. During the 1967 Six-Day War, he commanded a tank battalion, and in 1971 was promoted to 600th Brigade Commander.

The mission, though secondary, involved reorganization. The 407th Battalion commander, Lt.-Col. Oved Maoz, had suffered his brother being killed in action and his brother-in-law captured, so Raviv was ordered to demobilize him. He was replaced by his deputy, Captain Yeshayahu "Shaya" Beitel. Right after his assignment, Beitel was reassigned to the 14th Brigade's Command, under Amnon Reshef. He arrived at Tasa for Reshef's afternoon briefing, breathless, and was told his force should follow the 79th and 184th Battalions, and be used for mopping up the area between Tirtur and Akavish roads.

The brigade's other two battalions, namely the 409th and 410th, under Raviv, had a somewhat vaguely defined assignment. The planned deceptive attack had no specific territorial objectives, but only "pushing west while fighting" toward the Egyptian-held Missouri perimeter, advancing towards Televizia perimeter, formerly an Israeli Stronghold. As Sharon put it: "At 1700 hours, at Hamdiyya ridge, the 600th Brigade would initiate a head-on offensive towards Missouri, with two battalions only, supported by an artillery unit. Purpose: deception. Let it go as far as it gets."

After the war, the commanders of the 409th and 410th couldn't say what exactly their mission had been, either a deceptive attack or a combat patrol, aimed at raiding and intelligence gathering. After the war, when the 409th Battalion Commander, Maj. Ben Yitzhak, was asked whether he knew the purpose of that night ride, he said he still had no idea.

9. MATT'S FORCE

The battle-hardened 247th Reservist Paratroopers Brigade, under Col. Dani Matt arrived at the Southern Command on October 10th, and was engaged in minor tasks near the Mitla Pass, such as securing positions and chasing Egyptian units. Its somewhat elderly commander, at 45, was a legendary paratrooper. He had gone through the 1950s Reprisals, the 1956 Battle of the Mitla as a deputy battalion commander, had commanded the 80th Paratroopers Brigade in the Golan Heights in the Six-Day War, and the Regular Paratroopers Brigade in 1968. Since 1969, he had been commanding the 55th Brigade, reassigned as the 247th. Under Col. Mordechai "Motta" Gur, his predecessor as commander, it had conquered East Jerusalem in the 1967 Six-Day War. In addition to being a battle-hardened warrior, Matt was also a close friend of Major General Sharon.

Due to its unusual size, the brigade was split up, when its 564th Battalion, under Lt.-Col. Yossi Yaffe, was reassigned to reinforce the Baluza area, assigned mostly with securing the road to Fort Budapest. Later on, infantry forces, especially paratroopers, were increasingly needed to handle the AT missile attacks by Egyptian infantry. So a company under Capt. Benzion Weiner was sent to reinforce the 217th Armored Brigade.

The battalions remaining under Dani Matt were the 565th Battalion, commanded by the Bravery Award ("Ott Ha'oz") owner Lt.-Col. Dan Ziv; the 416th Battalion, commanded by Lt.-Col. Zvi "Zviki" Nur, the Brigade's Reconnaissance Battalion and Engineers Company. All of the commanders of these units, just like most of their men, were battle-hardened paratroopers.

During the first days of fighting, the brigade's men were just walking about the desert, looking for action in vain. Then, they were airlifted to Refidim, where they served as the Southern Command's reserve and were stationed in Baluza, where they had little to do. Thus, the job allotted to the brigade as part of the crossing campaign was to make up for many days of frustration.[*]

The brigade was trained to be the first part of the 143rd Division to cross the canal by boats, as early as in the prewar training. The plan was even submitted to Southern Command Commander Shmuel Gonen, when he assumed command. Therefore, the very redeployment of the brigade southwards was a sure sign the crossing was near.

When the brigade was positioned near the Mitla Pass there were several suggestions, some rather bizarre ones, on how to deploy it. For example, in October 11th, Gonen planned to assign a part of the brigade, about one battalion strong, with a combat patrol near the Chinese Farm, a rather suicidal mission, considering the size of Egyptian forces in the field. Sharon recalls how this mission was aborted: "On the night between the 10th and 11th of October, at 1900 hours, 2 paratrooper officers came

---

[*] For further details about the 247th Brigade's part in the War, see Israel Harel, *Operation Valiant* [in Hebrew], the Brigade's publication, 1974.

to me. One of them was the 247th Brigade's Reconnaissance Force Commander, a very nice fellow. When I asked them what they wanted, they told me they wanted permission for a patrol in Amir and Missouri perimeters. When I asked what for, they told me the 247th Brigade, under Southern Command's orders, should, the next day, carry out an infantry attack on these two perimeters! I felt really sorry for those guys. When asked whether they had ever been there, or had any acquaintance with the field, they told me they didn't. So I told them I was terribly sorry, but I couldn't authorize that patrol, since we had ambushing forces all over the place."

By early Friday, October 12th, Brigade Commander Danni Matt was especially flown to Dvela HQ, where he joined the Command's team planning the crossing. Meeting him in the conference room, the front commander greeted him, laying a hand on his shoulder and solemnly announcing that the brigade was given its original assignment, that of the crossing force, as part of the 143rd Division. Right afterward, the brigade commander and his staff members were told to board the helicopter flying Sharon back to his Tasa HQ. Then, together with the divisional staff, they started planning the crossing.

Practically, the 247th was the only brigade that had made long-term preparations for the crossing. It started preparing for it as early as Saturday, October 13th, when stationed at the Mitla Pass. On Sunday, October 14th, at midnight, it was ordered to move to the pre-crossing assembly zones, on the Refidim-Tasa road, about fifteen kilometers east of Tasa. While the brigade was waiting, its commander spent the 15th of October at operational briefings and divisional staff planning meetings, alongside Ariel Sharon.

Danni Matt and his staff struggled with two problems yet unsolved: one, the shortage of halftracks, and another one, the failure to meet the fording boats, by which they were to cross the 160 meter wide Suez Canal. Both problems reflect the chaotic logistics during the crossing campaign, yet also the Israeli Command's resolution to handle it. According to the plan, the boats were to arrive at the brigade's assembly zone, on October 15th, at 2200 hours. Yet they failed to come on time. After the war, the paratrooper commanders argued that the boat-carriers, by some misunderstanding of their orders, had arrived at a point twenty kilometers away from the road where the paratroopers were waiting for them. Whatever the reason may be, by 1430 hours, a few hours before H-hour, there was no boat in sight. So Danni Matt approached an officer named Nakhman ("Nakhchik"), gave him a jeep and a radio, as well as the boat-carriers' frequency, telling him to "look for the war, and find the boats." He found the boats three kilometers away from Tasa. Now the men had to link up with the boats.

On October 15th, at 1530 hours, Matt summoned his men together on a sand dune, presenting the crossing plan, while drawing the routes with a stick in the sand. In his words: "Objective: the IDF launching a counteroffensive, taking the war to Egyptian territory. The brigade would cross the canal first, securing a four-kilometer-wide bridgehead on the west bank, bounded by the Freshwater Canal. This should allow for the construction of the bridges to be used by the armored forces to cross. The brigade should advance behind the 14th Brigade, which should clear the east bank of Egyptian forces. On October 15th, at 2000 hours, the boats, with the Engineers Company, should be launched, and five minutes later, the first Israeli trooper should set foot on Egyptian soil."

The brigades' command was engaged with a scramble for half-tracks throughout the morning of October 15th. Thanks to the resourceful commander of the 565th Battalion Staff Company, who managed to snatch thirty vacant half-tracks from the Refidim canteen, the 565th Battalion had basic means of transportation, though far below the brigade's needs.

At 1600 hours, Major General Sharon complained to Southern Command staff about the insufficient number of half-tracks delivered. Chief of staff, Asher Levi, claimed at least some of them were delivered. They were both right. The shortage of half-tracks generated several difficulties: first, the men were overcrowded in the available vehicles, which reduced the 565th combat column to a practically non-combatant, vulnerable column. Secondly, 416th Battalion, under "Zviki" Nur, had to travel in unarmored vehicles, and therefore couldn't join the first wave of attack. Thirdly, it significantly reduced the crossing force's order of battle. So the plans were immediately adjusted. As 2nd deputy brigade commander Arik Achmon recalls, "At 1545 hours, I realized I could not muster my force, since my reconnaissance unit had no halftracks. I rushed to the brigade commander, reporting that to him. The battle plan was changed right away: Yedudah Bar, the 1st deputy brigade commander, undertook both the supervising of the boats' crossing, as well as the seizure and clearing of the bridgehead.* Meanwhile, Zviki Nur's battalion, too, was found to have had no half-tracks, and only a fraction of the brigade could be moved. In other words, after delivering the first crossing

---

*   Harel, ibid.

force, the available half-tracks had to cross back, to carry Nur's battalion forming the second wave. These changes had been communicated to the commanders audibly, shortly before the troops mounted the vehicles. At 1600 hours the brigade finally moved, without yet meeting the boats.

10. THE BRIDGES ARE ALMOST IN PLACE.

Three different fording technologies competed for the crossing: The Roller Bridge, Unifloat pontoons, and the Alligators. Of those, the Roller Bridge was definitely the favorite. It seemed to be the most available for immediate use, although it had been constructed at Yukon perimeter, some distance from the canal. Despite its availability, it had another "minor" problem: nobody was quite sure, though everybody hoped it could survive the entire twenty-seven kilometer long journey to the canal.

Lt.-Col. Shimon Ben-Shoshan, commander of the 421st Brigade's 257th Armored Battalion, assigned with delivering the Roller Bridge, had demonstrated that miracle of technology no earlier than October 14th, a day before D-Day. He was the only person to have ever seen a demonstration or training exercise using that bridge prior to the war. The October 14th training preparation took place at night, and involved a two or three kilometers long towing. Beside Ben-Shoshan's men, the deputy division commander, Col. Yaakov "Jacky" Even, Col. Menashe "Georgie" Gur, Deputy Chief Engineers Officer of the crossing campaign, Lt.-Col. Hannan "Johnny" Tenne, Southern Command Command's Engineers Officer, and other Engineering Corps officers, were all huddled next to the Bridge.

As Ben Shoshan recalls, "We summoned the entire battalion, and, with flashlights and a sketch, explained to them the bridge's features and construction, how to tow it and how this whole thing works. And it all happened in pitched dark, with firing from all directions. According to the procedure, the bridge should have been towed by no more than eight tanks, including the rear securing tank. Following Georgie's idea, we used ten tanks, believing it should work. When we went downhill, the bridge started rolling on and on. With nothing to stop it, it just ran over the tanks towing it. On top of that, the men were dead tired. By the time I gave the command: 'Get ready, move!,' three would have fallen asleep. In short, it was the bridge that pulled the tanks, instead of them pulling the bridge. We had many mishaps all the way. It had been running wild for three kilometers until we reached level ground. Then we managed to halt it, and camouflaged it in the morning."

The other fording means, Unifloat pontoons, were still parked about forty kilometers away from the assembly area, somewhere on Paduy Road, between Refidim and Artillery Road. That morning, the 264th Battalion's deputy commander, Maj. Ilan Maoz was sent there, with twelve tanks, to tow them. Meanwhile, the much more mobile Alligators Battalion made its way, laboriously, toward Tasa.

Col. Haim Erez who could see the wider picture, doubted whether he could deliver the required means within the available timeframe. He thought the crossing would have to be postponed for twenty-four hours, so he shared his views with Division Commander Sharon. To this, Sharon sarcastically replied that he feared two things might happen: "Either the Egyptians might change positions, or our leaders might change their mind. So we have to cross with whatever we've got."

* * *

After the sleepless night of October 14th, on the morning of October 15th, 257th Battalion was busy preparing for the towing. Ben Shoshan possessed twenty-four tanks; four bulldozers traveling ahead of the bridge, and another four behind it; a reconnaissance team in the van, clearing the road; APCs securing the flanks, and a horde of tractors on the left flank. It all amounted to a gigantic 100 meter wide column trying to reach the canal within six hours.

Meanwhile, the Unifloat pontoons of the 605th Regular Battalion, traveling to the canal from Baluza, northern Sinai, were bogged down on the north-south Kartisan Road, which was also jammed with Adan's 162nd Division's transportation units. Since it would take at least twelve pontoons to construct a crossable bridge, there were concerns about the pontoon reserve being insufficient, in case some of the 630th Battalion's twelve pontoons were damaged. The entire road between Yukon and Kartisan road, serving as the main logistics route, was stuffed with vehicles. "I must say that on that very night I already realized the pontoons wouldn't get to the tanks on time," Sharon would later confess.

The 605th Pontoon Battalion Commander Lt- Col. Leshem, had to deliver the pontoons from Baluza, up north, by the Kartisan road, in a sixty-kilometer-long journey, all the way to the assembly point at Yukon perimeter. After the war, he had a bellyful of complaints about that campaign. This is how he saw that drive: "Early in the morning of October 15th, I received the only order concerning the crossing. A dispatcher came from the HQ of Col. 'Alush' Noy, 275th Brigade Commander, telling me to get the pontoons to Tasa. It was the only command concerning the Crossing I had received throughout the entire war. The route from Baluza, where we parked the pontoons, to Tasa junction was sixty kilometers long. In all of our training sessions, it had taken two tanks to tow a pontoon, but there were just a handful of tanks in the entire Baluza sector. When the Division was ordered to allot us tanks for towing the pontoons, they did everything they could to not give us those tanks. They sent them bit by bit. Eventually, I only got eleven tanks for towing twelve pontoons, so I had to abandon one pontoon because I had no tank to tow it. The Paton tank proved a difficult towing vehicle. The pontoons were parked on sand surfaces, and one had to cross 200 meters of quicksand to get there. The 605th Battalion's main struggle was with towing all of the pontoons through the sands. All we were told to do was deliver the pontoons to Tasa, with no schedule or anything else. I estimated that the travel time would take fifteen hours, traffic jams not included. The pontoon-construction teams rode in buses following the pontoons. The tanks struggled with the towing, one pontoon running over a tank. On the morning of October 15th, the 162nd Division's logistics vehicles entered the road, and this is when it got disastrous. There was some 'general' who ordered that the pontoons be pushed off the road with bulldozers, so they got bogged down in the sand, and just 'stood their ground' for a couple of days. We couldn't pull them out even with six tanks. We tried to couple three bulldozers and more tanks to them, and four tanks had their towing hooks torn off. I kept yelling at the chief of my staff all the time, and he said 'Good Lord, I am willing to tow the pontoons with my bare hands, I am a healthy fellow.' Thus, only three pontoons joined the 630th Battalion in Tasa. Another five were left bogged down along the road."

* * *

So the hope of acquiring any available pontoons lay elsewhere. On October 15, at 1100 hours, Battalion Commander Giora Lev sent his deputy, Major Ilan Maoz, with twelve tanks to tow the pontoons of the 630th Battalion from the hellhole where they were gathered, tens of kilometers away from the Yukon assembly point. It involved towing them on the north-south road, then, along Akavish Road, all the way to Yukon, twenty-seven kilometers away from the canal. To that purpose Maoz was given tanks most of which he referred to as "dead." As he recalled: "We got to the assembly zone at about 1300 hours. I was met by the Engineers Battalion Deputy Commander who explained to me how it works: to let every tank approach a pontoon and tow it."

Two hours later, at about 1500 hours, the column started off, entering Paduy Road, then, to Mavdil Road, northwards, with no special difficulties. But then the battalion commander, Major Giora Lev, went on the radio telling his deputies to urgently join him on Akavish Road, adding that he didn't believe the force could get through, "since it's bedlam out there." About eight kilometers away from Tasa, the force had to stop. All kinds of units were gathered on the road, including elements of the 162nd Division, so the pontoons were stalled among the Divisional logistics columns and the 143rd Division's ammunition trucks.

As Maoz recalls: "What was jamming the road were mostly the logistics vehicles. I remember the driver of Armored Corps Commander wouldn't move his Gladiator Jeep aside. I gave the command to push all the vehicles jamming the road the hell out of there, just to let us through. At 1700 hours, I reached

Tasa Junction, on Akavish Road. About five kilometers away from Tasa, a helicopter landed carrying a grey-haired brigadier-general with a black beret and GHQ insignia [it was Uri Ben Ari]. He told me to stop, saying we were crossing tonight, and that the success of the crossing depends on me. He also promised to clear the road. I never saw him again."

By the time, he got to Tasa Junction, at 1800 hours, Maoz had only managed to deliver two pontoons, but by then one of the tank's towing cables was torn off, and the pontoon blocked the road. Getting the pontoon detached and cleared off the road was a complicated, time-consuming operation. All kinds of generals, including the chief engineer officer, were huddled around Maoz, all offering useless tips. One of them suggested a detour through the sands. When they tried it, they got bogged down. Maoz was desperate. Nothing seemed to be moving through the junction. Hours later, the column had gotten on to Akavish Road, but that, too, was absolutely jammed, with no vehicles getting through. "Occasionally", Maoz recalls, "I just shot to the side, to get through. It was that bad. Buses, mobile kitchens, and mobile water tanks, an entire world of vehicles just stood on that road."

Eventually, the pontoons got stuck a few kilometers west of Tasa, and were not able to meet the crossing's deadline.

* * *

The only unit capable of making the crossing, which had successfully made it to the Yukon storage area, on the morning of October 15th, was the Alligators battalion. As early as October 14th, their commander, Lt.-Col. Igal Yaniv, was summoned to Tasa for an operational briefing, where he was informed about the planned crossing operation. His battalion, which had been assembled a couple of days earlier, on Paduy Road, used its relative maneuverability and independence of towing vehicles effectively, in order to make itself fully available to the division. At 1700 hours, moving on its own, overtaking all kinds of obstacles, it reached Yukon, where it completed preparations for taking to the water, and was assigned to the 264th Armored Battalion. As one of its officers explained on a radio show following the war, "We always knew we would be the first to cross. We were mobile, self-reliant, and dependent on no one."

Haim Erez, the commander of the brigade in charge of the towing of the means of fording, had other challenges to deal with. In addition to the towing, navigating the Roller Bridge, launching it into the water, and determining the location for the launching.

Initially, the Roller Bridge was planned to be launched into the canal north of Tirtur Road, near its 95th kilometer. The trouble was that this route, except that segment, was not marked or prepared for traffic. To solve the direction problems, a special task force was formed, led by Col. Amazia "Pazi" Hen, formerly the commander of Shaked Reconnaissance Unit. Its job was to post road signs on the route, find the challenging parts, and deliver the bridge to its destination. It was to detect a sewage pipe on the east bank of the canal and mark the approach route to it.

Another problem emerged during the preparation of the road. It was entirely crisscrossed with ditches, and nobody knew how it had been affected by a week of fighting. Therefore, "Patzi's" force, which was to mark the road westwards, was to be followed by some bulldozer tanks, which were to prepare the road for traffic, filling up the ditches and clearing away obstacles.

In addition, there was the problem of delivering cumbersome, vulnerable units through enemy territory yet to be cleared. It meant they would have to be taken there during an armored nighttime attack, in which the tanks advance, leaving behind them pockets of resistance. It meant the brigade had to allot a considerable force to secure the fording machinery on their way to the waterfront. It referred mostly to the Roller Bridge, which took 12 tanks to tow, and another 12 tanks and an APC company to secure its flanks. Meanwhile, the Bridge was being delivered and secured, but not completely, since it had to be secured against landmines. Therefore, the bridge was coupled to a flail tank driving in front of it, followed by several bulldozer tanks planned to sweep for potential landmines with their buckets.

The fording units were to advance by two routes: the 257th Battalion, under Ben Shoshan, carrying the Roller Bridge, by Tirtur Road, to the launching point, 95.5 kilometers away; and the Alligators and Unifloat pontoons were to advance on Lexicon, Tirtur and Nahalah Roads, alongside the Paratroopers, in order to reach the crossing zone with enough time left to be used for securing the bridgehead. The 599th Battalion, under Maj. Ami Morag, was planned to advance on Tirtur Road, following the Roller Bridge, crossing the canal over it, and then dash forward, to seize the fords of the Freshwater Canal.

Now, after the plan's details had been agreed upon, Col. Erez told the deputy division commander: "I am taking charge of everything, asking for just one thing; assign the route-clearing to the divisional command." And route-clearing was the main challenge.

11. SHARON'S DECISION.

The clearing of the jammed routes was regarded as a major problem in Operation Valliant's command, yet it was by no means solved. Southern Command Command HQ hinted it was willing to take charge of the route-clearing and controlling the traffic, assigning this task to its Staff Officer, Col. Uri Bar Ratzon. After reaching the field of battle, he described what he saw this way: "Mavdil Route usually served Bren's maintenance units, which now had their supply and ordinance vehicles scattered all over the road. This was not to be thought of as something orderly. It was all mixed up, with the maintenance group and the brigades completely jamming the route.

"Whose fault was it? It was obvious: three divisions, as well as another ad-hoc one, were all operating here. All of the north-south routes of the Sinai were jammed to some extent. A fifteen ton truck, full of ammunition and fuel, stood alongside buses, mobile kitchens, canteens and every other kind of vehicle. The Front Command told me to deal with it, with no specific assignment. I was just charged with the Front Command's logistics, which empowered me to take control. The question was, could anyone have taken control? The answer was: no. No doubt, the responsibility for controlling the divisional combat was that of the Front Command's. Yet the Command couldn't have controlled all the roads in such an area. It was obvious. It had no means to do this job; no vehicles to move the traffic along the routes. I went to Refidim, where I knew there were some personnel whose job it was to lead columns. I met a fellow I knew there, whose job was to get the columns there from GHQ, and I knew these forces were under his command. I found their vehicles to have medium-range radios, so I assembled these units. Fortunately, I met some officers there whom I had known as my Officers Academy trainees long ago. They knew me, so at least I knew there were people whom I could talk to. So I assembled them, and the MP officer, giving them a sort of operational briefing. I had only five teams. I told them, our task was to guarantee the flow of traffic from Tasa all the way to the bridge crossing point. If we could muster more teams, we could try to control the north-south routes and the Refidim route as well."

Practically, controlling the traffic was almost exclusively the 143rd Division's responsibility. It was the 143rd who controlled the traffic teams under Col. David Maimon, and directed the movement of forces. Yet even that didn't prevent the chaos on the routes.

After the war, Gideon Altschuller, 143rd Division's Chief of Staff, testified that "it was absurd to think one could have delivered all that manpower, equipment, those vehicles of all kinds, all moving in different directions, through one route, and hope that it would go smoothly. It was absurd not to consider it in advance. For such a campaign, one should have built at least four or five parallel roads, to allow the troops to advance. Just taking care of all the logistics vehicles of three armored divisions is a terrible burden. Plus, we had to coordinate their movement with twenty pontoons travelling on the very same routes. Plus another armored division planned to move on those same routes to the bridgehead. And there were also command and control elements and the Front Command's maintenance units."

* * *

This was the situation as seen and recalled by Major General Sharon, a few minutes before the planned launch: "At 1600 hours it was obvious the pontoons wouldn't make it; the Roller Bridge was away from the canal, and only the Alligators could move on." Chief Engineer Officer Brig.-Gen. Ben Dov, described what he saw at 1700 hours, when riding a halftrack on Akavish Road, together with the 606th battalion commander and Col. David Laskov, of Yiftah Team:

"When we got to Tasa Junction, we had already seen some pontoons bogged down, amidst the long columns, some of Sharon's Division, and some of the 162nd Division, which had already started off. Amidst all that was Danni Matt's 247th Brigade, which was planned to cross the canal. And there were also supply, ammunition, artillery and other columns, all pouring into Akavish Road, heading for the canal."

Facing these circumstances, Major General Sharon had to decide whether to cross or not. He never had any doubts there must be a crossing, and that it was his division which should be crossing. As he recalled it: "There were a lot of hesitations throughout the campaign, at the front. At 1500 hours, an hour before departure, I told Bar Lev that all routes, north of Tasa were jammed, and that the pontoons were stuck. We'd been towing the pontoons for two days, trying, in vain, to get them onto Akavish Road. So Bar Lev asked me, 'What do you suggest?'". Sharon explains that he had gathered from this that Bar Lev was leaving it up to his discretion. As he explained it, "The die was cast." According to Sharon, he told Bar Lev: "It's tonight, for sure."

* * *

Sharon's decision to cross at all cost was triggered by not only his character. He had more than enough reasons to assume it could be done despite all challenges. Before departure, Sharon asked his deputy, Col. "Jacky" Even: "What is in place?"

"The Roller Bridge and the Alligators," Even replied.

Indeed, by 1500 hours it was clear that the Alligators had managed to reach Akavish Road, and the Roller Bridge had been fully prepared at the Yukon perimeter. The division's commanders were confident of the operational plan. The 14th Brigade, planned, in Phase I, to clear the launching zone of enemy forces and secure the approach routes, advancing eastwards; and the 600th Brigade, planned, in Phase II, to carry out the deceptive attack, assume their launching positions, and be at high alert. According to Intelligence reports, there were no indications of the Egyptian Army anticipating an Israeli attack, and surprise seemed achievable.

As Sharon recalled, "We knew that the Egyptian 16th Division had not changed its position, and that the 21st Division had lost over 100 tanks the day before. We knew exactly how it was arrayed. We also knew there were no enemy forces west of the canal. Therefore, I realized that any delay or change of the plan might result in us facing some armored brigade or battalion across the canal. This would have made the Crossing much costlier. So, I stepped into the decision-maker's shoes, deciding I must cross at once, since, so I thought, once we had a foothold on the other bank, no matter how tiny, we would have a great opportunity to develop our offensive maneuvers. Our trouble was breaking through Egyptian forces, so I think this logic was right. I believed that we should operate in a manner that kept the routes clear. It was unthinkable for us to be stopped during the most critical part of the campaign because of some unit's logistics vehicles.

"So I told Haim Bar Lev that I believed that the pontoons would not make it, since the roads were jammed. We discussed whether we should attack that night. I told Haim I would check it out once again. I was planning to move at 1600 hours, with my HQ, preparing for an attack planned to be initiated at 1700 hours. At 1545 hours, it was reported to me that the Alligators had gotten through and were ready to go. That same moment I told Haim that the Gillois were on their way, and that we already had the Roller Bridge. The pontoons wouldn't make it, so I would initiate the attack that night. Haim told me he thought the same, so we started off on the attack."

PART 3:

THE IDF IS
ON THE WEST BANK

1. THAT HOARSE, FAMILIAR VOICE.

143rd Division, October 16, 1700:
Operation Valiant started with a deception maneuver assigned to the 410th Battalion of the 600th Brigade, commanded by Maj. (res.) Yehudah Geller. Geller led his battalion westward to the Egyptian positions, near the abandoned Televizia stronghold, which had been taken by the Egyptians at the beginning of the war. From this position, the Battalion was to threaten an Egyptian force positioned west of the stronghold, in an area codenamed Missouri. The purpose of the attack was to make the Egyptian commander believe he was facing a westbound Israeli head-on attack, thus diverting him from what was going on in his rear, near Deversoir, formerly Fort Matzmed. The 14th Brigade, under Amnon Reshef, was to penetrate that area, advancing northwards, in order to secure a corridor for the crossing and threaten the rear of the Egyptian perimeter in Missouri.

As Col. (ret.) Yehudah Geller, commander of the 410th Battalion of the 600th Brigade later recalled, "We started off from

Akavish-Caspi Road by nightfall, heading northwest, at about 1700 hours. We crossed Tirtur Road near the abandoned Fort Televizia. We had tanks only, moving in very close formation, a column of companies, with me in the center. When we got to Televizia, we suddenly saw hundreds of (Egyptian) infantrymen running north in a panic."*

Division Commander Sharon got an initial report from 600th Brigade Commander, Col. Tuvia Raviv, about "raging fires" and panic among the Egyptians.

Southern Command HQ concluded the Egyptians had swallowed the bait. At 2100 hours, Chief of General Staff Elazar shared his appraisal of the situation with his deputy, Major General Tal. Both of them believed the enemy misunderstood the maneuvers in the crossing area.

Yet the feat of the 410th Battalion ended with a misadventure, when, on its way back to the launching point on Hamdiyah Hill, it found itself in a minefield.

As Geller recalls, "We drove on westward, fast, heading for the canal. It was dark, and suddenly, a tank hit a landmine. We found ourselves in a minefield. When we tried to move in a single column, another six tanks hit landmines, and could not be recovered. We got one man killed. The rest of the battalion managed to retreat to the Artillery Road, and from there, to Hamdiyah Hill, the brigade's assembly point, after a twenty kilometer night ride."** Yet this feat was just a sideshow.

---

*   An interview with Col. (ret.) Yehudah Geller
**   An interview with Col. (ret.) Yehudah Geller

The 600ᵗʰ Brigade's deception maneuver on the night between the 15ᵗʰ and 16ᵗʰ of October:
Nearly the entire Israeli High Command gathered in Dvelah HQ, including the Chief of General Staff and Defense Minister Dayan, who had made his entrance at 1745 hours. The tension ran high. Everything depended on the performance of Sharon's division. Using the communication devices attached to the walls, connected to the various brigades and field HQs, the attendees tried to keep up with the forces' movements, shifting the tactical markings on the gigantic maps covering the walls, accordingly. Communication with Sharon was carried out through Southern Command Commander Lt.-Gen. (res.) Haim Bar Lev and Front Commander Shmuel Gonen. The Chief of General Staff, David Elazar, only rarely joined in the communications: even at that critical moment one could sense the bad blood between General Sharon and his superiors. For some reason, Elazar considered it a proper time to enlighten the Defense Minister about Sharon's problematic behavior, including his habit of holding briefings for journalists and disobeying orders.* He referred, among other things, to a series of conflicts that had surfaced, mostly, on October 9ᵗʰ, when the Chief of General Staff and the Commander of Southern Command felt that Sharon was waging his private war. It wasn't the last time "the Sharon issue" was privately discussed between the Chief of General Staff and the Defense Minister during the crossing campaign. Dayan, as his biographer, Arieh Bar-On reported, was not happy to hear such words at that phase of the campaign. He also abhorred the sight of reporters and newspaper editors invited to Southern Command's HQ to hear

---

*   Bar On, p.185

high-ranking officers slandering Sharon. It seemed the major players had already gotten deep into a post-war public image battle. Yet the campaign's demands were more pressing.

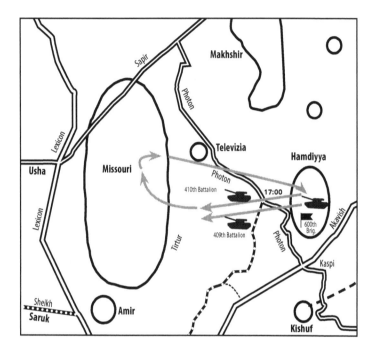

Shmuel Gonen, on his last briefing to the Defense Minister, before the forces were launched, estimated that the first Israeli tank would cross the canal even before 2200 hours; the first bridge would be launched into the water right after the bridgehead was secured and a corridor to it was secured; and that about 100 rubber boats, a number sufficient to carry the Paratroopers Brigade, would be launched into the water at 1900 hours. All these estimations were highly optimistic, and eventually proved to be wishful thinking.

That night belonged to the 143rd Division Commander, Major General Sharon. Nearly all major decisions made throughout the night were made by him. He controlled his forces from an APC in the front, alongside his Operations Officer, his Intelligence officer, Col. Sagi; Brig.-Gen Avraham "Abrasha" Tamir, and next to journalist Uri Dan. He was in control of the smallest details in the field, following his philosophy that a general may tell his subordinates what to do, but only if he is in the frontline, getting a firsthand impression of what is going on in the field. It was not just about setting an example, but a concept of generalship that to make a difference a commander must be in the most critical location for the success of the operation. "Though it was quite a challenge," Sharon would later confess, "I assumed I needed to be at the crossing zone, trusting my brigade commanders to get along on their own, everywhere else… The clearer that the subordinates can discern the general task, and the more they are aware that it is their responsibility and that they are expected to show initiative, the greater are the chances for success."

He also believed in giving the junior commanders a free hand. In his words, "You should brief them before the fight, and try not to interfere during the actual fighting, or to over-control them. If your subordinates are in trouble, they'll ask for your help. The greatest and most dangerous mistake is for commanders in the rear to dictate the smallest operational details. This is what bred all the misunderstandings between me and the Southern Command."

Sharon believed that the Command should have a control unit in the field, near the frontline, to coordinate the efforts of the two divisions planned to cross the canal. Nonetheless, he believed that the Front Command was unbearably interfering in his battlefield decisions.

Sharon's HQ usually moved on Akavish Road close to the vanguard where most of his forces were advancing toward the canal. Sometimes, he went even further than that. By dawn of October 16th, he appeared in person at the Matzmed perimeter, directing the fording forces from there. His familiar, hoarse, yet reassuring voice became just another element of that night.

By night, the complicated battle became difficult to read, and the division commander relied on reports of forces engaging the enemy and on his eyes, which struggled to peer through the dark. Meanwhile, he also attentively listened to sounds from the radio in his command APC. One of them was the voice of the front commander, urging him to keep up with the schedule. Others were calls for support and occasionally, for a rescue. On top of the terrible burden of a constantly malfunctioning communication system and the pressing need for solutions or to give commands to deal with the evolving situation, one had to clearly read the incoherent battle and correctly detect the difficulties suffered by the forces in the field. Above all, one needed resolution. And indeed, Sharon bet all his chips on one decisive move in the entire campaign: getting some kind of foothold on the west bank of the canal during that night. This affected all his decisions, regarding both the transportation routes as well as the advancement of forces across the canal. Sharon intentionally preferred to gain a foothold on the west bank, while postponing the clearing of the approach routes. It was a bet, but, so he believed, a calculated one. Yet the Southern Command officers, who grew increasingly concerned by the insufficient width of the causeway and the insufficiently cleared approach routes, did not share his thinking. This led to disagreements that would haunt the crossing campaign till its very end.

The deputy division commander, Col. Yaakov "Jacky" Even, was assigned with the overall responsibility for delivering the fording equipment to the canal. He had been an Armored Corps man through and through ever since his first day in uniform, back in 1951. During the 1956 Suez campaign he led a tank company and was awarded the Southern Command Commander's Decoration. In 1965, he started the first Israeli Patton tank battalion, of the 7th Armored Brigade. During the 1967 Six-Day War, he commanded the 520th Armored Brigade, which dashed through the Mitla Pass heading for Ras-Sudr. During the War of Attrition, he already held command of the 7th Brigade, the cream of the crop of the Israeli Armored Corps, and in 1973 he was made the deputy of ex-paratrooper Sharon, the 143rd Division commander. The encounter between the Armored Corps man and the paratrooper bred mutual respect resulting in productive cooperation.

Col. Even formed his ad hoc HQ on the night of October 15th, by mustering GHQ Col. Simha Maoz, Paratroopers Col. Amos Neeman, Major Ilan Oko, and a Signal Corps officer. That group rode during that night in an APC, along Akavish Road, handling all kinds of malfunctions, delays, and occasional problems. Col. Even spent most of that time near the Roller Bridge, but during later stages of the campaign he led the Alligators' column and the paratroopers' column. The most critical decision he had to make and carry out, according to Sharon's reading of the battlefield, while coordinating it with 421st Brigade Commander Hain Erez, was which of the fording means were to be moved, depending on their position on the roads and their movability.

Yet the problem was not just the technicality of movability, but also the routes' capability of sustaining all that traffic.

Throughout the twenty-four hours of crossing, one could feel the absence of a single command controlling the traffic, prioritizing movement and overcoming traffic jams. Southern Command charged several officers with handling the unbearable bottlenecks on the routes going to the Tasa end of Akavish Road, but their efforts proved to be fruitless.

Col. Even, as we said, saw that chaos first hand. Using his old acquaintances, he formed a control group made of some officers, including some senior in age and rank, who were mustered to his HQ or gathered there nearly by accident, such as Col. David Maimon. Even ordered them to take to the field and make sure the traffic ran free on the east-west road, Akavish, the main route to the canal. That group was an improvised unit, which the Division started ad hoc, and its performance was fitting of those circumstances. It resulted in a disastrous traffic jam with hundreds of vehicles: civilian buses, supplies, water trucks, and ammunition trucks, ambulances and jeeps, all stuck head-to-tail, unable to get off the road, jamming the already too narrow road. Making their way through all that, were the gigantic columns of combat vehicles—halftracks, tanks and Command cars. The forces towing the gargantuan pontoons, suffered most from the jamming of their routes, since anytime they got off the road it took a struggle to get them back on the route. Occasionally, these struggles ended with the pontoons left off the road. After the war, Gideon Altschuller, 143rd Division's Chief of Staff reflected on this frustrating situation in this way: "It was absurd to think one could have delivered all that manpower, those vehicles, and that equipment, of all kinds, all moving in different directions, through one route, while hoping that it would go smoothly." The traffic jam on the way to the canal was strongly impressed on the memory of all those driving toward it from those hours onward. Yet Major General Gonen saw it otherwise, explaining in retrospect that "We had a traffic controlling body, commanded by the Front's Chief of Staff. Yet it failed due to poor discipline." That is, due to a lack of prioritizing and to the crowded routes. All the while, the forces kept moving westward.

2. AS IF ALL HELL BROKE LOOSE.

14th Brigade, October 15, 1815 hours:
By the last rays of the setting sun, Col. Amnon Reshef, took a final look at the long armored column, arrayed by battalions, advancing from the Yukon perimeter toward the Brigade's assembly point at the 56th kilometer of Artillery Road. He trusted the enormous force in his possession, of nearly 100 tanks, and elite infantry troops, to carry out its assignment. As mentioned above, Reshef was assigned with securing the corridor for the crossing between Usha Road, in the north, and the abandoned Fort Lakekan—in the south, twelve kilometers away. The planned bridgehead, on the Perimeter of Fort Matzmet, north of the Great Bitter Lake, was in the middle. The 14th Brigade was to clear this perimeter of enemy forces, while advancing northward. Simultaneously, it was to move westward, clearing Akavish and Tirtur roads, the routes connecting the corridor to the crossing zone.

Reshef expected no unusual difficulties in seizing the East Bank. According to the latest intelligence report, there were no Egyptian armored forces along the north-south Lexicon Road, at least not at the Nahala-Lexicon and Nahala-Tirtur junctions, which connected Lexicon to the canal.

Reshef's operational theater was known as the Chinese Farm, a name IDF men fighting in Sinai had given to a farm located

east of the area where the canal continues north of the Great
Bitter Lake. It was the site of the Bitter Lakes Project, planned
by UNRWA and the Egyptian Government, for the settling of
homeless Bedouins and demobilized soldiers. It was planned
to be built in an area of about 8,400 acres, called the Farming
Strip. The plan was to build villages and farming centers,
irrigated by the Freshwater Canal running west of the Suez
Canal. Two large pump houses and tens of one-floor houses
were built in the Farm. On the IDF's operational maps it was
codenamed Amir, located south of the perimeter codenamed
Missouri. When the IDF occupied it, in the 1967 Six-Day War,
the troopers mistook the Japanese inscriptions on the pumps
for Chinese, thus naming the area the Chinese Farm. Yet in
1973, the IDF made much graver mistakes concerning this
perimeter.

The Chinese Farm boundaries were Sheikh Road on the
north, Yahfan Road in the south, Akavish-Tirtur Junction in
the east and Lexicon Road in the west. It was an upside-down
triangular area with its base in the north and its tip pointing
southwards. Its base was about six kilometers long, and its
western side, aligned with Lexicon Road, was about fifteen
kilometers long, making its area about fifty sq. km. it was all
crisscrossed with tens of irrigation ditches, the total length of
which was about 140 kilometers.*

---

*   14th Brigade's official website.

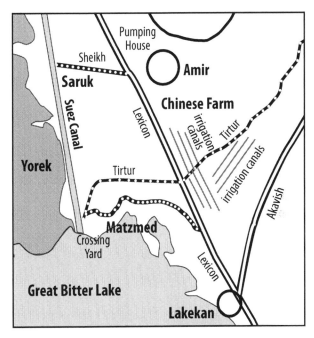

The Chinese Farm Diagram

At 1805 hours, exactly as planned, the 14th Brigade started advancing from its assembly point at the 56th kilometer of Artillery Road, about twelve kilometers east of the Crossing Compound. The armored vehicles drove straight, on rough roads, until they entered the east-west Lexicon Road. The 87th Reconnaissance Battalion, under Maj. Yoav Brome, led the armored column comprised of four armored battalions and three battalion-strong infantry forces. As mentioned above, the 87th was well acquainted with the route: six days earlier it had stealthily reached the waterfront near the abandoned Fort Lakekan, south of abandoned Fort Matzmed, thus revealing the breach between the second and third Egyptian Armies, between Fort Botzer and Akavish Road. On the morning of October

15th, it had already carried out a preliminary reconnoiter of the planned route, to verify its passibility.

Brome was the battalion's second commander. A single child, born in Kibbutz Shfayim, and a teacher in his civilian occupation, he had been already decorated for bravery as a Golani Infantry Brigade officer for his actions in the 1962 raid on Nuqeib on the Syrian held Golan Heights. At the conclusion of an Armored Corps war game, Major General Adan had referred to him as the best officer he had ever met. When war broke out, Brome was in the United States, yet he hastily returned to Israel, on October 8th, and was assigned to replace the Battalion Commander, Lt.-Col. Benzi Carmeli. The latter was killed at Hamdiyya Hill, while the Battalion was defending the Artillery Road, during the misfortunate battles of October 8th.

Driving toward Lexicon during such a dark night, was a serious navigation and movement challenge. Phosphorous rounds fired by an artillery battery at the abandoned Fort Lakekan illuminated their destination, making it easier to detect, yet the irrigation ditches crisscrossing the road impeded the vehicles. At 2200 hours the 87th Reconnaissance Battalion reached Lexicon Road, headed north, drove by Lakekan twenty minutes later, and carried out its assignment. Three of its companies split up, heading west by Sheikh, Nahalah and Tirtur Roads connecting Lexicon and the canal. The Battalion quite easily assumed positions north of the planned crossing zone at Matzmed perimeter. At 2045 hours, Brome reported that advancement on Shik road was unobstructed, and that his force's mission, securing the west flank of Lexicon Road, had been accomplished.*

---

*   14th Brigade's Radio network.
**   14th Brigade's Radio network.

Following the reconnaissance battalion, the armored column dashed on with its three armored battalions, the 79th, under Amram Mitzna, the 184th, under Avraham Almog, and the 407th under Yeshayahu Beitel, following each other. They were followed by the half-track mounted Shaked Reconnaissance Battalion, under Lt.-Col. Moshe Spector. He was told his main task was clearing the area after the armored forces broke through, so he was not too concerned. As he recalled, "I fully briefed my men, with a map only, with no aerial photographs or Intelligence reports. We thought, let's get up and go, and we'll manage." He was also given an Officers Academy cadets' company. In the rear, half-track mounted, was the 582nd Paratroopers Battalion.

Not all men of the brigade knew exactly what their assignments were, mostly because of the intense schedule. As Maj. Natan Shunari, 582nd Paratroopers Battalion, recalls, he was ordered to move at 1700 hours, "But I didn't know what our task or objective was, just that we were to join the 14th Brigade. With nine half-tracks, we started chasing the brigade, the brigade commander constantly hurrying us up to catch up with it." The unarmored reconnaissance jeeps and recoilless gun jeeps, just like the civilian buses, were left behind, under Battalion Deputy Commander Maj (later Knesset member) Imri Ron.

At 2000 hours, the 79th Battalion, under Lt.-Col. Amram Mitzna, reached Lexicon Road, with Amnon Reshef's Brigade HQ advancing close to it, and started pushing north. "No exchange of fire," Reshef reported to Sharon. "The brigade still maintains the element of surprise."**

By 2020 hours, all of the other tank battalions had reached Lexicon Road as well (the infantry and 582nd Paratroopers

Battalion arrived later). The brigade moved on for about an hour, nearly unobstructed, in a column heading north on the north-south Lexicon Road. In the words of one officer, "It was like a hot knife through butter." "We held our fire in order to maximize our penetration," as the brigade deputy commander explained post factum.

At 2035 hours, Amnon Reshef reported from Nahala-Lexicon Junction about some exchange of fire. But they hadn't yet engaged the Egyptian force lying in wait for them, further on, northwest of Lexicon-Tirtur Junction, and for the time being enjoyed their night sleep. The shots reported by Reshef were probably fired by the tank gunner of the 87th Brigade's 2nd Company commander, Captain Rafi Bar Lev. He was the Front Command's nephew, and had just destroyed three Egyptian tanks. (The engagement took place on Sheikh Road, about 500 meters west of Lexicon Road). It was probably the very first shots that the brigade fired in that battle.

By 2100 hours, all seemed to be going smoothly. Col. Reshef reported to Sharon that his vanguard 87th Reconnaissance Battalion, had reached the Sheikh-Lexicon Junction, four kilometers north of Matzmed, meeting with no intense opposition.* The 79th Battalion, under Mitzna, drove by Lexicon-Tirtur unopposed, on its way to secure the corridor's northern defenses, on Usha Road, eight kilometers north of Lexicon Tirtur Road. The brigade commander was contented to watch it: the Egyptians were taken by surprise and were still

---

* 143rd Division's Radio network.
** Ibid.

misreading the situation. Another force had already reached Fort Matzmed, the planned launching point of the crossing. Contrary to expectations, the Egyptian 16th Division HQ wasn't there. Reshef planned to deploy the Shaked Elite Infantry Battalion, under Lt.-Col. Spector, to search the area.** The brigade commander's HQ, which followed the 79th Battalion, as well, had crossed the Lexicon-Tirtur Junction unobstructed.

Now, the 184th Battalion, twenty-one tanks strong, under Lt.-Col. Avraham Almog, had to cross the Junction, helping the 79th Battalion securing the corridor's north. For Almog, it was his second time around in the battalion. He had already commanded it before the war, and reassumed command after the former commander, Lt.-Col. Shaul Shalev, had been killed on October 9th.

The communication networks kept silent, but then, at 2121 hours, Almog suddenly broke radio silence, reporting to the brigade commander, with alarm, about fierce fighting at the Junction. "I was taking on hellish short-range fire from an AT defensive position," he later recalled. What had alerted that position? Probably a shell fired by Captain Rami Matan, the commander of the 79th Battalion's 7th Company, at shadows he had spotted to his right while crossing the Junction. The scene at once came alive, with long volleys of tank guns being fired, the explosions of AT and rounds fired by other weapons, coming mostly from east of Lexicon-Tirtur Junction, "as if all hell broke loose." Ten tanks of the 184th Battalion were hit immediately, with some of them hitting landmines. Tanks engaged each other at very close range, everyone just shooting everyone else. Battalion Commander Almog believed it was merely an ambush, not realizing yet that it was a dug in defense. His tank was hit, and he struggled to control his force. Only two tanks obeyed his order to push north, another seven joining them later. His communication with his company leaders was cut off. Injured men jumped from their tanks, yet at the moment, nobody stopped to evacuate them, and the wounded cried for help. One tank had been crying for help over the radio for a long time. By the time the battalion commander got to Sheikh Road, north of the Chinese Farm buildings, he was left with half of his force. The other half was fighting for its survival at the Lexicon-Tirtur Junction. By then it was already clear that something had gone wrong (see map).

* * *

The 407th Armored Battalion, the fourth in the order of movement, under its new commander, Captain Yeshayahu Beitel, was assigned with clearing the Akavish and Tirtur routes, and moving eastward. Yet even before it reached Lexicon Road, the tank of 2nd Company commander, Captain Gideon Giladi, fell into a ditch, thus disrupting the schedule. When it arrived near abandoned Fort Lakekan, heading north, the battalion suffered its first enemy fire. As Beitel recalls, "We only saw flashes; shells were flying all over, and to this very day, I cannot figure out who fired them. The firing was totally chaotic. You couldn't see who or what you were firing at." The battalion just fired in response to fire. Here, its companies were to split up, starting to clear the routes. One was to clear Akavish Road, and another one Tirtur Road. Akavish Road was easily detectible, being marked and paved; but Tirtur was a dirt road, difficult to spot through the dust and dark and under incessant fire, although it could be discerned by two tanks of the 184th Battalion which were on fire. The lead company, under Giladi, missed the right turn leading to the road, and when it turned back, its tanks started taking hits. It was a hard time for the new battalion commander. As he recalled, "When we turned back, starting to look for the Junction, we were hit, and I was injured as well." He had to wait in his tank for three hours to be evacuated.

The 407th Battalion's 1st Company, under chessmaster Captain Ehud Gross, operated according to plan, advancing, while firing, eastward, on Akavish Road, until its connection to Tirtur Road, where it reported Akavish was drivable. Under the brigade commander's orders, it turned back to Lakekan, to wait for further orders. However since Tirtur was not cleared yet, Akavish, for another two days, remained under threat of Egyptian forces positioned north of it. The question as to whether Akavish was actually cleared at the time, and what kind of vehicles could get through it, remained the subject of controversy throughout the war as well as after it.

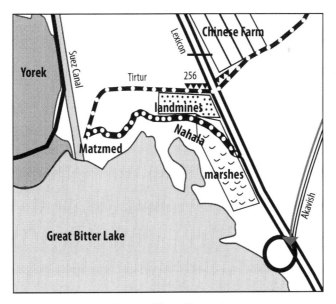

Lexicon-Tirtur Junction

Lexicon-Tirtur Junction started looking like a killing zone. The 407th Battalion suffered many casualties, right where the 184th Battalion, which had driven through that junction before, had some of its tanks torched. Another company, under Captain Gabi Vardi, securing the Shaked infantry battalion and the so-called Shmulik Force Paratroopers, was pinned down at the Lexicon-Nahala Junction, two kilometers south of the Lexicon-Turtur trap. Vardi, turning west, led the infantry forces toward the canal, by Tirtur Road, but a half-track filled with Shaked men, which blew up behind his tank, blocked the road for many hours. Eventually, Vardi spent that entire night regrouping his forces and firing at more or less detected sources of firing.

By 2130 hours, the vanguard, 79th Battalion under Lt.-Col. Mitzna, which had managed to pass the Lexicon-Tirtur Junction safely, reached the area south of Usha Road, connecting Lexicon Road to the canal, about nine kilometers north of Matzmed Yard. At that point, the battalion was to deploy its armored vehicles to secure the north of the corridor, yet the Egyptians responded quickly, with a southbound counterattack on the vanguard force. Egyptian tanks emerged at a few meters range, and a fierce battle ensued. Company Commander Israel (Iber) Ben Ari was killed, probably by the blast of a shell he had fired at an Egyptian tank ten meters away. This was typical of the entire battle. Rami Matan, 7th Company commander, watched as an Egyptian soldier got on his tank, while he was driving north, to ask for a cigarette. Rami just threw a grenade at the Egyptian, killing him. As Lieutenant Yiftah Yaakov recalls, "First, we fired at ammunition and fuel depots, so everything caught fire and the scene was lit up in a moment. You could see scores of

Egyptian trucks, and other vehicles and men, but only a few tanks."*

More tanks of Amram Mitzna's battalion caught fire, with officers and men moving from one tank to another, fighting on. Some gathered in trenches along the road. Just eight tanks, under Mitzna, managed to reach the planned objective—Usha Junction. The companies had to regroup. As it turned out, the battalion had overextended itself, considering its strength. As Mitzna later explained, "It was difficult to control the battalion then. I asked the brigade commander for permission to retreat south, to Sheikh Road, five kilometers from Matzmed, for regrouping. He granted my request. At 2200 hours, on the move, I was wounded and handed over the command to my deputy, Maj. Nathan Ben Ari." Mitzna would later recall: "A few meters away, three Egyptian tanks emerged. We hit two of them and I saw the third one rotating its turret. It was right in front of me: A shell was immediately fired at us." Their tank caught fire. His operation officer, Lt. Amos Melzter and the gunner were killed, and Mitzna was blown to the ground. He sustained a serious knee injury and had shell fragments piercing his back and hands. Brigade Commander Reshef, approaching Mitzna's tank, found him lying inside, incapacitated. As he explained it, "I kissed him on his head and sent his tank crew to the evacuation point at abandoned Fort Lakekan."

The brigade commander's tank, too, actively participated in the fighting. As one combatant recalled: "After my tank had been hit, I mounted the brigade commander's tank, which was nearby. Suddenly, three Egyptian tanks

---

* Ohayon, *We're Still There*, p.143.

approached us, and the brigade commander hit them all."*
The withdrawal southwards, from Usha Road to Sheikh
Road, took another toll: another two tanks were set ablaze,
including that of Lieutenant Yiftah Yaakov. Both he and his
crew were seriously injured. Yiftah, Yitzchak Rabin's cousin,
was left in a trench beside his tank, partially unconscious,
his entire body charred. Egyptian soldiers were lying around
him, and it was difficult to tell who was who. As tank driver
Berti Ohayon (later an Israeli police commissioner) recalled:
"We were resolved to rescue Yiftah. I started slowly walking,
bending down, from one trench to another. Wounded
Egyptians and Israelis lay side by side, difficult to tell one
from another. I just whispered to whomever I saw 'are you
Jewish?' assuming an Israeli would respond. All the while,
the firing went on. In one trench, I spotted a wounded man
lying alone, his face black with soot. I instinctively asked:
Are you Jewish? 'Yes,' he sighed, 'it's hard to be Jewish'." It
was Yiftah, and Bertie dragged him to the nearby evacuation
point. When the evacuation was over, the 79th Battalion had
just five tanks left, out of the original twenty-two. According
to plan, this force was to secure the northern boundary of
the corridor to the crossing zone. The surviving tanks set up
a defense perimeter north of Sheikh Road.

At about 2200 hours, Mitzna's 79th Battalion, positioned on
Sheikh Road was reinforced by the decimated 184th Battalion,
under Almog, deployed north of the Amir perimeter and north
of Lexicon Road, at the very heart of the Chinese Farm. That
area was found to be overrun with enemy tanks, some dug in

---

*   Ohayon, *We're Still There*, p.147.

with turret emplacements, while others, on the move, as well as with infantry men with ample AT weapons.

The 14ᵗʰ Brigade commander, Col. Reshef, soon realized something had gone wrong. At his position south of Shiekh Road, next to Mitzna's and Almog's battalions in the north, relatively some distance from the impassable Lexicon-Tirtur Junction, he saw his planned assignment was now rather insignificant, compared to the very survival of his brigade. This is how he would describe what he saw: "Ammunition dumps, hundreds of trucks and a lot of artillery batteries that the Egyptians had abandoned, kept blowing up all around us. Egyptian infantrymen were running between our tanks, hitting them with RPGs. Many men were running away. It all felt like a beehive…tanks milling around, four or five Egyptian tanks, occasionally starting counterattacks, at ranges as close as 200 or 300 meters up to half a meter. Occasionally, when a tank had no room to move its turret, they asked a tank nearby to fire at the tank in front of them. When the battle was over, we saw that some tanks had fired on each other at a range of is few as ten to twenty centimeters. We deployed two battalions along the Sheikh-Lexicon junction. While the main Junction south of us, the Lexicon-Tirtur, was still blocked, I realized we must clear Tirtur Road to let the Roller Bridge through."*

The top priority was evacuating the numerous wounded, scattered along the road but mostly at the junction, and the regrouping of crews who had had their armored vehicles

---

* An Interview with Maj.-Gen. (res.) Amnon Reshef.

destroyed: tanks and other vehicles roamed around, leaderless, detached from their units, and officers and men looked to join a formation. At 2200 Reshef ordered Maj. Shmuel "Shmulik" Arad, who commanded a two-company strong elite force of inexperienced paratroopers, named after him, to move north and help rescue the wounded. Later on, he also assigned the two company strong Shaked Battalion, under its battalion commander, to the evacuation effort. A half-track full of Shaked's men, under Company Commander Eli Sagi, which had spearheaded the advancement along the Nahala Road, had sustained a direct hit, with all nine men on board killed. The burning half-track blocked the narrow road running between the dunes and marshes. The combatants desperately looked for a safe way out, to survive and to evacuate the many casualties from the Lexicon-Tirtur Junction. An attempt by deputy battalion commander, Maj. Yuval Dvir, to circumvent the ambushing force at the junction resulted in his half-track being hit. Then, Dvir ordered his men, for whom it was their baptism of fire, to assume positions and to fire on the Egyptian forces.

As he later recalled, "We had our own peculiar war at the Junction, firing at the Egyptians with small arms, scratching some paint off the sides of the tanks."* Battalion Commander Spector rushed to the Junction and started evacuating wounded men from the many vehicles scattered about. He counted fourteen tanks and six half-tracks hit. When it was realized that his efforts were of no use, he was ordered to retrieve anything he could for regrouping near Fort Lakekan. As (later) Brig.—Gen. Spector would confess, "It felt unpleasant that night. Honestly

---

*   Uri Milstein, *Shaked,* p.316.

speaking, I felt helpless, unable to do nearly anything to get us out of the grim state we had got into."

After the war, the 6th Company of the Brigade's 202nd Battalion, which was a part of Shmulik Force, recorded its experience of that night:

"When we reached Tirtur Road, all hell broke loose, with us left behind the armored column. The enemy, recovering from the initial surprise, deployed an AT ambushing force at the Junction, so we and the tanks drove into the trap. We took on hellish fire, with mortar shells pouring like rain, falling a few meters from our half-tracks, 'Shmel' and Sagger AT missiles flying around all the time, as well as tank guns and small arms firing, an entire concert. The tanks did most of the fighting, constantly firing on the move. We felt like kittens being attacked by tigers. It was horribly dark, so even when we fired, occasionally, at suspected sources of firing, we saw nothing. Bullets pelleted the walls of our half-track. twelve tanks were hit around us, and two halftracks of Shaked were directly hit, with everybody on board killed. We just froze still, fearing the torrent of mortar shells. While advancing and retreating, our half-tracks bumped into each other. Terrible screams to be careful and 'hold it!' could be heard on all sides, we just kept praying that our half-track wouldn't get hit. We had some injured men, so we started evacuating them to the first aid station, and kept moving between the tanks, to avoid being targeted. We failed to accomplish our mission. We reached neither the Amir perimeter nor Chinese Farm, nor did we clear the area. Yet we allowed other forces to cross the canal. The clashes at the Junction went on all night long, but we, under cover of the fog, disengaged the enemy, retreating to the shores of the Bitter Lake to regroup."*

Sharon kept impatiently looking at his watch, worried mostly by the disrupted schedule, in the form of Dani Matt's Paratroopers' impeded advance on the Akavish road and the obstruction of the 630th Pontoon Battalion moving on the same road. On top of that, the delivery of the Roller Bridge on the Tirtur Road had also been impeded (see map): **

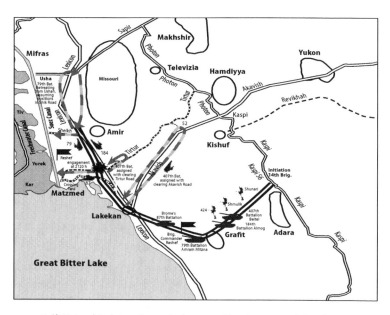

14th Brigade's drive, the night between October 15 and October 16

---

* From the *Course Graduation Book* of *202nd Battalion/ 6th Company*, 1974.
** 143rd Division's Radio network.

3. GET ON THE BUS, WE'RE GOING TO WAR!

247ᵗʰ Brigade, October 15, 1630 hours:

The force that was planned to make the first crossing, the 247ᵗʰ Paratroopers Brigade under Dani Matt, was positioned thirty kilometers east of Tasa, about sixty kilometers away from the canal. Their departure was planned for 1630. Since the brigade possessed just fifty-eight half-tracks, only the 565ᵗʰ Battalion, under Dan Ziv rode in them, with all other men going to war onboard buses. Their initial assignment was to link up with the rubber boats delivered by the Engineering Corps, supposedly waiting for them at Akavish Road. Their advancement was nerve-wracking, slow, and troublesome. Both Divisional as well as Brigade HQ had been rushing Matt, and it felt like, in his words, "The ground was burning under our feet." The brigade covered the thirty kilometer distance to Tasa in the reasonable time of two and a half hours. Yet when it entered Akavish Road, the one going to the canal, it met with a challenging obstruction, in the form of hundreds of vehicles of all kinds jamming the road. As Matt recalled:

"We had to beg, yell and force our way through the jammed junction, driving one half-track at a time. The hope of launching the first boat by 2000 hours was doomed right from the start. Now, the question was whether we could make it at all."[*]

Col. David Maimon, too, was concerned with this question. He offered his good offices to 143ʳᵈ Division HQ in an

---

[*]   Israel Harel, *Operation Valiant,* a restricted booklet issued by the 247ᵗʰ Brigade.

attempt to regulate the massive westbound traffic, crowding the narrow Akavish Road. All he had was a Jeep, another officer, and a flashlight. On the night of October 15th, at 1900 hours, he was ordered by Division Deputy Commander Yaakov "Jacky" Even to get to the Junction, and make sure two things happened: the pontoons entered the road unobstructed, and, that a "small detachment" of the Paratroopers Brigade entered the road before the pontoons, in order not to be blocked by the latter.

Maimon recalls he got about 200 meters north of Tasa Junction, his planned destination, and this is what he witnessed: "The road was entirely jammed by vehicles driving in both directions, with no way of moving back or forth out of it. Eleven pontoons, those of the 630th Battalion advancing north, had already occupied the Junction. One, critically significant later on, was stalled in that very Junction. I realized the most critical thing to do was to let through the combat force planned for the fording of the canal."

Maimon was beginning a dash to Refidim, when he was surprised to see a huge motorized column. It was Danni Matt's Paratroopers Brigade, who had yet to cross through the Tasa Junction heading for Akavish Road. As he recalls, "I asked the brigade's deputy commander what the hell he was doing there, so he told me he had his entire brigade following him, on board buses, jeeps, half-tracks, you name it. Using my flashlight, I commanded the junction keeping everyone else out of it, letting through one half-track at a time, and no other units. Then the brigade was finally able to move on. While we drove, I asked the deputy commander whether they had any unarmored vehicles. He told me they had over ten buses. It would be a challenge, to get the troop-loaded buses through that road. So we took a tractor and a bulldozer and began pushing bogged down buses. I think it took us over ninety minutes to get the entire brigade through the junction."

Thus, for over an hour and a half, the brigade had been held up at the Tasa Junction, until it managed to turn all its half-tracks with their fronts facing westward, onto Akavish Road. But the troubles weren't over yet.

With his flashlight, Col. Maimon struggled to direct the hordes of vehicles competing for the use of the road: Including Matt's Paratroopers, Ordnance Corps vehicles, Engineering Corp vehicles and the 630th tank-towed Pontoon Battalion, each pontoon was sixty tons in weight and over five meters wide.

In his words: "I had returned to Tasa Junction to allow the pontoons to get through, and up until 2330 hours, we'd been maneuvering the pontoons in an attempt to steer them from Mavdil to Akavish roads. It was a sharp turn, and it didn't go smoothly. One pontoon got stranded in the Junction, and a tank, coupled to it to pull it out, had its tow ring broken. We tried another tank, and failed. Finally, we coupled two tanks to it, and managed to pull it. It was about midnight when the pontoons started entering Akavish Road. I left the place at 0130 hours, when Uri Bar Ratzon got there, as well as the chief of military police and all kinds of characters best suited to deal with the situation." It took Maimon six and a half hours to handle the Tasa Traffic Jam.

As a result, at 2030 hours, the Paratroopers Brigade assigned for the Crossing, was still on Akavish Road, thirty kilometers away from the canal. As its commander, Dani Matt had realized even earlier, the goal of launching the first rubber boat by 2000 hours had become long since unrealistic. His commanders, at all levels, started urging Matt to make haste, to compensate for the delay in the schedule. Finally, at about 2100 hours, after covering four kilometers in three hours, the brigade started off to meet the Boat Company, which had been stopped at the 66th kilometer of Akavish Road.* It took another hour and a half for the boats to be inflated and hauled onto the half-tracks. Thirty-four out of the sixty ready boats were loaded onto the half-tracks. The men were crammed in-between the boats, twenty-five in each vehicle designed to carry ten. The boats were loaded, in two layers, one on top of the other, with the upper layer of boats occupied by the boat skippers.

Naveh would later recall: "They met us at about 2100 hours. We loaded the boats in two layers, two boats in each half-track, with me and my crew in the upper boat."** The company commander, Maj. Giron, elaborated: "It was a fantastic, Fellini-style scene: the half-tracks looking like some monstrous ducks on wheels. We were all trapped inside, unable to move a muscle or do anything."***

Needless to say, the entire column was unable to fight back if attacked. Yet the force kept moving on, the brigade reconnaissance force and the Division Deputy Commander's HQ laboriously clearing the road.

The delay kept building up: it wasn't until 2220 hours that Col. Matt reported that he had reached the Akavish Road and Artillery Road junction, and had joined the tank company of the 599th Battalion, called Harif Force, which had been assigned

---

* 143rd Division's Radio network.
** An interview with Maj. (ret.) Ayalon Naveh.
*** Giron, in an interview on the phone.

with escorting his force all the way to the canal. The traffic through the overcrowded junction resumed at 2200 hours, and there were still miles to go.

Dvelah HQ, 2230 Hours:

Those were nerve-wracking hours for the decision-makers in Dvelah: with no specific issue to attend to, the Chief of General Staff "Dado" Elazar found time to discuss politics with the Defense Minister, asking him to "keep it low" when dealing with the government, just report that we have a foothold across the canal. The task of updating the already overly-tense ministers he assigned to his deputy, Major General Tal. There was still no good news, the major problem being falling behind schedule. As Dayan complained, "I have been dealing with the Sinai for the last seventeen years, and never did I like the idea of reaching the canal. It took me seventeen years to make me want to reach it,"* alluding to his disapproval of reaching the Suez in the 1967 Six-Day War.

The communications between the Southern Command commander and the 143rd division commander, Major General Sharon, were frequently severed, since Sharon had to constantly relocate, to avoid the sporadic shelling. Occasionally, shell fire could be heard through the radio.

At about 2230 hours, Sharon reported that the Akavish Road was cleared, yet fierce fighting was still taking place at the Lexicon-Tirtur Junction. He also reported that he had had to halt the Paratroopers Brigade, since Akavish Road hadn't

---

* Bartov, *Dado*, II, p.236.

been completely cleared, and that he had considered deploying additional forces to breach the blocked junction. Nonetheless, "The enemy forces are breaking down," he reported. At the time it was still wishful thinking.

That had been enough to alarm HQ. It was mostly the Defense Minister who raised concerns: "If," Dayan had asked Elazar, "the fording is stuck, then when will the next phase take place?" "We will be wiser in an hour," "Dado" replied.

For Dayan, that wasn't good enough, so he inquired whether the crossing campaign had already gone beyond the point of no return, or should one consider other options. Dayan, though advocating the move, was haunted by doubts. And he wasn't the only one.

Major General Gonen suggested throwing Adan's 162nd Division into the battle as well. The Defense Minister demanded an estimation as to how many nighttime hours were left for delivering the force. Bar Lev reassuringly said that there were another seven hours of nighttime. If they reached the canal by 0400 hours, he said, they could cross it within an hour, "provided the infantry has already crossed."

"What if we don't?!" Dayan insisted.

"We can do it by day as well," someone suggested.

Bar Lev decided: "I think we can cross and have a bridge in place by the morning. If we haven't, we'll make a decision at 0300 hours." The Chief of General Staff, as well, believed that at this stage there was no point in considering the recall of forces. Yet they kept vacillating. Responding to Sharon's request for additional tanks, Dayan remarked, "Arik might complain that he lacks tanks for the breakthrough, while at the same time reporting that the enemy is breaking down, and see no contradiction between these reports."*

4: A WALL OF ANTI-TANK MISSILES AT LEXICON-TIRTUR JUNCTION.

Toward midnight, the 14th Brigade commander, Col. Reshef, realized he must reassess the situation. At 2330 hours, Maj. "Shmulik" Arad, leader of Shmulik Force, reported he had finished evacuating the injured men from Lexicon-Tirtur Junction, and that the battle for breaching it had been resumed. He had also had to shorten the lines of his northern periphery, having succumbed to the Egyptian pressure on his two lead battalions, and had retreated to Shiekh Road. What is worse, the blocked Lexicon-Tirtur Junction threatened to cause the entire crossing campaign to fail, and the corridor was extremely narrow. Therefore, Reshef had to clear the blocked junction, clear a route, and regroup his disarrayed forces, having only a short period of time in which to accomplish this and with increasingly dwindling forces.

The division commander, Sharon too was aware of the challenge that was evolving at the junction, and was trying to muster additional forces to help the 14th Brigade. Meanwhile, he ordered Reshef to hold a line north of Shiekh Road, at Lexicon Road.

The question as to what stopped the forces advance toward the canal and at what point the enemy seized the junction, remains unanswered to this very day. The routes for advancing had been selected in accordance with intelligence reports, that

---

* Bar On, *Moshe Dayan*, p.186.

there were few enemy forces in the area. So when had the anti-tank defense perimeters that the brigade had had to face, been formed? Obviously, the Lexicon-Tirtur Junction defense perimeter had been formed during the morning and afternoon of October 15th, as suggested by aerial photos post-war analysis. The Egyptians, most probably, deployed during that night, or even earlier, anti-tank-equipped infantry and a few tanks in the Chinese Farm irrigation ditches along Akavish and Tirtur roads, turning the junction into a real defensive perimeter, as the 14th Brigade was to find out.

When the morning fogs faded away, Major Zamir, the Cadets Force commander, could see what had held him back the night before: at the junction, he discovered an anti-tank defense consisting of four dug-in T-62 tanks, with four anti-tank missile-carrying jeeps between them, in addition to an entrenched commando force rich in anti-tank weaponry. There were another two tanks positioned on both sides, closing the trap on the forces which got caught in the ambush. In addition, numerous Sagger anti-tank missiles and RPG launchers had been deployed along Tirtur Road. IDF forces trying to clear the route the night after were surprised to find, in the irrigation ditches near the 42nd kilometer of Tirtur, a dug in Egyptian infantry battalion with ample anti-tank weapons. None of these had ever been mentioned in intelligence reports preceding the campaign.

The tank crewmen of the 79th and 184th Battalions had easily crossed the junction earlier that night, reached Usha Road, and headed north, only suffering resistance south of the Missouri perimeter, the location of the Egyptian 16th Division's logistics center. It consisted of trucks, artillery batteries and only a few tanks. Yet the Egyptians had responded quickly, attempting to close the breach in their lines during the night by redeploying an armored force of the 24ᵗʰ Division. This was probably the force which the 79ᵗʰ Battalion, under Mitzna, and the 184ᵗʰ, under Almog, had faced. The combatants' reports reveal that total chaos ensued, marked by engagements at extremely close range. There were incidents of Egyptian tanks driving into Israeli columns and in some cases, the opposing forces only detected each other at a distance of a few meters. So the withdrawal to Shiekh Road somewhat disentangled the two forces.

* * *

421ˢᵗ Brigade, October 15, 2300 hours:
While the 14ᵗʰ Brigade had been exhausting itself in the battle for the Junction, and the Paratroopers Brigade had been struggling to make its way to the launching point, the gigantic column delivering the three types of fording equipment kept rolling on, heading for the canal, under the direct command of Col. Hail Erez. The success of the many maneuvers that had been planned for the crossing depended on the Roller Bridge arriving in time. That "marvel of technology" was parked at the Yukon perimeter, with all kinds of field and engineering officers messing with it.

The reason so many top brass members were gathered there was that the Roller Bridge had never been towed for such a distance on such a terrain, under combat conditions. Its 200 meters of length and 400 ton weight had to be delivered several kilometers, under wartime conditions, and, if possible, according to schedule. Finally, it had to be delivered to the crossing point, 95.5 kilometers from the north end of the canal. (During the night of October 15ᵗʰ, the Bridge had only moved a few kilometers from Yukon perimeter).

For the first two kilometers of its journey, the bridge traveled at eight kilometers per hour. Then, it was impeded by all kinds of obstacles. First, two damaged APCs standing by the road; then, a large pit on the left of the road, which took a long time to cover up. But mostly, it was due to rough terrain. It took a great effort from the tanks to tow it across the dunes, both uphill as well as downhill. More and more tanks were coupled to it, in an attempt to pull it through, which resulted in numerous malfunctions. Nonetheless, for the first hours of the journey, it seemed to move, though slowly. At 0120 hours Sharon ordered his second in command, "Jacky" Even, who was in charge of delivering the bridge to stop at the 52nd kilometer of Akavish Road, where Tirtur Road begins. That was wishful thinking: the Roller Bridge was still far away.

* * *

Half an hour after departure, at 2330 hours division deputy commander, Col. Even, who headed the column towing the Roller Bridge, and who was stalled at the 5th kilometer of Akavish Road, felt that it was necessary to consider using alternative fording means. He stressed to Sharon that Tirtur Road, the point to which the bridge was to advance, was still blocked and that instead the pontoons should be redeplo yed from the south, through Akavish Road. Sharon approved, yet the pontoons proved to be troublesome as well.

At 2100 hours Ilan Maoz, 264th Battalion deputy commander, carrying the eleven pontoons of 630th Battalion, encountered Col. Maimon, who was directing traffic through Tasa Junction using his flashlight. The pontoons were advancing northward, and would have to turn left at the junction, to enter Akavish

Road, which led to the canal. At that moment, Maimon was busy getting the 247th Brigade, the brigade assigned with securing the bridgehead, through the Junction. This was the order of movement for which he was responsible: first of all, Danni Matt's forces, and then the remaining force. So he ordered Maoz to get his pontoons off the road. Maoz became stressed. His superior, Maj. Giora Lev, heading the Alligators column, urged him to link up with him. Through his earphones he heard his divisional chief of staff yelling "Ilan! Ilan! Where are you!?" In order to allow the long column of paratroopers, which also contained buses and jeeps, to get through, it was necessary to uncouple the front pontoon from its tank and get it off the road. Now, the command group was ordering him to get the coupled pontoons off the road. The rest of the pontoons had halted. Some were bogged down in the sand off the road, while others couldn't handle the sharp turn. It was dark and a dense fog covered the road. Maoz, losing all track of time, desperately reported to his superior, as he later explained, "We'll make it in a couple of days," and suggested that he abandon the pontoons and join him. Battalion Commander Lev told him to do just that, hoping to complete his tanks strength. While uncoupling the tanks from the pontoons, as his superior had ordered, he received a frantic order from Col. Gideon Altschuller: Division commander orders all pontoons delivered, at all cost!" Having no choice, Maoz began the exhausting work of retrieving and recoupling the pontoons. By midnight the advance was resumed, yet only on the following morning did his last company commander leave Tasa Junction, heading onto Akavish Road. And then the struggle to pass through Akavish Road began.

At midnight, though the pontoons, after being coupled,

uncoupled and recoupled were ready to be towed, the division commander had to reassess the order of movement of the fording machinery. The only means accessible for the crossing, under the strain of an increasingly pressing schedule, were the Alligators. Though they had been planned to cross last, they were the only reasonable option at the moment. So Sharon asked his deputy, who happened to be standing next to the Engineering Corps commander at that moment, whether he could get to Lexicon Road in thirty minutes. Col. Even explained that the pontoons were stalled, while the Alligators, "have some bugs, yet they can be handled."

Sharon: It's getting late. Get going immediately, with the "trailers" [i.e. Roller Bridge]. Who is handling the "softies" [Alligators]?

Even: Those who brought them.

Sharon: Can they move quickly?

Even: They are moving quickly.

Sharon: We should deliver the "softies" by Akavish Road, and the "trailer," by Tirtur Road.

It wasn't just technical malfunctions which halted the Roller Bridge. Tirtur Road was blocked, and it didn't seem it would be cleared soon. Its blocking rendered the Roller Bridge's route useless. So Sharon had to order his deputy to stop the Roller Bridge at the 52nd kilometer of Akavish Road, before it entered Tirtur Road. An elementary calculation caused Sharon to realize that the option of launching the Roller Bridge early in the morning was becoming unreal. At that point, it would have taken at least four hours of unobstructed towing to get the bridge to its launching point, at kilometer 95.5, north of Matzmed. Those towing the bridge had already realized it was falling behind. At one point it had taken sixteen tanks to tow it, and towing on such a terrain required a level of operational accuracy for which the unit had not been trained. At 0115 hours, while the bridge was being pulled down a high dune, the front rollers ran over the two towing tanks, and it took great effort and resourcefulness to free the tanks from under the heavy "monster." Nevertheless, the tanks were recovered within an hour, unharmed, and the towing continued smoothly, at least for a while.

Meanwhile, Even reported to Sharon that the Alligators were making their way to the canal. That was the first good news of that night. As Col. Even recalls, "All of the communication networks were silent, with nobody breathing a word. Suddenly, the Roller Bridge was halted, since the Tirtur junction was blocked, the pontoons being wherever they might be. So Arik asked me what we had in the field. I told him we had Alligators. He asked where they were, so I told him they were with me. Then he ordered, 'Man them and get them here.' It was a critical decision. So I took the Alligators' battalion commander with me, and reached Arik's APC at the 52nd kilometer of Akavish Road, with the entire battalion following me. Then he assumed command of the force, and I left him, to handle my other jobs."

5. "YOU MAY CALL IT ACAPULCO."

247th Brigade, October 16, 0115 hours, Matzmed Yard:

At midnight, Danni Matt, 257th Brigade commander, reported to Dvelah HQ that he was a kilometer and a half away from the canal. Though it was good news, HQ staff still saw the glass as half empty. At 0300 hours, the General Chief of Staff confessed his concerns to those around him, saying he had his reservations about launching the Paratroopers into the water on rubber boats alone, without the assistance of the Alligators. Bal Lev, reassured him, saying that the Alligators were on their way. Major General Gonen even ordered Major General Adan, commander of the 162nd Division waiting for the bridging machinery, to advance his troops. Tension in the HQ was running high in anticipation of the 247th Brigade's approach to the canal.

At 0100, Sharon, attempting to reassure Bar Lev, told him that Danni Matt was "driving forward, and it's all quiet on the other bank."

"What about the Roller Bridge?" Bar Lev insisted.

Sharon: "There is still one section of Tirtur Road we haven't cleared yet. I expect we'll manage it before daybreak. The going is tedious for many reasons, but it's going to be OK. We are advancing the 'softies' [Alligators], and I'm clearing Tirtur from the rear. Just give me an hour and I'll get the 'trailer' [Roller Bridge] through."*

Indeed, at 0115 hours the Paratroopers Brigade commander confirmed that his route to the canal was for the most part unobstructed. A few minutes later the lead force, under his deputy, Yehuda Bar, turned at Lexicon-Nahala Junction westward, heading for the canal, reaching Matzmed Yard shortly afterwards.

The eastern part of the bridgehead consisted of a "yard," a compound of about 500 meters by 500 meters, located on the northern boundary of Fort Matzmed, surrounded by a rectangular embankment. Its area was designed to include three bridges, as well as their approach routes, both westbound as

---

*   *Southern Command Command Operations Log.*

well as eastbound ones. The bridges were planned to be placed 200 meters from each other, while another bridge, the Roller Bridge, was planned to be erected a kilometer up north, 95.5 kilometers from the northern end of the canal. The entire compound, constructed way back when Sharon had been Southern Command Commander, was designed to serve as a base for all those troops assigned with guaranteeing the flow of traffic across the canal.

Approaching the canal, the Paratroopers were amazed at the silence: one could actually hear the ripple of waves coming from the canal. It was only disturbed by the sound of distant explosions. It was hard to believe that the 14th Brigade was fighting for its survival just about 800 meters away. Upon arrival, 2nd Company of the 416th Battalion, dismounted its half-tracks, and started searching the Yard for the enemy. Brigade deputy commander, Lt.-Col. Bar, together with Col. Nachman Sirkin, marked out the two planned launching sites, codenamed Red and Green. Brigade HQ assumed its position along the embankment. Suddenly, shells fired from the east and broke the silence, mortally wounding deputy company commander David Vazah, and injuring other troops.* At 0120 hours, after the deputy brigade commander had authorized the crossing, the rubber boats were unloaded, and the brigade's engineering force started up the steep embankment, with the boats on their backs.

From 0120 to 0130 hours, all senior commanders followed the dramatic events unfolding on the banks of the canal. Sharon, when hearing on the radio, at 0120 hours the code

---

* The shells were fired by Israeli forces.

word "aquarium," which stood for "the boats are in the water," asked Col. Matt whether he had reached the other bank yet. Before Matt had enough time to reply and Sharon quickly announced to the men in Dvelah that the canal had been crossed. A few minutes ahead of the use of the agreed upon code word Acapulco, standing for "The boats have reached the west bank," Sharon stated, "You may call it Acapulco."

One of the first six rubber boats the Engineers Company had launched, that of deputy company commander Mano, began sinking immediately. The engines, too, proved difficult to start. Yet all these adversities failed to stop the fording force.

As Boat Company deputy commander, Captain Eylon Naveh recalls, "The entire launch was carried out under completely peaceful, war-game-like conditions, with nobody opposing us. Yet it took some time for the engines to start. It is still disputed as to who was on board the first boat. It seems everybody was, but me. The launching perimeter was divided into two parts, one under me, and the other under the other company's commander, Captain Elhanan Pas. I was left at the launching point. Then, we started an orderly fording from two launching points, back and forth, taking six men at a time. We were lucky not to meet with any opposition on the other bank."*

On October 16th, at 0132 hours, seven minutes after the code word "aquarium" had been reported on the radio, the boat of Lt.

---

*   An interview with Maj.(ret.) Elon Naveh, 2006.

**   The diary of Sergeant Yaakov Priel, who served at Dvelah (ff. "Priel's Diary").

Eli Cohen, (later an ambassador), was the first to reach the west bank of the Suez Canal. The forces breached the embankment with explosives, letting the first wave of the crossing force gain a foothold and mark the routes.

As brigade commander, Col. Dani Matt, later recalled, "We only said one word: Acapulco, which quickly spread over the communication networks of the entire army. One could practically hear the sigh of relief in Dvela all the way to the GHQ Compound in Tel Aviv." Bar Lev hastily reported to Major General Aharon "Araleh" Yariv in the GHQ, saying: "I have good news for you, Araleh. The IDF is on the west bank. It's been long overdue, but we did it."[**]

The entire Southern Command had been listening to the 143rd Divison's communications. They heard Sharon tempering the euphoria, saying "There is still an area we haven't cleared, but we will, and the bridge is advancing like mad."

Gonen: Will you get through it in an hour?

Sharon: We will, we'll manage. The Roller Bridge is at the 52nd kilometer of Akavish Road, and it will make it here in thirty minutes. I have some problems with some anti-tank defense perimeters. We have many casualties.

Gonen: Wish you all the best.[*]

The commanders started showering him with congratulations, some grudgingly, and others, wholeheartedly.

Sharon, questioningly: How are they doing elsewhere?

Gonen: More or less the same as you. All are doing well!

Dayan: Arik, there is no elsewhere.

---

[*]   Ronen Bergman, *Real Time*, p. 229.
[**]   ibid.

Sharon, trying to exploit his success, suggested that Bar Lev deploy a detachment of Adan's division in support. Bar Lev replied, "I believe you'll manage as is. If you don't, then we'll give you Adan's force which hasn't crossed." **

The Southern Command Command HQ, too, was overwhelmed with momentary relief and joy. Lieutenant-General David Elazar found time to address Journalist Aviezer Golan, stating: "This is a decisive battle which might turn the tide at the Egyptian Front. This is the turning point of this war… If ever the historians that record it wonder how we did it, they will find that it was due to the greatest demonstration of chutzpa ever."

Two hours later, Col. Matt himself crossed westward, and Gonen radioed him in person:

Gonen: Gonen 103 here, congrats.

Matt: Matt 20, thanks.

Gonen: Here, talk to my superior.

Chief of General Staff, Elazar: 99 here. How does it feel?

Matt: Great.

Chief of General Staff: Congrats, congrats! Over and out!

With this, more or less, the congratulatory part of that night ended.

Right after the Engineers Company had completed marking the area, through 565th Battalion, under Dan Ziv, started fording the canal, with boats, just as planned, quickly moving from one bank to the other.

At 0140 hours, the 14th Brigade commander told Paratroopers Brigade Commander Danni Matt not to deploy his half-tracks, which were heading east on Tirtur Road, since the Tirtur junction ambush had not been resolved yet.* At 0230 hours, Brigade HQ crossed the canal; fifteen minutes later Matt reported that, despite taking some casualties, he had met with no real opposition. By dawn of Tuesday, October 16th, the fording force had already occupied a considerable area, stretching four kilometers north, one kilometer south and three kilometers west of the landing point, all the way to the Freshwater Canal.

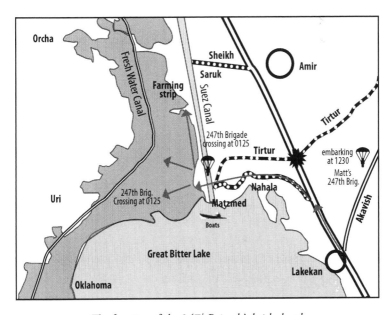

The forming of the 247th Brigade's bridgehead,
October 16, from 1300 to 0600 hours

---

* 143rd Division radio network. As a result, the half-tracks, unloaded, drove back by the Nahalah-Akavish road, without delivering another round of troops, as planned.

6. A MISREADING OF THE BATTLE.

Dvelah HQ, October 16, 0300 hours:

As the situation became clearer, the mood in Dvelah turned gray. After the war, Major General Gonen confessed; "At 0300 we learned we had no bridges in the field: the Roller Bridge being stalled on Akavish road. I have to say that this road was under the 143rd Division's responsibility. By 0300 hours we found out that the bridge was some distance from its destination, while both Uri Ben Ari and Asher Levy were busy clearing the road."

Gonen shared with Sharon his grave concern about the Roller Bridge lagging behind. Sharon told him to relax. There were problems; the road was full of holes due to the heavy shelling. He said that he could get there quickly. In his words, "The beginning is always the hardest part of such jobs. Once we clear this blockage here, it will run smoothly. Some eyebrows were raised among the Front Command over this statement.

Meanwhile, an unplanned discussion developed at Dvelah HQ, with Defense Minister Dayan suggesting recalling the Paratroopers since "with no bridges, there's no crossing." All of the other attendees disapproved. As they said, "If we don't make it tomorrow, we'll make it the next day." So it was decided to proceed.

Sharon had no misgivings. In his words, "I believed that once Matt reached the west bank, we couldn't hold it."

At 0400 hours, Sharon reported a malfunction of the Roller Bridge which might take an hour to handle, and that he was quickly advancing the Alligators, "hoping to deliver some vehicles. All quiet on the Western Front." Gonen pressed him to try harder to deliver the Roller Bridge and to try advancing the pontoons. He said it was "most critical" to get as many pieces (as possible) across the canal. This conversation took place a few minutes after another failed attempt by the 14th Brigade to break through the Junction. As Sharon angrily explained it to the Front Command's HQ, "The 14th Brigade is engaged at Lexicon-Tirtur Junction. The 'Big Thing' [Roller Bridge] is delayed." "Our major problem is the battle for the junction. I guess we'll overcome it shortly. You misread the battle. Currently, there is fierce fighting at the junction, with everybody engaged in it. We must bring an end to it. This blocked junction is keeping us from delivering the Big Thing."*

Alligators Battalion, Matzmed Yard, October 16th 0445 hours:

"Do you know where Matzmed is?" Major General Sharon asked the 264th Armored Battalion commander, Maj. Giora Lev, whom he encountered on Akavish Road. That young officer, despite not knowing where Matzmed was, said he did. Lev was less than confident that these monstrous looking vehicles, called Alligators, could save the day. "Well," Sharon ordered him, "form a column and get there fast. Engineering Corps should be waiting for you there."**

Sharon realized that time was against him, his element of surprise fading away, threatening the success of the entire crossing. His fear of the breach in the Egyptian lines being closed by counterattack was based on a real threat, mostly to the north. Therefore, he had to deploy as many forces as possible, without delay, through the bottleneck at the Akavish-

----

*   Ronen Bergman, *Real Time*, p. 233.
**   Brig.-Gen. (res.) Giora Lev, in an interview.

Lexicon Junction, disregarding the machinery delivery priority list. It called for his personal interference in moves critical for the success of the crossing campaign. His winning cards, therefore, were the Alligators, and the 264th Armored Battalion escorting them, under Lev. The small column, consisting of Lev's tanks, the Alligators, and the division commander's APC in the rear, at 0400 hours, dashed toward Matzmed. To its surprise, the route was relatively clear all the way from the 52nd kilometer of Akavish Road to the abandoned Fort Lakekan. Occasionally, the road was blocked by burning tanks, attesting to the fierce fighting which had taken place a few hours earlier. Bulldozer tanks, leading the column, were clearing them off the road. Reaching Lakekan, the column turned north, along the shores of the Great Bitter, anxiously looking for the entrance to Nahalah, in order to avoid the threatened Tirtur Road.

Suddenly, they spotted a massive Caterpillar D9 tractor, which had probably come the wrong way. "Which way to Tasa?!", the driver asked, desperately. "Follow me," Lev told him, joining him to the force. As they were approaching Matzmed, Lev spotted, through his binoculars, the sticks marking the crossing yard. Sharon radioed him directions himself:

Sharon: You, turn right, getting your tanks into the Yard, but stay by the gate. I'll be right behind you, telling you exactly what to do. This is the space between the two compounds.

Giora Lev: This is 1. I have stopped.

143rd Div. Operations Officer: This is 42. We're right behind you.

Sharon: This is 40. Get one of the engineering vehicles, where you see lamps.*

---

* 421st Brigade radio network. Quoted on 421st Brigade's website

Battalion Commander Giora Lev drove into the Yard, wondering where exactly was the point in the embankment where the breach for the Alligators should be made. Sharon pointed to a couple of red bricks he had prepared in advance, to mark where the embankment got thinner. "Where's the heavy machinery?" Lev wondered. Two bulldozer tanks were mustered right away, but their buckets merely scratched the embankment.

"After working for a long time, we decided to use the tractor operator who had been looking for Tasa (the D9 tractor)," Giora Lev recalled. "It worked perfectly, and at 0500 hours, after forty-five minutes of work, the embankment was breached wide enough to let the Alligators through."

While the bulldozers were working on the breach, the Alligators were speeding on to the launching point. Missing, in their haste, the turn to the crossing area, they went on a little north of it, but soon correcting their mistake. The Alligators Battalion entered the Yard at 0445 hours, waiting for its turn.* The vehicles were deployed, their crews started inflating their buoys and preparing for launching right away. It was silent all around, with no firing or shelling heard. As Lev, then a major, later explained, "Suddenly, the Alligators men told me they could not operate their vehicles, since they needed diesel fuel. So somebody, somehow, managed to find a diesel fuel tanker. It just popped up out of the blue. After filling up all the Alligators, we used the rest of the diesel for our tanks. We managed to inflate all the Alligators, and took to the water even before daybreak. But then the Alligators Battalion explained to me that the Gillois, or Alligator, is nearly the same

---

*   421ˢᵗ Brigade's Radio network, at 0400 hours. Quoted on the 421ˢᵗ Brigade's website.

size as a M48 tank, but ten centimeters narrower, and must be boarded by driving backwards. I estimated that it would be daybreak within fifteen minutes, and that it would be safer by day." At 0630 hours, the first Alligator rolled into the Suez Canal through the breach in the embankment.

A while later, Sharon reported to the Dvela HQ that he was at Matzmed in person and had witnessed the 14th Brigade engaged in a heavy tank battle. In his words, "I might get there to help them, since I've got ten tanks here."

Here Gonen saw a chance to play with Sharon:

Gonen: Let Bren cross first. Meanwhile, you regroup and cross following him.

Sharon: Hear you loud and clear. No problem, I can cross too. No problem.

Gonen: Get ready. I am ordering Bren to get ready to cross.

Sharon: The trouble is that right now we have nothing to cross the water with.

Gonen: Well, when we do have it.

Sharon: Obviously. Let Bren cross first, I might cross second. It doesn't matter.

Gonen: What matters is that we secure and expand the corridor.

Sharon: We're holding up.*

---

*   162nd Division's Communication Network, at 0445 hours. Alligators Battalion Commander reporting to Front Command's Engineer Officer: "The first vehicle's in the yard. When will it get into the water?"; "I don't know", the latter replied. Yet about an hour later, at 05:57 hours, he reported: "We made one breach in the wall. The yellow [civilian tractor] is working on in, the other one can't. Completion estimated in 15 minutes."

** Bar On, *Moshe Dayan*, p.188.

Gonen, optimistically, ordered Adan: "Get ready to cross first, at my command. After you cross, regroup in Marktzera, on the west bank, and wait for Haim Erez's 421st Brigade to cross."

Yet the battle for the crossing was far from over, and it would take another forty hours for Adan to set foot on the west bank of the Suez. Referring to this, the Defense Minister's adjutant remarked: "I heard all of the top brass members, even the Chief of General Staff, mulling, first and foremost, over how to keep Sharon from crossing first, thus snatching away all the glory."** Yet Bar On's words are not supported by any of the GHQ conversations records.

7. SHUNARI'S FORCE GETS TRAPPED.

800 meters north of the relatively quiet Matzmed Yard, Col. Amnon Reshef, with his disintegrating brigade, was still struggling with the jammed Lexicon-Tirtur Junction. He realized his top priority must be the clearing of the junction and Tirtur Road. As mentioned above, from his position south of the Missouri perimeter, he had hit three enemy tanks at a range of fifty meters.* Regrouping for yet another attack on that goddamned junction, he ordered Maj. Yoav Brome, 87th Reconnaissance battalion commander, positioned two kilometers west of the junction, to attack its rear, heading eastwards. The two companies strong battalion had seven

---

*   His exact position was codenamed Purple 140, west of Lexicon Road
     and north of the Chinese Farm and Shiekh Road.
**   87th Battalion's website; the story of Yair Litwitz, quoted on the 14th
     Brigade's website.

tanks, and the same number of APCs. Overcoming several problems, Brome reached the junction with three additional tanks.

As one of the battalion's officers recalled, "The force started advancing toward the junction, with the battalion commander's tank in the center, 1st Company on the left flank, and 3rd Company on the right flank. Right after we passed the junction, we started facing hellfire. Battalion Commander Yoav Brome, was killed immediately, and both of the company commanders' tanks were hit. Many vehicles and men were hit as well, the remnants of the battalion retreating to the 50th kilometer of Tirtur Road. The deputy battalion commander, being a Reconnaissance man, didn't feel capable of commanding the Battalion, so it remained without command, and practically ceased to exist as a fighting force." **

While the 1st Company tanks picked up the survivors, the 87th Battalion was struck off from the brigade's strength, and the brigade commander scattered its remnants among various battalions.

Sharon kept pressuring Reshef to throw the 582nd Paratroopers Battalion, under Natan Shunari, into the effort of clearing the road. A few minutes later, Sharon suggested a daytime attack, since the nighttime fight seemed to get chaotic. Reshef recommended against committing more forces, since the crowdedness within the theater of combat might expose troops to friendly fire. Therefore, Reshef prepared for a defense along Shiekh Road, and kept reporting he had taken many casualties and had hardly any vehicles left intact.

At 0400 hours Reshef ordered his deputy, Lieutenant-Colonel Eitan Arieli, to assume command of the 407th Battalion's 1st Company, and clear the junction. He planned for the 582nd Battalion and another company to follow him and mop up the junction. Yet this plan went wrong right from the start: the brigade deputy commander's forces proved slow in regrouping, and after yet another failure, the force retreated to Lexicon Road. Then, one of the most tragic battles that night took place.

The 582nd AT Paratroopers Battalion got involved in it almost by accident. Being a part of a brigade stationed up north, it just went to the front looking for action. It was a close-knit group of old paratroopers, veterans of the 1950s Reprisals Operations, the 1956 Battle of the Mitla Pass, and the victorious 1967 Battle for Jerusalem. Its fresh commander, Natan Shunari, born in Kibbutz Beit Hashita, had mustered up all sorts of old acquaintances, including the man who started the unit, Maj. Micha Kapusta. The commander's acquaintance with Sharon, and a roadside encounter with the 14th Brigade commander on the morning of October 15th, had gotten the battalion attached to Reshef's forces, with its men hardly informed about their task. The unarmored recoilless gun-carrying jeeps, under battalion deputy commander, Maj. (future parliamentarian) Imri Ron, were assigned with defending the southern approach of Fort Lakekan. The half-track mounted troops waited near Lexicon-Tirtur Junction. By 0400 hours, after all armored assaults had been spent, Reshef tried to breach the junction and Tirtur Road using this battle-hardened force.

As Maj. Natan Shunari, 582nd Airborne AT Battalion recalls, "Reshef told me to assume command of Gideon GIadi's force, and clear the junction by an eastbound attack. I had no idea what forces were defending the junction, otherwise, I would've never gone there." The plan was to clear the junction with an infantry force following the tanks and half-tracks breaching it open. In his words, "Some guys and I went to check out the junction. We saw a great fire burning there, and a lot of vehicles hit by landmines. People were busy rescuing injured men all around us. Two tanks were burning in the junction itself. We came back, reported what we saw, and waited. I had no intention of a head-on assault on the junction. The heavy firing was not in the junction itself, but a few hundred meters behind it."

At about 0430, the small column started off eastward, on Tirtur Road. It was spearheaded by Captain Gideon Giladi, with eight tanks mustered from remnants of various units, followed by Shunari's men, riding in six half-tracks. A few minutes later, Giladi reported to Shunari that the road was clear and that he was advancing, with his deputy with him. When Shunari wondered where the rest of the force was, Giladi replied, "They were scattered." To Shunari, it seemed like a loss of control, with tanks just driving back and forth without instructions.

The following testimony of an officer of Giladi's company illustrates the chaotic nature of the battle for the junction at that time: "At one point we formed a column with Gideon leading, and I followed him. After we started off, Gideon's tank hit a landmine to the right of the road, so he mounted another tank. Now, the deputy company commander was leading the column, with Gideon following him. They ordered us to attack Tirtur. Missing the turn taken by Gideon and his second-in-command, I kept driving north, and after a while I noticed that I was all alone. Realizing my mistake, I drove back to the junction, finding nobody there. As I found out later, the tank following me had fallen into a ditch, its crew dismounting and abandoning it. Failing to communicate with either the battalion commander or his deputy, I couldn't make a decision, so I stayed at the junction until daybreak. I kept carefully following exactly what the other vehicles were doing. Whenever other tanks drove forward or backward, so did I."

The fate of Company Commander Giladi and his second-in-command in their last moments is still unknown. While driving eastward, Shunari noticed two of their tanks beside Tirtur Road, burnt out with the entire crew dead, some inside the tanks and others along the road. Giladi was posthumously awarded with the Medal of Bravery for his actions.

The six paratrooper carrying half-tracks maneuvered their way between the tanks' remains, with Shunari and Maj. Micha Kapusta manning the forward vehicle. The battalion commander's brother, Yehiel, who had come back from the States to serve in the war, was in one of the other vehicles. Lt. Yoni Kaplan, alongside Dr. Naftali Hadas and his medical team rode in the rear half-track.

As Hadas recalled, "Our half-track was terribly crowded, with 14 paratroopers practically on top of each other. I was also exhausted from a night of attending to the wounded. Still, we were extremely thrilled." All of a sudden, Hadas spotted a comet-like blinking light on the ramp alongside the road, approaching the half-track at an enormous speed, and hitting it with an alarming crash. It was followed by artillery fire coming from scores of guns. His half-track, as well as other of the vehicles, was immediately set on fire.* Natan Shunari would later recall: "A few hundred meters away from the junction

---

*   Shimon Nurieli, *The Night of the Chinese Farm Breakthrough*, IDF Chief Education Officer Publications, September 1975, p. 40.

we started taking on hellish fire, on both our north and south flanks. The force had entered into a trap. At one point I told the men: 'The fire is too heavy, just get the hell out of here to the east,' to get away from this perimeter which I knew nothing about." The fire mainly came from north of the road, from Amir perimeter. All of the half-tracks reported sustaining fire and casualties. Shunari and another lead half-track managed to break out to the east of the killing zone. Consequently, three half-tracks reached safety while another three were left behind, each struggling on its own. They continued to receive multiple hits while their crews attempted to rescue themselves.

As Shunari later explained, "From that moment on, I was essentially out of touch with the other half-tracks. I ordered the three half-tracks near me to go back and see what they could do… the first of those three was hit by a missile, and its crew abandoned it. After I had seen we could not go back, I realized that each vehicle was fighting on its own to maneuver its retreat toward Akavish. This was not carried out by my orders, since my communications had already been cut, but under orders of each vehicle's commander."

The paratroopers tried to escape back to Akavish Road, but the Egyptians had encircled them. As Noah Kinarti recalls. "We saw a deep ditch and got in, seeing the Egyptians rushing at us fifty meters away, yelling: Get the Jews!" By that point, the force had collapsed into small bands of individuals each fighting their own war.

Shunari, who suddenly found himself left with only the two half-tracks that were still near him, detached from the rest of his force, sped to the east end of the road, all the while crying out for help to the 14th Brigade commander. At 0530 hours he reported his men were encircled at Tirtur junction, and asked the brigade commander to rescue him out of the junction. At 0545 hours, he reported four of his vehicles were destroyed at the junction, and asked for immediate tank support. At 0615 Shunari cried: "We are under tank attack, the going is tough. Request for urgent artillery, tanks, and aircraft support. Cannot disengage, many casualties. It's urgent! My entire force is getting killed off; they are practically on top of me! Why can't you throw in tanks faster?! The brigade commander's reply was, 'We have no tanks here, or aircraft'."

As Shunari recalled it, "Actually, they did try to help me later on, but got knocked back and retreated, though they knew we we're trapped there....By morning, the entire route was covered with a dense fog. This was our salvation, but I kept asking where the hell the tanks were. Once the fog lifted we took on hellfire. Actually, we got out of there in broad daylight, at 0700 hours, with just two half-tracks, with enemy infantry and tanks chasing us along the road."*

The 582nd Battalion's jeep mounted recoilless gun force, under the deputy battalion commander, Maj. Imri Ron, attempted a rescue attack on the west flank of the road as well, but was halted, by the division commander's order.** Once he reached the medevac point near Yukon perimeter, the 582nd Battalion commander tried to re-muster his scattered flock and assess the damages: these were grave. His troops were scattered all over the place, each man making his own way back to Israeli lines. As one survivor, who managed to reach the Israeli lines near Fort Lakekan, reported, "Once we reached our lines, I found the 14th Brigade deputy commander,

---

*   14th Brigade's Radio Network, 0647 hours. Quoted on 14th Brigade's website.

**   Col. (ret.) Imri Ron, in an interview, 206.

and told him we had men and an officer left out there. He replied: 'We all know about you, even the Chief of General Staff does. But I'm sorry to say, there's nothing we can do. I got in there with five tanks, and got out with just two,' he was all smeared with blood and dirt, so I said nothing." Eventually, Maj. Shunari had a bellyful of complaints about being sent to the lion's den with insufficient information and forces. His battalions had twenty-five men killed that night. Among them were his brother, Yehiel; Israel Schindler, a decorated veteran from the 1967 Battle for Jerusalem; Dudu Aharon, whose brother, Hanoch, was killed three hours earlier, in Tirtur Road; and an equal number of wounded.

Indeed, some attempts had been made to rescue the battered force. At 0515 hours, the 14th Brigade's commander had ordered his deputy to send the company which had cleared Akavish Road to yet another northward attack on the junction, to reach Titur and rescue the casualties of the 852nd Battalion and Giladi's force. Deputy Brigade Commander Lt.-Col. Ariely, reached the junction, but, after having three tanks hit, including his own, turned back, leaving three tanks of the 407th Battalion under Ehud Gross.

At 0500 hours, Col. Reshef reported to the division commander regarding the state of things, asking him to assign him a portion of the neighboring 421st Brigade, under Haim Erez, in order to rescue the hard pressed 582nd Battalion, which was scattered along Tirtur Road. Sharon approved, so now Reshef's division mustered its already overstrained resources for the rescue. After talking it over with the 421st Brigade commander, the latter lent the 14th Brigade the 599th Battalion, under Maj. Ami Morag.*

---

* For an account of this battle, see also Bergman, *Real Time,* pp. 246-252.

Between 0400 and 0700 hours there were actually two battles being fought over the junction and Tirtur Road. One was the attempted rescue by the 599th Battalion under Morag, and another, at the 43rd kilometer of Tirtur, by the survivors of the 582nd Reconnaissance Battalion struggling to retreat, some on foot while others on board the surviving half-tracks; some heading eastward, others westward, for Lakekan. All the while, the junction and Tirtur Road remained impassable.

At 0600, it was reported to the Southern Command Command that the Roller Bridge had broken apart, while being towed over a dune, when the tork of the towing tank and braking tank were out of balance. This also had the effect of shaking the morale of the Front Command. A few hours later Deputy Chief of General Staff Major General Tal, took out his frustration on the Southern Command commander demanding: "Did we get the pontoons?! Did the bridge not make it because it was broken, or because of the traffic jam?! Why didn't they deliver it in three separate sections, in accordance with procedure?! That was terribly wrong of them." At that point, the Roller Bridge was out of the picture.

Shunari's attempt to break through the junction, October 16, 0500 hours:

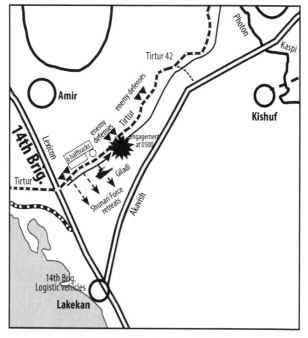

Dvelah HQ, October 16 0506 hours:

The day dawning on the desert was shrouded with a dense fog, making it difficult for the decision makers gathered at Dvelah to see the situation clearly. At 0615 hours, Defense Minister Dayan reported to the Prime Minister in Tel Aviv, from the HQ, about the complicated situation: "We haven't got a bridge yet, but there are no enemy tanks across the Canal, so there is no danger of us being cut off. Our forces have reached the beachfront, including the paratroopers battalion on the west bank. We intend not to recall them and are supporting them with our tanks from the east bank. This is because we want to build the bridge in daylight, or, if we have to, by night. However, we do not want to relinquish our bridgehead across the canal. We lost forty men yesterday there, so currently, we are not doing any worse. Heavy tank battles are still on. But we have enough tanks. We'll throw in aircraft and the enemy will probably use artillery. There are no complications, but there is a wedge of some Egyptian tanks, so we cannot get on with the bridge until we clear them out."

The senior commanders had mixed feelings. Dayan said one critical sentence, reflecting everyone's feeling: "We do not want to lose the bridgehead," and his tone is saying, "yes, but," inferred from the failed attempt to bridge the canal. Though the arrival of Alligators was some comfort, the Southern Command could hardly call it a bridgehead. Bar Lev reported, "The paratroopers are on the west bank, securing the passages across the Freshwater Canal; we have one Alligator launched, and we'll soon start fording tanks. Arik requested another brigade, but this is absurd. Maybe we'll send it, if it's inevitable."

Then, the Chief of General Staff revealed his feelings about last night's battles, stating "there was a lot of politics mixed up all the time." He was probably referring to the subtle quarrels over assignments. Sergeant Yaakov Priel, who watched the scene as a common serviceman in the HQ, recorded in his diary that "this morning, the atmosphere was grave and tense, diametrically different to the one during the early hours of the campaign."

Nevertheless, the Paratroopers were across the canal, in the Yard, the Alligators were ready to launch, and the embankment was being breached. Yet the junction was still blocked, and the battle raged on.

PART 4:

A DEADLY CROSSROADS.

1. NO ONE'S GETTING OUT OF HERE ALIVE!

Pontoon Battalion, Artillery Road, October 16, 0630 Hours:
Early in the morning, the pontoon column, commanded by
Lt.-Col. Avi Zohar and towed by Ilan Maoz's tanks, reached
the 55th kilometer of Akavish Road, about two kilometers away
from the Akavish-Artillery Road Junction. It had only traveled
twelve kilometers away from its outset, Tasa, and was still about
seventeen kilometers away from the canal. On the roadside,
Zohar met the 143rd Division deputy commander, Yaakov
"Jacky" Even, who ordered him to keep moving on Akavish
Road, all the way to the launching point. The column was led
by four bulldozer tanks. Near the Akavish-Tirtur Junction, one
of them was torched by a missile, and all of the others took
cover in the empty irrigation ditches along the roadside.

Akavish proved too risky for delivering the pontoons. The
column, drawing the inevitable conclusion, made a stop near
the Akavish-Caspi Junction, about fourteen kilometers short of
its destination. Nearly at the same time, at 0605, the Sisyphean
journey of the Roller Bridge reached its breaking point, literally,

at the 55th kilometer of Akavish Road. The bridge only was towed five kilometers, from Yukon. It broke down due to poor coordination between the towing and pushing tanks, during the climbing of a dune. A desperate tank battalion commander, Ben Shoshan, reported to Even that the bridge would take a long time to repair. "So uncouple it and leave," Even ordered. His brigade commander, Haim Erez, overheard it from his position at the waterfront, and told him "come, we're crossing." So Ben Shoshan abandoned the bridge.

The situation on the morning of October 16th was the following: at the 55th kilometer of Akavish Road, the roller bridge had broken down. Near it, the pontoon column, as well, had been forced to halt. The 14th Brigade had failed to secure Tirtur Road, so the Egyptians deployed north of it were threatening the narrow corridor that had been secured between Tirtur and Akavish, the two roads that were to be used in the crossing.

Despite the foothold that the paratroopers had gained on the west bank, the senior staff gathered at Dvelah HQ were disappointed. In addition to the Front commanders, the main conference room was occupied by the Chief of General Staff and the Defense Minister, who had been following the events throughout the night. At 0615 hours, after a tense, sleepless night, the Defense Minister, trying to reassure the Prime Minister, told her he was not concerned about the paratroopers on the west bank being cut off. In his words: "I am positive that what we need most of all is defeating the Egyptians, and the way to do it is crossing the canal".* As agreed upon by the High Command members the night before, the politicians

---

*   Bartov, *Dado,* p.239.

were only updated on a need to know basis, without too many details. High ranking military officers received a completely different report: at 0630 hours, the Chief of General Staff Elazar phoned his deputy, Major General Tal, informing him that the IDF had missed a rare opportunity to freely storm all over the west bank of the canal while the enemy deployed no forces to oppose it. We may have no second chance like this, Elazar deplored: "We have failed to exploit the element of surprise, and our achievements will be smaller than they could have been." Elazar also portayed this partial disappointment in his reports to the Government and the Knesset's Foreign Affairs and Defense Committee. This attitude also affected some of his decisions made during that day, such as reassigning some tasks from the 143rd to 162nd Division. This impression was shared by the rest of the Southern Command commanders. Yet General Sharon, the fording force's commander, completely disagreed, adhering to his philosophy.

When asked whether to proceed with the crossing, he categorically approved, yet some doubted whether his division could handle its assignment, considering the nightmarish consequences of the previous night's fighting. Addressing this concern, he asked the Front commander, Lt.-Gen. Bar Lev, for support of 162nd Division elements. But Bar Lev turned him down. Now Sharon had no choice but to muster the remaining available elements of his forces.

* * *

While the Chief of General Staff was updating his deputy, he received reports about the first Alligator entering the canal and that Giora Lev's armored forces were being delivered, in turns, to the west bank. It meant that the elements of an armored forces bridgehead had been created. This only intensified the dilemmas of the Chief of General Staff and Southern Command commanders. Dvela HQ conference room had witnessed a hot debate on whether the bridgehead formed was sustainable enough to allow for proceeding with the original plan. There was the growing impression that the forces of the 143rd Division had been exhausted, and that the 162nd Division, under Maj.-Gen. Adan, had to be called up for the road clearing operation. The relatively small detachment holding the west bank bridgehead posed a hamlet style dilemma for the decision- makers: should they recall it, due to the absence of bridges, or throw in more forces?

Nonetheless, the main fighting that morning was being waged over the roads. There was a pressing, undisputed need to uncork the Lexicon-Tirtur Junction bottleneck.

"This is what we had achieved," Major General Sharon concluded, considering the glass half full: "we have had achievements on the west bank, as well as on the east bank. Though Tirtur Road is yet to be cleared, still Akavish Road is secured. We failed to secure a few kilometers wide corridor, as expected, and we could have done more on this night."

14th Brigade, Lexicon-Tirtur Junction, October 16:

It was difficult to discern the results of the fighting over Lexicon through the dense morning fog of October 16. Yet none could avoid the sights imprinted in the minds of so many: pairs of tanks, an Israeli tank facing an Egyptian tank, each a few meters from the other, both smoking, entangled like some dueling medieval knights; according to one count, there were twelve Israeli tanks and six other armored vehicles hit near the junction, all a short distance from each other. The grounds of the Chinese Farm were strewn with vehicles of all types: tanks, APCs, troop-carriers, missile carriers, and corpse-carriers, hit and burnt, both Israeli and Egyptian. The 14th Brigade had lost over fifty tanks and about 120 men that night, yet the goddamned junction was still impassible. The 14th Brigade seemed exhausted after having attacked it five times. Though that night was marked by a clear drawback, it still witnessed one significant success. Covered by the tenacious fighting of the 14th Brigade, the Paratroopers Brigade had managed to cross the canal nearly unobstructed.

At daybreak, Col. Reshef, 14th Brigade Commander, drove his tank south, to the 50th kilometer of Tirtur Road, west of Lexicon Road, near the Yard, to get a first-hand impression of what was going on at the junction. Doing a quick calculation, the commander soon realized his force had decreased to a fraction of its former strength. Of his four battalion strong armored force, only two reduced battalions and some other remnants survived. Judging from the morning count, his two battalions had just about forty tanks left, of the 97 departing yesterday from the 56th kilometer of Caspi Road. What was worse, most of his commanders had been killed: Col. (posthumously) Yoav Brome, 87th Reconnaissance Battalion: Maj. Rafi Bar Lev, a company commander of that battalion; Captain Gideon Giladi, a company commander of 407th Battalion; Eliezer Caspi, a company commander of 184th Battalion and Ben Ari, a company commander of 79th Battalion. Yeshayahu Beitel, who had replaced the 407th Battalion commander, and Lt.-Col. Amram Mitzna, 79th Battalion commander, were wounded. The force had to regroup.

At 0530 hours, Reshef revealed to Sharon his feeling of having reached the limits of his strength. Though Sharon continued to press for the clearing of the route, Reshef admitted to difficulties. In his words, "Sorry, I am observing the scene closely, and doing my best to score some achievements." "I know," Sharon said emphatically.

Due to the withdrawal of the 79th and 184th Battalions, which had been assigned to secure the north flank of the corridor, from Usha Road southward to near to Shiekh Road, the corridor had been significantly narrowed, and its width now seemed insufficient to sustain the massive stream of traffic expected to pass through it. But Sharon stated that "we clearly have just one challenge, and that is crushing the enemy force near Lexicon-Tirtur."

However, there were more tasks yet to be carried out. The situation was as hazy as the foggy air. At that moment, fog was a major factor. On the one hand, it offered cover to the troops for their retreat, yet it also made the spotting of friendly forces, vehicles and the enemy, difficult. As Lt.-Col. Almog recalled, "The 184th Battalion, advanced, at daybreak, through a dense fog, through which you couldn't see the tip of your nose. The dense fog made it difficult to navigate and detect enemy forces. At the 254th kilometer of Lexicon, we spotted an Egyptian tank a few meters away, and my intelligence officer just mowed down its crew with his Uzi."*

The 79th Armored Battalion was exhausted and needed a respite. As Natan Ben Ari, who replaced the battalion

---

*   Ehud Michaelson, *Operation Valiant,* p.279.
**   Ohayon, *We're Still There,* p.184.

commander described it, "By morning, our strength included the remnants of our battalion, one company strong; the remnants of the 87th Battalion, one company strong, and a company of the 600th Brigade's 407th Battalion."

By 0700 hours, Reshef allowed this ragtag battalion to disengage and retreat, through Matzmed, to Fort Lakekan, to regroup. At 0745 hours, reaching Lakekan, the men dismounted their tanks, and looked around in disbelief. Of an initial twenty strong tank force, just five had survived, and not all of them were intact. Company Commander Bertie Ohayon told of one sight that would not leave his mind – of a Company Commander sitting in the sand, head bowed, covering his face with his hands.**

* * *

The dwindled 184th Battalion, which had spent the night with just five operational tanks, was left on Sheikh Road to secure the north flank. In the morning, the deputy managed to retrieve another six tanks left behind, increasing the battalion's strength to eleven tanks, each of which had survived its own infernal night.* Obviously, that battalion needed a respite as well. As Brig.-Gen. (ret.) Benny Taran later recalled: "It was at the Chinese Farm that I first sensed fear. My mouth was parched, and I sensed it was my end, that we weren't getting out of here alive. It was a mishmash of damaged tanks and vehicles, with

---

*   For the 184th Battalion's fighting in the Chinese Farm, see Michaelson, pp.256-267.

**   Ibid, p.272.

*** Ibid, p.280

the occasional tank blowing up. A terrible sight." **

Thirteen men of the 184th Battalion were killed in that battle. Yet in the morning, Almog wrote his wife: "We're doing great….the Egyptians are broken…it was a hard night's fight, the veritable inferno, but victory is as good as won."***

Reshef disbanded Beitel's 407th Armored Battalion and Brome's 87th Reconnaissance Battalion, which now had no commanders and few tanks left, reassigning their surviving men and company commanders to various armored battalions where the command had survived. These battalions were temporarily stricken from the order of battle. Infantry battalions needed regrouping as well. Most of them were withdrawn to the rear at Fort Lakekan, where some of the 143rd Division's logistics elements were stationed, for recuperation and regrouping.

Both Sharon and Reshef started looking for additional forces for breaching the road. The only available force was the 599th Battalion of Haim Erez's brigade, under Maj. Ami Morag. It was planned for them to cross the canal first. They weren't in charge of any fording machinery, yet were forced into the reserve unit due to the events that night. Now they were being reassigned to the operation under Reshef.

Maj. Ami Morag, an infantry officer reassigned to the Armored Corps after the 1967 Six-Day War, had already had his share of ordeals since the war had broken out. In October 9th he had led his battalion in an attack on the Egyptian occupied Fort Hamutal, which was threatening the central section of Artillery Road. The attack had failed, nearly wiping out his entire battalion, and seriously traumatizing the commander. Now he was being called to help in the rescue of Maj.Natan Shunari's men who had been seriously hit, as well as to participate in yet another attempt at clearing the road of Egyptian anti-tank men. This time, he was to advance westward. He met Shunari, who was still shocked by the results of that night's events, at Akavish-Tirtur Junction. Mounting Morag's tank, Shunari explained to Morag that he must hurry to Tirtur, to save his unit's numerous casualties. Before the tank was able to advance, the entire force suffered a volley of missiles, probably fired from positions north of Tirtur Road, and Shunari ran from the tank. Morag wondered aloud, on the radio, whether or not it might be pointless to enter the junction, yet Reshef clearly ordered him saying "You must clear the road."

At about 0700, the force under Maj. Ami Morag began its short yet fierce adventure. With a column of no more than six tanks, manned by officers only, he attempted a breakthrough westward, on Titur Road. But, to avoid the intense missile fire, all six tanks had to take cover in a roadside depression, which lay in a dead spot not reachable by Egyptian anti-tank units. Occasionally, the force tried to assume positions and detect the source of fire, but in vain.

As Morag recalled, "I told the 14th Brigade commander that I couldn't see any way that we could break through, except by dealing with the Chinese Farm, because to get there was as good as committing suicide. He replied he just wanted a breakthrough in the road. When trying to take to the road, I had some missiles fired at my tank, which I managed to evade, by driving backwards. I clearly detected missile launches coming from the southern edge of Missouri perimeter. I reported to Reshef that I spotted missile launches from there, requesting artillery fire on that position. He told me that he would order a battalion of the 600th Brigade, stationed in Hamdiyah, to push them southward, so I could get up to the road."

Reshef requested and was given reinforcements from the 600th Brigade, in the form of the 409th Battalion. However, taking hits from several missiles and having one tank hit, the battalion retreated. At about 0900 hours, Morag started to take action. In his words, "We were taking artillery fire all the time, doing poorly…whenever we moved out of the depression, missiles were launched at us. It feels terrible to be stuck in a pit after getting used to mobile warfare. So my artillery fire support officer, told me: I'll give you artillery and Katyusha fire, so you can break through to that road.' I replied I thought it was suicidal, yet we would do it…"

"The moment we got to the road, we took on a hail of missiles. We darting between the raining missiles, firing constantly. I knew exactly where to aim, and every shot counted. We also didn't have to choose ammunition, since we were targeting infantry. We launched whatever we could fit in the breech, either armor piercing or high explosive squash head. It was a two and a half kilometer mad ride, during which I spent nearly all of my ammo supply, as well as five 0.3 caliber browning belts. We were just driving along the road, spotting the Egyptians in the Chinese Farm's ditches. There were hordes of them there, a few meters away, who kept firing RPG rockets and machinegun fire at us. All the while, missiles kept flying. I couldn't reach Lexicon-Tirtur Junction, because near the 42nd kilometer of Tirtur Road, it was blocked by the remains of half-tracks and Patton tanks (the traces of Shunari's force). I pulled off to the left, hitting a deep ditch—my tank driver felt it strongly. I told him to pull back. We pulled to the left, heading east, but I saw we were getting nowhere, since there were ditches and enemy all over, firing at us constantly. We had one tank knocked out right as we emerged from the ditch, and evaded their rockets by veering to the left and right. The wind was working to our advantage, giving us a kind of smoke screen on our right…we drove fast, firing with whatever we had, even Uzis, like mad, both left and right. One tank was hit by a missile right away and retreated into the depression. The deputy company commander's tank was hit and stopped. We were facing one of the irrigation canals in the Chinese Farm, and I somehow managed to jump across it. I then descended a small bluff, I watched as my tanks followed me, one by one. In the end, four of our original tanks survived. Then, Reshef radioed me, asking for my position, but I replied that I couldn't speak. We were all soaked with sweat and exhausted. It was sheer madness. Until this very day I don't understand how we got out of there."* The traumatic experience of Morag clearly indicates that the Egyptians were strongly defending the perimeter north of Tirtur, and could be a threat, from their trenches, against Akavish Road as well. At about 1000 hours, Morag advanced as far as the 43rd kilometer of Tirtur Road, but couldn't make it to Lexicon, so he turned south, heading for Akavish, got out of the killing zone and retreated to the 53rd kilometer of Akavish Road. Though he managed to drive down the road, he failed to clear it."

In retrospect, Morag noticed, "Though it seemed like an attempt to clear Tirtur Road, but, checking around, one could have seen other ways to do that. We were strongly affected by this experience, and I had many meetings with my deputy, in an attempted to analyze what went on there. Our conclusion

---

*   B.Z. Kedar, *The Story of 97th Battalion*, restricted publication, 1975, pp.70-73.

was there were other ways of clearing the Chinese Farm, and it was eventually used, but a little too late," he said enigmatically.

* * *

At about 0730 hours, while 143rd Division was trying to pull itself together, coping with the effects of that disastrous night, Front Commander Shmuel Gonen decided to get a firsthand impression of the division's condition. So he flew to the abandoned Kishuf stronghold, two kilometers south of Akavish Road, where the 162nd Divison's HQ was quartered in a group of tents. There, he tried to see with his very eyes whether Akavish Road was cleared.

While he was traveling there, Bar Lev was running the Command from Dvelah HQ. He tried to question Sharon about his condition. The latter was still working out the blocking. Bar Lev's main concern was when the 162nd Division could be delivered across the canal.

Bar Lev: What is the schedule for the handling the containment?

Sharon: I have enough forces to handle it.

Bar Lev: Do your best, ASAP.

One inevitable decision that Front Commander Bar Lev made was to relieve Sharon of some of his assignments, to let him focus on setting up the bridgehead. Following the breakdown of the Roller Bridge, he asked 162nd Division commander, Major General Adan, to help by towing the pontoons planned to construct the bridge. Meanwhile, he made a remark implying a major change of plan: "Lexicon-Tirtur Junction is blocked. Arik handles it. At the 42nd kilometer of Tirtur Road, our infantry suffered an enemy tank attack. If possible, step it up and knock out some of their tanks, to avoid humiliation. Let your right flank determine what can be done. Arik fears the Roller Bridge is not intact. Due to that, it's most important to advance the pontoons."

Adan was puzzled. For the last few hours, his division had been all set to cross the canal. He wasn't thrilled about assigning forces to the fight over the junction or any other assignments that might disperse his forces.

* * *

At 0800 hours, at the western end of Tirtur Road, 14th Brigade commander, Amnon Reshef, mustered an ad hoc force out of the remnants of the 87th and 407th battalions, and dashed northeastward to storm the impregnable junction. His assault came to a halt about one kilometer north of the junction, after hitting eight enemy tanks, when his tanks ran out of ammunition. Yet an hour later, Reshef was able to report to Sharon, with some relief: "I'm holding the junction." Though somewhat uncorked, the bottleneck still remained. At 1100 hours, Reshef reported that his brigade was critically short of ammo and fuel. In actuality, its main effort was now being redirected from carrying out new offensives to defending accomplishments.

2. BERGER BEGS FOR PERMISSION TO CROSS.

421st Brigade, Matzmed Yard:

The Alligators, escorted by the 264th Battalion under Giora Lev, reached Matzmed Yard at 0400 hours. At 0615, Alligators

Battalion commander, Col. Yaniv, reported they are ready to take to the water, and ten minutes later the first Alligator was launched into the canal. Fifteen Alligators were launched, in groups of three joined together to form a two-way raft. This was the very moment Maj. Lev had been waiting for. His reduced force consisted of only ten tanks, the rest were stuck with the Unifloat pontoons, far behind. Once the first Alligator was launched, they had a tight schedule. As Lev recalls: "When I reached the Yard, the division commander ordered me to cross the canal at once and operate under the paratroopers commander. Then, Bar Lev radioed me to remind me of the following. He said, 'This is 1000.' Pretending not to recognize him, I told him to wait. He replied, 'Operate under 9.' I didn't recognize 9. It was Danni Matt. By then, we had already mounted the floated rafts, and Company Commander [future ambassador] Yossi Berger begged me, crying, for the honor of crossing first. I said: 'Hold it, maybe the division commander wants to cross first.' When I asked Sharon, he said, 'No way. I'd love to, but I must remain here.' Meanwhile, Berger sneaked between my tank and the raft, stating: 'I'm here anyway, so why can't you let me in?!' The mounting of the rafts went smoothly, with the battalion commander directing each tank's mounting personally. I, too, directed the tank drivers over the radio. It was the very first time we drove on board these rafts."

The tanks climbed the rafts one by one. By 0815 hours, the entire ten tank strong force was already on the west bank of the Suez. The tanks were ordered to follow the tracks left by Berger's tank. As Lev recalls, "After thirty or forty meters, we faced another embankment, one that was difficult to get through. So we just rammed it, driving backwards and forwards, and breached it."

* * *

Reaching the 52nd kilometer of Akavish Road, Maj. Ami Morag tried to gain some respite after his fiasco of attempting to clear Tirtur Road. At about 0830 hours, while the Alligators were crossing the canal, he spotted a long westbound column advancing on Akavish Road. It was led by the 257th Armored Battalion, under Lt.-Col. Shimon Ben Shoshan, which had abandoned the broken Roller Bridge and advanced with Erez's 421st Brigade's HQ to link up with Giora Lev on the west bank. Following it, on board buses, was the 2nd Paratroopers Battalion, under Lt.-Col. Zviki Nur, of Danni Matt's brigade. They, too, were planned to take part in the canal crossing. As Morag later recalled, "I saw missiles aimed at them, so I alerted Ben Shoshan. He just thanked me, and then his tank was hit by a missile and he was wounded." Ben Shoshan would spend the entire following year in several hospitals. Due to the missile volley hitting Ben Shoshan's tank and another four tanks, Erez ordered the paratroopers back to the 55th kilometer of Akavish Road. Zviki argued, yet finally had to obey his brigade commander. "It was the right thing to do," Erez recalled, "or else we would have taken heavy casualties. Erez pulled himself together, contacted the 257th Battalion's radio network and dashed forward on Akavish Road toward Fort Lakekan. He reported to Sharon that Akavish Road was "dangerously impassable."

The brigade commander's force and Ben Shoshan's eighteen tanks, didn't tarry in Lakekan, their objective being to cross the canal westward, and to link up with Maj. Lev's force. When Erez entered Matzmed Yard, at 0900 hours, it was quiet. While a few hundred meters away two armies were entangled in a deadly embrace, at Matzmed one could just go fishing on the canal bank. At 0930 hours he met Sharon in the Yard. The latter assigned him with a surrealistically daring task: to get deep behind the Egyptian lines and destroy six anti-aircraft missile bases. As Erez later recalled: "Intelligence was scant. We only knew that nothing but seventy tanks stood between us and Cairo. Nobody could give me any information. We were also asked to capture one missile intact. These bases were positioned on Vardit Road. All I knew was that in addition to the missiles, every such base has between 250 and 300 men."

At 1030 hours, Col. Erez joined Giora Lev's force, and the combined 257th and 264th battalions made up a twenty tank and ten APC strong task force, under the direct command of Lev and the brigade commanders HQ.

* * *

While the battles for the roads and junctions were raging on, the officers at Dvelah HQ tried to assess where they stood. At 0830 hours, the Chief of General Staff decided to go back to GHQ compound. He and the Defense Minister agreed to redeploy the 35th Brigade, under Col. Uzi Yairi, from the Ras Sudr area to the crossing zone. This was a response both to the need for additional forces to clear the roads, as well as Sharon's division's partial setback.

At this stage, Dayan, like the rest of the men at the HQ, estimated that "only thirty percent of the plan has been realized." The blocked Junction haunted Dayan, so he asked, "ex cathedra" the Front commanders, whether Adan's 162nd Division should be thrown in. Front Commander Bar Lev replied that Sharon was regrouping and could fend for himself.

Yet it was obvious that the 143rd Division was exhausted by the night's fighting over the roads. At 1140 hours, HQ personnel heard Sharon radioing Bar Lev: "Amnon is out of fuel and ammo. We must hold that line, and we have nobody to hold it. It's rough going, but it's going. We've entered Tirtur Road westward and eastward." Yet at 1145 hours, he reported to Gonen that "the attack failed. The Egyptians are launching suicide attacks. I cannot use airstrikes since we have casualties."

162nd Division, near Tasa, between the 15th and 16th of October:

The men of the 162nd Brigade, gathered at the assembly zones on the north-south roads near Tasa, were in for a surprise: Yafa Yarkoni, the singer who was known for her entertaining of all IDF warriors, was standing on a tank lit by the headlights of two command cars, performing her best hits. Soon all of the men were inspired to join in a sing-along.

The division commander used the evening hour to personally address his men. Lit by a jeep's headlights, standing on a tank, loudspeaker in hand, he tried to breath a fresh fighting spirit into his men, getting them to share his sense that the battle was about to turn in their favor. At 0145 hours, the brigade headed for its assembly zone. Not far away, Sharon's men were already engaged in fierce fighting.

During all that night, Adan's division prepared for the crossing, without any hurrying up. As mentioned above, it was planned that he would cross the canal after the 143rd had secured a bridgehead, and then carry out a southward flanking maneuver, heading for the city of Suez. H-hour was set for October 16th, at daybreak. As the hour approached, the division commander arrayed his troops. The 162nd Division was to reach Suez within twenty-four hours,

188 | AMIRAM EZOV

thrusting through Gnefa hills. It was to have no tasks on the east bank. As Adan recalled, "I asserted the importance of quickly gaining a foothold in the rugged Gnefa hillside, and that we should leave the Egyptians a way out of the city, westward, in order not to harden their expected resistance."* Despite the relatively flexible planning, no alternative plans were drawn in case the securing of the bridgehead and the corridor by the 143rd Division went wrong. Intelligence reports alerted Adan about possible commando ambushes at the roads and passes and possible damage to logistic support elements. Yet he, as we said, only looked straight ahead, at the canal.

To "Bren's" discontent, his division had been reduced to just two brigades, the 460th and 217th, with a total strength of 145 tanks. The 500th Brigade, under Col. Aryeh Keren, was held as the Front Command's reserve.

Adan's armored columns moved south of Akavish Road, carefully avoiding traffic jams. Some of the unarmored vehicles, led by deputy division commander, Brig.-Gen. Dov Tamari, traveled on the road. Division HQ's APC, too, advanced along the road, to closely watch the advancement of 143rd Division.

* * *

Adan was strongly affected by what he had seen on the road: "I realized the road was just jammed with traffic. I stopped by the broken Roller Bridge, and was told it would take hours to repair. I found Haim Razon, one of the best ordnance technicians of

---

*   Adan, *On Both Banks*, p.187.
**   ibid., p.200.

the Armored Corps, sending him with a technical team to help the repair works."* By daybreak, the HQ assumed position near the abandoned Fort Kishuf, waiting for further orders.

At about 0500 hours, the Front Command informed Adan he was to cross the canal first, but should wait for the command.** The division's operations officer had started making the wake-up calls and delivering the deployment orders to the brigades.

By then, the vanguard of the 460th Brigade, under Gabi Amir, already faced Caspi-Artillery Road. At 0600 hours, 217th Brigade, under Col. Natan Nir, reached the 59th kilometer of Revicha Road, and joined the waiting division.

Twenty minutes later, Adan was updated by Major General Gonen, who was on his way to his HQ, about "a traffic jam on Lexicon and Tirtur roads which we couldn't work out, and therefore, we cannot keep towing the bridge. Arik wants you to give him a brigade, but we want you to get with full force to Makztera zone, on the west bank." If he only listened carefully, Adan should have noticed here signs that his division's task was about to change, since there was a lot of work to do on the east bank, before one could dash westward.***

Late in the morning, Brig.- Gen. Uri Ben Ari, deputy front

*   Adan, *On Both Banks*, p.200.
**   Ibid, p.200.
***   At 0620 hours, Gonen reminded Adan, "When in Maktzerah, don't forget to deal with all those things that are giving Benny (Air force Commander) a hard time. The softies [Alligators] are already afloat and prepared."
**** Adan, *On Both Banks*, p.201.

commander, flew to 162nd HQ near Kishuf, followed shortly by Maj. Gen. Gonen. "Bren" asked Ben Ari, his superior from the old days, "what was going on here"!?" To this, Ben Ari replied, "Give me a break, Bren buddy, it's a delicate issue. Let's talk about it after the war." Adan asked him no more about it. Instead, he ordered his deputy, Dov "Dovik" Tamari to handle the towing of the pontoons waiting at the 55th kilometer of Akavish Road.*[4]

When Gonen reached HQ, Adan asked him as well. Gonen told him Sharon didn't deliver. He couldn't see what went wrong with Sharon in that war. Bren took it as an inappropriate overreaction, but preferred not to respond.*

Gonen and Tamari went on driving on Akavish Road, in order to see for themselves what was going on at the Chinese Farm. Suddenly, a lone tank appeared in front of them. Gonen ordered it to halt and mounted, spotting a hole in its turret and two dead men on the floor. When asked what had happened, the surviving crew told how they took an anti-tank missile on Akavish Road. Driving on, Tamari and Gonen climbed Hamdyah hill, where they dismounted and travelled on foot a few kilometers, to an observation point. They could only pray that no Egyptian missile launcher had set his sights on them while reaching the observation point. They watched as missiles were being launched at the 600th Brigade's tanks. Suddenly, they spotted an Egyptian tank turning its gun toward them, at a distance of 1500 meters. "He'll miss," Tamari said. Indeed, the tank fired and missed. "So what did I learn from this whole

---

*   Adan, *On Both Banks*, p.201.

tour?!" Gonen asked rhetorically. "That the Egyptians hold the Chinese Farm, and that Tirtur and Akavish roads are blocked. In other words, I found out the state of things in the field was not what I thought before. We got paratroopers on the west bank, and the Roller Bridge is nearly fixed. Of the pontoons, we have four or five, and the only thing stopping us is enemy forces."

When he was back in Bren's HQ, Gonen warned the 162nd Division commander that he would have to fight for the east part of the bridgehead. The major obstacle to advancing the fording machinery was found out to be not technical malfunctions, but that the Akavish and Tirtur routes were being blocked by the enemy. Gonen couldn't figure out all that from received reports, but had to see it with his very own eyes.

Gonen considered the blocked roads and the lack of a bridge unnecessary risks which Southern Command shouldn't have run. "These are not calculated risks," he said, even the supposedly cleared Akavish Road could not have qualified as a secured route.

Sharon disagreed, obviously. In his words: "Counting all the damaged vehicles along Akavish Road, I found there were no more than thirty-eight, although hundreds of vehicles had traveled on it. Though the road is not fully cleared, it is at least passable by armored vehicles. We could have delivered another armored brigade to the west bank, and formed a more substantial ford, with no obstructions. We could have deployed armored vehicles there. See, I got there in my Wagoneer on Friday morning. Though it was shelled down in the Yard, yet it got there."

The 162nd Brigade was still waiting for a decision, its commander hoping that no changes were being made in the plan. At about 1000 hours Defense Minister Dayan's helicopter landed at Kishuf. The minister crawled under an APC, and fell asleep. Adan started growing impatient, pressing the front commander to allow him to advance his troops. Gonen, giving him some allowance, let him advance one of the 460th Brigade's battalions, and to order the rest of the forces to standby for action, nothing more.

Adan quickly delivered Gonen's command down to the 460th Brigade commander, Gabi Amir, and further down, to Col. Amir Yafe, the 198th Battalion commander. That battalion was to be the first to move. The armored battalion started off at 0945 hours, advancing from the 55th kilometer of Caspi Road straight through the dunes, to the canal. At 1100 hours, the seventeen strong tank battalion reached Matzmed Yard. Right after spotting a breach in the embankment, the battalion commander started getting his tanks on board the Alligators. He only got two vehicles on board when 143rd Divison Commander Sharon approached him, ordering him to get his vehicles off the Alligator. When Yaffeh wondered what the matter was, Sharon explained: "Front Command forbids delivering any more tanks to the west bank."

As Adan recalled: "Sharon called me at 1145 hours, reporting the prohibiting order, and went on: ' Amnon has been fighting all night like hell. He had grave losses. His remaining tanks are engaged, but low on fuel and ammo. I request you leave me Amir's battalion so let Amnon regroup.' I granted it at once."*

Adan, *On Both Banks*, p.201.
**   Hillel Carmeli in an interview. See also Yishay Wexler and Yehuda Tal, *198th Battalion in the Yom Kippur War*, Ministry of Defense Press, 2002, p.93.

Sharon subordinated Yaffe's battalion to the 14th Brigade, and ordered it to relieve the 184th Battalion under Almog, who were holding with their last bit of strength, the north flank of the crossing corridor, along Shiekh Road.

Sharon's old signal officer, Lt.-Col. Hillel Carmeli, recognized, among those arriving with the 198th Battalion, his son, Shmuel, a tank crewman. After a short conversation, the son went on with the northbound force. Due to poor coordination, he received an all too "warm" welcome: the battalion which they relieved, the 184th, failing to recognize the approaching force, fired at it, hitting one tank and seriously injuring three men. One of those was Shmuel. "I ran to the medevac point," Hillel later recalled, "where I hardly recognized him. He had stomach, leg, and tailbone injuries which nearly gave him a permanent paralysis. He was evacuated to the rear in a half-track, yet it wasn't before evening that he reached a hospital, in Tel Aviv. I had no idea where he was. It was my nephew who found him there. Today he is a chemistry professor, walking on crutches, and the father of three." **

The 198th Battalion assumed positions between the Chinese Farm, codenamed Amir, and the canal. Soon it intensely engaged enemy forces trying to cut off the bridgehead from the north. The 184th retreated for regrouping, and at about 1200 hours, the north flank of the crossing corridor was secured.

GHQ Compound Room, Tel Aviv, October 16, 1000 Hours: "Dado", the Chief of General Staff, was absent from the GHQ for nearly 24 hours. He came back there very exhausted, frustrated and enraged. Summoning all High Command members, he poured out his bile on them. Though praising the plan, he was disappointed by the performance. He believed the Egyptians misread the maneuver, failing until then to close the breach with more considerable forces. The paratroopers and tanks had successfully penetrated the breach, with no significant opposition.

As Elazar recalled: "In the middle of this wild ride, there was a small blockage, first considered an ambush, and then an anti-tank defensive perimeter. Nevertheless, there was that little trouble, or maybe it was more than little. I cannot figure it out until this very day. Anyway, our forces were in a mess all night, and it took daylight to make things clear. By morning that defense proved stronger than we had suspected. It had anti-tank weapons, missiles and even some tanks. So we had to get disentangled, withdraw, regroup and charge…we kept telling Sharon to get it over with, and he kept replying that he needed one of Bren's brigades….When finally he was told to wait for Bren, he said he had a sufficient force, and other things which I never heard of, in all the wars I've been through. His reports all that night were overconfident, with no real info. At some point I just asked him: 'Just tell me how it is going.' To this he replied: 'Don't worry, you have nothing to fear, everything we'll be fine.' 'Who said anything about fear, we're all fearless. Just tell me how it is going?!' So we were being had all night. In a word, it was one mess up after another. Mind you, we didn't engage the enemy. Until 0900 hours the enemy hadn't known what hit them, and maybe they didn't get it until that very moment…."*

Now the Chief of General Staff went on updating his audience: "So far, we have twenty-eight tanks on the west bank already,

---

* Bartov, *Dado,* p.240.

yet not one bridge across the canal. It is all because of that tiny blockage." He assumed the bridges would be advancing toward the canal within four hours.

"We had two bridges that could be delivered in the afternoon. Yet the situation was deplorable. The Egyptians still hadn't figured it out, and here we had an open space, up for grabs, so it tortured my heart. If we had only had a bridge across the canal by 1000 hours, Bren would have stepped in and caused complete havoc. Bren had been given clear orders— to spot the AA missile batteries, raid them here, and knock them out with artillery there. Then the road would have been open to the Air Force. It would have been heaven on earth."

His deputy, Major General Tal, tried to comfort him. To this Elazar replied: "Hold it, I haven't lost this war yet. It just hurts my heart. If there was ever a golden opportunity missed, this was it. But let bygones be bygones. I'm not looking to be consoled. Right now we have the paras and a twenty-eight tank strong force, which should make a dash for the missiles and start going wild. That would make things much easier. This is where Danni Matts' force and the tanks are. Here is where Matt will secure a stronghold, with ten tanks. From here, a force of sixteen tanks and APCs will launch a raid. Today, between 1500 and 1600 hours—to be on the safe side, Bren's division will cross over to the west bank. It will not face strong defenses, yet not the open undefended space it would have faced last night. Therefore, they will not do it in one blow, just expand the foothold tonight, and tomorrow we will rise to see that the IDF has a substantial foothold west of the Suez. It won't be the brilliant blitz we wanted it to be, but that's it."

Deputy: "It will still happen. This is what Churchill referred to as 'the turn of the tide.'"

To this Elazar replied: "It will be the turn, indeed, I don't know of what, but there will be a turn."

* * *

Now the Chief of General Staff referred mostly to Major General Sharon, the 143rd Division commander, who he accused of ambiguous reports to the Front Command, making it hard for them to reach decisions. Somehow, Lt.-Gen. Elazar had failed to realize the catastrophic nature of the battles being waged over the junctions and roads, blaming the ill-conducted fighting on Sharon. His main concern was the lack of exploitation of the successes that already been achieved. For him the greatest fiasco had been the failure to erect a bridge. This had been the main challenge, he believed. At any rate, though it allowed the Chief of General Staff to give vent to his frustrations, the delayed schedule might have called for an adjustment of plans. Nonetheless, he kept to his initial plan: clearing the AA missiles in order to allow the IAF to do its best, and then building the bridge and completing the planned maneuver.

3. TIRTUR ROAD IS BLOCKED.

564th Battalion, west bank of the Suez, October 16, 0700 hours:

At 0700 hours, on the morning of October 16, Giora Lev's sixteen tank strong force joined Danni Matt's paras on the west bank. Nobody met them, except the cheers of the exhausted paratroopers, or gave them any assignment. Suddenly, a paratroopers' battalion commander jumped on the tank company commander's tank, telling him "Let's ride along the road to see what's up." So the company leader took the paratrooper for a ride through the trees. Spotting some men, he fired an anti-personnel Squash Head projectile, killing one and injuring another two. The three were found out to be Israeli paratroopers. "From then on, I ordered him to fire at assaulting armored vehicles or infantry only," Lev recalled. Then, two disoriented Egyptian APCs emerged opposite him, charging ahead, and he knocked out both of them. The Egyptians had no idea of what was facing them.

Meanwhile, Southern Command Commander Bar Lev, concerned about the insufficient width of the bridgehead on the west bank as well, ordered Matt to expand it all the way to Masecha Road, along the Freshwater Canal. At 0740 hours, Bar Lev authorized Sharon to deploy more tanks on the west bank, as long as his division could overcome the anti-tank defense perimeter using its own resources. He considered the deployment of the additional forces of the 421st Brigade a worthy way of maximally using an opportunity. There were no disagreements between Sharon, the 143rd Division commander and his superiors, about the necessity to proceed with the crossing. They only argued about the sufficient width of the corridor. While Sharon believed it was sufficient already, the High Command considered its current width too risky for further crossing. The Front Commander kept reminding of the need to suppress the AA missile bases first, since the future corridor must be cleared for the Air Force as well.

On the morning of October 16th, Danni Matt's paratrooper force was ordered to consolidate their foothold west of the canal. After the heartwarming encounter with Lev's tanks, which had just passed by, they were ordered to secure a defensive perimeter in a four kilometer radius from the landing point, clearing it of Egyptian forces. This order was more the result of confusion, rather than any attempt to advance the force.

Lev's tank force slightly boosted the confidence of Matt's force, which consisted of 700 paratroopers, the 565th Reconnaissance Battalion, under Lt.-Col. Dan Ziv, and the Brigade's Engineer Force. The bus mounted 416th Battalion, under Zviki Nur, was recalled after the buses had been proven to be easy prey for the Egyptian AT-men along Akavish Road. It only rejoined the force on the night of October 16th. Another component of the brigade, under Lt.-Col. Yossi Fredkin, was left on the east bank, to secure the Matzmed Yard. At 1000 hours, Matt was ordered to seize Deversoir Airbase, and did it without any casualties, finding it nearly deserted by the completely surprised Egyptian force. Yet the peaceful air greeting the brigade was soon rent with sporadic clashes and first casualties. Nonetheless, the day in general was marked with little action.

After the war, Col. Matt lectured about his emotions back then: "Though the hills around us were swarming with Egyptians, we felt, on October the 16th, that they were utterly confused and that we could push on." That impression fomented, among the troops, the sense of being abandoned, but also confidence that the IDF armored hordes would be joining them soon.

East bank of the Suez, Matzmed Yard, October 16, midday

By midday of October 16th, "Arik" Sharon was in the Yard, dealing with three major tasks: first of all, securing the approach routes to the Yard; secondly, checking the Egyptian southward pressure on Shiekh Road; thirdly, accomplishing the mission assigned to the Paratrooper Brigade on the west bank. On top of that, he also had to secure and organize a perimeter allowing the delivery of thousands of vehicles westwards. Gradually realizing that his tasks were by far disproportionate to his forces' strength, he was forced to somewhat reassess the situation. Nevertheless, he didn't quit for a single moment the aggressive approach marking his conduct since the beginning of the crossing campaign. He also grew increasingly critical of his superiors. In his words: "If only some officer more senior than a division commander was here, not just for a few minutes—and I suspect nobody lacking of courage, gentlemen—and saw what was going on….I think they would have just misread the battle."

Sharon's major complaint was against the halting of the crossing on October 16th, until the canal was bridged. But he also resented Southern Command constantly meddling with his command of his division. By that night, they had not allowed any significant force to cross the canal. In Sharon's words, "We got another tank here and there, from the 421st Brigade; about twenty-five tanks in total. We had more tanks on the ground, but they didn't allow us to get them across the canal."

Sharon held that since he was with his forces on the west bank anyway, it was just reasonable to place him in charge of all the forces on the west bank, leaving the 162nd Division on the east bank. Such suggestions, probably, did not win the approval of any of the front commanders. At that stage, the Front Command stuck to the original plan, reluctant to reassign troops and missions. So Sharon's pleas to concentrate his forces west of the Suez were repeatedly denied.

* * *

At 1100 hours, Bar Lev ordered Sharon to stop delivering tanks to the established bridgehead, before the raft bridge had been launched. Bar Lev considered the securing of the bridgehead far from accomplished. "So far, we have casualties, and no secured route. The question is," he asked Sharon, "can you handle your assignments on your own, or do you need support? I shall keep Bren from crossing as long as we have no bridge. We cannot deliver a very large force to the west."

* * *

At 1115 hours, The Chief of General Staff received a phone call, after a short rest in his small room in the GHQ Compound. It was his deputy, Major General Tal. He reported Bar Lev's request to use the 162nd Brigade for clearing the corridor to the east bank. The Chief of General Staff granted it. But he clearly understood it meant straying from the original plan. It reflected Southern Command's belief that the success of the Crossing depended on the clearing of the route and the securing of the perimeters commanding the approach to the Chinese Farm, codenamed Amir, and the perimeter codenamed Missouri. At the same time, Gonen ordered Adan: "Halt all advancement for a while, and make sure the 198th Battalion, under Amir Yaffeh, does not enter the water."

The Front Command's HQ reassessed the developments: the bright side was the successful fording of 247th Brigade, which managed to secure a bridgehead on the west bank; the fact that an armored element of 421st Brigade had crossed; the partial clearing of Akavish Road, and the securing of a narrow crossing corridor. The darker side was, mostly, the waning of the 14th Brigade's offensive momentum, the failure to clear Tirtur Road, and the failure, so far, to erect a bridge over the canal.

Forty minutes later, Sharon updated Bar Lev about his forces' progress: Erez's forces were on assignment on the west bank; Reshef was doing his best to do away with the Tirtur impasse, but his men were low on fuel and ammo; as he explained: "The line must be held, but there's nobody who can hold it. The going is tough, but it's going." By that time, Gonen was back at HQ from a visit of Bren's forces, and had the following radio conversation with Sharon:

Gonen: Arik, I assigned Bren with clearing Akavish and Tirtur Roads. Your job is to seize the Chinese Farm and the (area to the) south of Missouri (perimeter).

Sharon: But right now we have run out of everything.

Gonen: So let Bren clear the roads. You can get fuel and ammo and seize the Farm.

Sharon: OK.

Gonen: Good. And stop deploying any more forces across the canal.

Sharon: What did you say?

Gonen: Deploy no more forces across the canal.

Sharon: I've stopped already.

Gonen: Where are you, physically?

Sharon: At the beachhead.

Gonen: You should be east of the canal

Sharon: I am, and so is my HQ.

Gonen: Will you deliver the Trailer [Roller Bridge] also?

Sharon: It's broken, there's nothing to deliver.

Gonen: It's repaired. I saw it.

Sharon: I'll get it for you.

Gonen: Good. And let Dovik [Tamari] deliver the R [rafts].
Sharon: What?
Gonen: Let Dovik, under Bren, deliver the R. Meanwhile, you secure the Trailer.
Sharon: Does Even know about this?
Gonen: He does, I visited him, with Dovik.
Sharon: OK.
Gonen: So, to repeat: Your sector is the Chinese Farm, all the way to the beachhead. Bren should clear both roads, and you will secure them later. You deliver the fuel and ammo, deliver and place the trailer, while Bren delivers the R. Is it all clear?
Sharon: Yes.
Gonen: Thank you. Did you write it down?

* * *

Sharon found this pill hard to swallow. The gulf between him and Southern Command widened as the campaign went on.

For some reason, the Command also grew concerned about the orders of the 143rd Division commander to his troops. Much to Sharon's fury, his superiors started communicating directly with his subordinates. For example, at 1400 hours, a concerned Southern Command commander directly contacted the 14th Brigade commander, asking him about his orders from his direct superior. He also told the 600th Brigade commander, Tuvia Raviv, to report to him when he was ordered to cross the canal, and that he was not to cross without updating him.*

This clearly suggests that Southern Command feared that

---

*   Bartov, *Dado*, p.200.

Sharon might bet all of his assets on an immediate crossing, while the Command preferred to act slowly but surely. Gonen also ordered Sharon to restrict the Erez's Force raid to about ten kilometers west of the canal, not beyond Havit Road. But it didn't turn out that way.

At about 1200 hours Dvelah HQ gave the following order to Maj.-Gen. Adan, 162nd Division commander: "Arik should remain in charge of the bridgehead, and also secure the Farm. The trouble is he is out of fuel and ammo. You clear Akavish and Tirtur Roads and deliver the R [rafts], while he will deliver the Trailer [Roller Bridge]." Though it was only a temporary change of plan, made without abandoning the original one, it had many consequences. In practicality it meant that the Front Command preferred to commit both brigades to clearing the roads. According to this approach, the securing of a corridor and the bridging of the canal were preconditions for proceeding with the crossing. So now, Southern Command ordered the crossing forces to halt, and divided the tasks between the forces.

These decisions resulted from the decision-makers' meeting convened by Bar Lev in the main conference room of Dvela HQ. Bar Lev had presented the attendees with several options, two of which he declined right away: one was to abort the crossing, "since we haven't used up all our resources." The other one was to proceed with the crossing when the canal was not yet bridged and the approach routes were under constant threat. Even if 300 tanks got across the canal, Bar Lev had argued, there was no guarantee that such a force could score substantial achievements. So Bar Lev offered a third option, which he advocated: proceed with the original plan, but with a different order of battle and using a different schedule. This plan could guarantee a secured bridgehead and allow for the development of a three division strong offensive. Major General Gonen, who spoke following Bar Lev, agreed with his superior: "So we disagree, which is the better way. Arik presented a clear case for proceeding with the crossing even without a bridge: the Egyptian defenses having collapsed and not yet recovered; we could seize them later. But, suppose we deliver the forces across the canal, the enemy could throw in forces, and we'll be facing a counteroffensive on our north as well as our south flanks. If it succeeds, and if the other (Egyptian) division crosses the canal, we'll be encircled, thus losing not just the crossing campaign, but the entire war. This should be our thinking."

Sharon would later criticize that decision: "I believe this was the greatest missed opportunity of the entire war: for thirty-six hours, not only were no forces delivered across the canal, but there weren't any clear directions on how a force more than one division strong could be concentrated and moved. I think this was the most critical decision to have been made during the crossing campaign."

The disagreements among the commanders were intense, with neither side bothering to conceal their depth or importance from each other or from chance audiences. They were expressed with harsh words, reflecting mutual suspicion and long-standing resentments.

Choosing the third option presented by the front commander meant that the crossing by the 162nd Division would be postponed until a corridor at least four kilometers wide was established against Egyptian counter attacks on the north and south flanks.

The Front Command assigned the two divisions the following tasks: clearing the blocking of Lexicon-Tirtur Junction; securing the corridor, at least all the way to Shiekh Road, and pushing the south flank of the Egyptian 16th Division north; and clearing

Tirtur Road so as to allow for the transportation of the bridging equipment and logistics vehicles. All this was to be accomplished without disturbing the execution of the original plan, by which the 162nd Division was to dash across the canal and then southwards. What allowed for both the deviation from the original plan as well as its subsequent execution was the mustering of additional forces, beyond the present order of battle.

162nd Division, Akavish and Tirtur Roads, October 16. 1700 hours:

As mentioned above, that afternoon Dvela HQ ordered Adan's division to clear Akavish and Tirtur Roads, but something went wrong right from the start, either because the order wasn't clear, or due to a wavering execution.

Later, Brig.-Gen. Uri Ben Ari described it as follows: "On October 16, at 1100 hours, the 162nd Division was ordered to clear Akavish and Tirtur roads. The Front Command had been informed of the ongoing battle throughout the day. By 1700 hours, we learned that our attack had failed, so the Front Command threw in the 35th Brigade. So how is it that despite of the order to clear these roads, the Division never attacked them at all?!"

The going had been sluggish right from the start: Adan sent the 217th Brigade, under Natan "Natke" Nir, to try clearing the routes by a southwesterly attack, but he, too, thought his forces had halted for unclear reasons.[*]

At 1345 hours, Adan spotted clouds of dust north of the

---

[*]   Adan, *On Both Banks*, p.202.

206 | AMIRAM EZOV

Chinese Farm, raised by enemy tanks moving southeast. He supposed that the enemy was developing a counterattack on the 217th Brigade, and chose to meet it at the defensive positions. Eventually, the enemy force turned away, to the north. Later on, Nir tried to resume his attack, but ordered his forces to slow down after two of his tanks were hit by Sagger missiles launched from ditches at the Farm. Then, 162nd HQ received a most alarming report from a deputy brigade commander of 143rd Division: "First of all, carefully avoid firing, since he has men, some of whom were injured, in the Farm's ditches, near the 51st kilometer of Akavish road. Secondly, the hill north of the 42nd kilometer of Tirtur Road is teeming with missile launching infantry. This also goes for the ditches between the Farm's buildings and the 42nd kilometer of Tirtur Road."

One cannot say how the Division's operations officer used this essential information, but obviously, Col. Nir was less than enthusiastic about leaving his positions for what he called "*the enemy's killing zone."*

The 217th Brigade's useless maneuvers, either due to its extended stay in its positions, or due to its reluctance to enter a killing zone, went on until 1600 hours. In a later interview, Brig.-Gen. (Res.)Natan Nir confessed: "It was a terrible mess, through no fault of mine. I had no clear orders. I was just trying to keep my tanks intact, so I didn't want to assume inferior positions. The Saggers still had a serious impact on us, although we had already learned to deal with them by October 15th."**

The Front Command wasn't too happy either: at 1530 hours

* Natan Nir, *Natke*, 201, p.178.

Ben Ari urged Adan: "Bren buddy, if you can't get it over by day, you won't by night either. So step it up!"

By twilight, the Division's operations officer was wondering why Col. Nir had withdrawn his tanks to defensive positions. At the time, Nir was furious, and responded: "That's outrageous. I just don't want to lose vehicles, but they think we can't handle it!" "How typically Latin American of you," the operations officer responded (although Nir was born in pre-World War II Warsaw), commenting on his tantrum. At 1700 hours, during incidental conversation, one operations officer asked another how it was going on the roads. His coarse yet accurate reply was "Shit!" Even four hours after he was ordered to, the 217th Brigade commander had not yet advanced his force, so Adan concluded his forces were just being wasted, and the solution was to employ another tactic and other forces. In his words, "I reported the situation to the Front Command, suggesting we should clear the area by night, with an infantry force. They approved, and told me an airborne infantry should be deployed in my sector, for a nighttime attack."*

In his book, Adan offers one more reason for his forces' staying in defensive positions: "Eventually, I concluded that the armored elements of the 21st Egyptian Division were trying to lure us into a trap where the missile launchers could take us on."* Elsewhere he concludes: "1730 hours: Natke reported he couldn't carry on, and was withdrawing to bivouac on Caspi Road. 460th Brigade was withdrawing too. This was the end of that phase."

---

*   Adan, On Both Banks, p.202.
** Brig.-Gen (res.) Natan Nir, in an interview.

Probably Adan's decisions were not made on purely tactical grounds. He was trying to have it both ways. His major concern was maintaining his force without straying from the original plan. He had a clear set of priorities, such as his division's original assignment. By comparison, the new task of delivering the rafts didn't involve the diverting of considerable troops, and he had no choice, anyway.

So that evening's bottom line was: Tirtur Road was still impassible for Israeli forces.

4. MORDECHAI TAKES OVER.

890th Paratroopers Battalion, Ras Sudr, morning of October 16th: On the morning of October 16th, the 890th Paratroopers Battalion of the 35th Regular Brigade, under Lt.-Col. Yitzchak Mordechai, was with the rest of the brigade at Ras Sudr, in the southern Sinai, on routine security duties. His officers and men felt as if they were missing the war, but they did not.

On the morning of October 16th, the battalion was assigned to an operation near Sharm El-Sheikh. While the men were preparing, Brigade commander, Col. Uzi Yairi, arrived at A-Tur by air, revealing to Mordechai that the battalion had been reassigned. Now it was to take part in clearing the approach routes to the canal. He also said he had to fly right away to Tasa to receive new orders, and that the transportation planes for delivering the battalion were on their way.

Col. Yairi took it for granted that his elite brigade should bear most of the brunt of the battle. After commanding numerous operations of the Special Forces unit from 1967 to 1969, and serving as Chief of General Staff Bar Lev's assistant, he was made, in 1972, the Airborne Brigade Commander. To his frustration, his elite force, which spearheaded all of the IDF's campaigns and operations, hadn't shown its mettle yet.

Thus, at 1300 hours, Southern Command subordinated the brigade to the 162nd Division, for a yet unspecified mission. The timeframe was tight: the force had to study the assignment, receive intelligence reports, deploy its battalions in their launching points, get ready and accomplish the mission—all during that night.

The regular Paratroopers were deployed as a result of the disappointing performance of the armored forces when facing the Sagger defenses in the ditches crisscrossing the plains north of Tirtur Road. The Command supposed that so-called "tank-hunters" were better handled with infantry forces. It also preferred to save the strength of armored 162nd Brigade for missions west of the canal, instead of using it up in the battles over the roads.

The 890th Battalion was flown in to the Refidim Airfield, about 30 kilometers east of Tasa. Mordechai tried to contact the brigade commander, but failed: Yairi was in the middle of a journey to Adan's HQ, for detailed operational briefing.

As Mordechai recalled later: "Even before I was back in my battalion, the deputy brigade commander told me: "You were called, so get your men on the buses and start off for Tasa immediately. The brigade commander is waiting for you. Take whatever you can." So we crammed about sixty or seventy men in a bus, and took off for Tasa."

This short amount of time for combat preparation, which also resulted in the battalion support fire company being left at

Ras Sudr, marked not only the standing operations procedure of the 890th Battalion, but of the entire brigade.*

At 1600 hours, the Front commander himself called the 35th Brigade commander, to make it clear how critical his mission was. Yairi and Bar Lev's close relation could be traced back to Bar Lev's serving as Chief of General Staff, when Yairi was his assistant. So Bar Lev told him: "Our condition is pretty tough. We managed to deliver forces across the canal, including some tanks, but the plan was not just a counteroffensive, but a decisive maneuver which can only take place if we have a real bridge. Take an operational map, so I can make it clearer. The bridging machinery was planned to be delivered through Akavish and Tirtur Roads, but that gentleman [Sharon], started fooling around with raids, so the Egyptians, following their routes, managed to creep south. So now these roads are impassable, with them knocking out every single tank, or vehicle, with their Shmels [Sagger anti-tank (AT) missiles]. Our hope rests in resuming our original tactic, by attempting to clear Tirtur and Akavish Roads. Right now, Bren's division is trying to clear them using a southwesterly attack, between the 53rd kilometer of Akavish Road and Lexicon Road. The trouble is this area is full of ditches, some enemy tanks and AT launching infantry. Arik tried to clear them this morning but was pushed back. We just have to get the bridges and deliver forces across. Since the ground is cut by trenches, and it is about to get dark, we would like you to be supported by Bren. You cannot finish the job by day, so do it by night. Now look, Uzi, your men will be here

---

*   The 332nd Mortar Battalion, under Lt.-Col. Yaakov Zur, was also attached to the brigade, but due to haste, it was left in the central Sinai.

in, say, two hours. Now, go down Akavish Road, and, at its 55th kilometer, you should meet your friend Dovik, Bren's deputy. Bren, himself, is in the field. When you get to Dovik, we'll tell Bren to brief you. You'll have a little more than an hour's daylight to check things out and learn about tactics from the boys. The enemy force is ordinary infantry, who crept up here by day since Arik failed to keep a watch. We're hitting them with a lot of airstrikes that should last until nightfall, so by tonight they won't be doing very well. Once we clear the road, we can begin what should be a decisive maneuver. So Dovik is waiting for you at the 55th kilometer of Akavish Road, and we'll inform him you're coming. Meanwhile Bren is making progress, so you may be able to convince him to lend you some tanks."[*]

These briefing contained, beside instructions, hints intended for the listener's ears only, such as the front commander's gossip like reference to the failures of the 143rd Division commander. He bluntly expressed his disapproval of Sharon's charging forward, while abandoning his logistics elements behind. He openly blamed Sharon for the Egyptian effectiveness in the blocking of the crossing corridor, while giving much greater credit to Adan's ineffective attempt to clear the roads. He referred to Yairi's opponent as "ordinary infantry forces, with no special elements." It was on his narrow shoulders that Bar Lev placed the success of the entire campaign.

If the road clearing attempts were to fail, the forces, which had already crossed the canal would have to be recalled. If this

---

[*]   Maozyah Segal, *Sand-Level Testimonies,* Modan Publishing House, 2007, p.76.

was the case, Yairi had little doubt regarding the importance and urgency of his job.

At 1500 hours, Dvelah HQ made another assessment of the situation. In addition to the regular decision-makers, the meeting was also attended by Maj.-Gen. Rehavam Zeevi, the Chief of General Staff's special assistant. Gonen presented the Front Command's view: "We are trying to clear the Akavish and Tirtur Roads, using Yairi's and Bren's forces, since Arik couldn't handle the job on his own. The precondition for the forces crossing is an intact bridge. If we can deliver neither the bridge nor the rafts, we must recall the forces. If we manage to get the rafts only, we can keep the force west of the canal. But Alligators alone are insufficient."

Gonen and Sharon kept arguing with each other. Sharon protested the halting of the forces and what he called "the piled up preconditions" the Front Command had set for proceeding with the crossing. Yet Gonen was resolved: "Arik, first of all, we've got to have a bridge over there. With no bridge, we can only deliver limited forces. Therefore, we must get through the Akavish and Tirtur roads. Currently, the question is whether we can do it. Make sure your boys [421st Brigade] do nothing foolish in Matt's sector. So we have work to do, Arik, and we wish you all the best. Bear in mind the key is the bridging machinery."

* * *

By 1720 hours, Chief of General Staff Elazar had returned to his room at the GHQ Compound, and following a short rest was updated regarding developments at the front. He looked grim, and rumors were heard that he had suffered a heart attack, was not able to function, and had even stopped directing the war.* At 1830 hours, he convened a meeting of the members of the High Command. The chief of Military Intelligence reported that by that morning, the Egyptians had still misread the situation: Egyptian Intelligence was mostly warning against a threat to the 16th Division's flank in the Chinese Farm. In other words, they were focused on the east bank. Since early afternoon they had been making initial efforts to attack the breaching force and Bridgehead, mostly by airstrikes.

The Chief of Staff couldn't help commenting, that "despite the excellent initial conditions, our last night's achievements were very incomplete." Yet he optimistically stated that there was no reason to feel the entire campaign was a failure, and expressed his reassurance from the Egyptians still being confused. "So, the major success I have been expecting wasn't achieved, yet a minor one was, and we have a chance of expanding it."

At the same time, another conference was being held at Dvelah HQ, attended by the Defense Minister who had gotten back to the HQ at 1730 hours. Gonen gave an exhaustive report about the morning's fighting over the roads, gibing at Sharon: "I left the field after Arik had reported the Farm was no problem. Well, he wasn't able to finish it off in one hour, as he had said." Gonen also reported that twenty-six tanks (actually, there were twenty-eight) under Haim Erez had already crossed the canal, and were destroying SAM bases. Regarding the roads, Gonen expressed his hope of the 35th Brigade clearing them, at last. Later on, Bar Lev argued that currently, the Command had no intention to recall the forces from the west bank. In his words, "We have

---

*   Bartov, *Dado*, p.254.

decided to keep advancing the bridges. If Uzi successfully clears the road, we can resume our original plan. Otherwise, we shall recall the half-tracks by night, and we'll have twenty-six tanks and infantry there. It would be better if we could launch the rafts, and the best of all would be if we could erect a bridge."

The Chief of General Staff shared the view of the Southern Command commanders: the crossing maneuver must be proceeded with and developed on the west bank. By executing this plan we could threaten the enemy flanks and rear, and roll up the Egyptians from their east bank positions.

Now, the permission to speak was granted to Chief of Manpower Directorate Maj.-Gen. Herzl Shafir, who reported the toll of war so far: 844 dead; 3700 injured; 251 MIA, mostly captured; 86 definite POWs. It was a difficult moment, which might have inspired the Defense Minister to ask why an infantry force (referring to the 35th Brigade) should be sent to clear the Chinese Farm, "After all, whatever Uzi can achieve, a single aircraft could do, with cluster bombs." Still, Dayan remarked, he advocated an infantry force operation, in a well restricted sector, and with air support, allowing the delivering of the Bridge.

Dayan repeated his skepticism about the effectiveness of using the 890th Battalion later on, in a phone call to Brig.-Gen. Uri Ben Ari:

Dayan: Has Bren met Yairi already?

Ben Ari: He has.

Dayan: I just want to make sure they agree on a very restricted field of operations.

Dayan: They'll operate between the two roads.

Dayan: Their only objective is clearing the roads. The bridge carriers will follow them immediately.

Even later on, at 2300 hours, during a GHQ conference, Dayan doubted the effectiveness of using the 890th Battalion on its own.

Dayan: Bren was crying his eyes out over the Shmel [Sagger]-firing infantry in the Chinese Farm.

Elazar: Uzi will take them on.

Dayan: Yes, but he cannot clear the scene unsupported.

Elazar: Intelligence reports that the Egyptians intend to withdraw from the Chinese Farm. The Air Force has dropped 200 cluster bombs on them. Maybe this will clear the road.

Dayan: The objective must be delivering the bridges as soon as the road is cleared, even if it is blocked again right afterward. Uzi and Bren should also advance, but they certainly cannot clear the entire field themselves. I told them they must create a situation in which we can safely strike the Egyptians with cluster bombs. It will be more effective than whatever Uzi can do."

* * *

At 1600 hours, 35th Brigade Commander Col. Uzi Yairi arrived at Tasa, with his deputy, Amnon Lipkin-Shahak and other officers, and started begging for information about his mission. He asked, inter alia, an Intelligence officer of the 87th Reconnaissance Battalion, who had already spent some time at the Chinese Farm.* That officer informed him the Farm is held by Egyptian forces who had already inflicted heavy casualties, both in killed and wounded, on the IDF. Yairi was ordered to

---

*   Segal, p. 77.

216 | AMIRAM EZOV

report right away to 162nd Division HQ, three kilometers south of the Kishuf perimeter.

Meanwhile, Gonen reported to Adan that he is sending him Uzi's force: "Maybe you, outflanking them with tanks, and Uzi, moving along the bank of the canal, could do away with Tirtur." He ordered Bren to get Yairi's force prepared for combat and to use them in a nighttime tank-supported attack. He warned Adan that "unless we clear Akavish and Tirtur roads, we cannot deliver the rafts and Roller Bridge."

As mentioned above, the division was to deliver the pontoons, even before carrying out its main task—crossing the canal and carry out its mission on the west bank.

The Paratroopers Brigade commander had to go through quite an ordeal on his way to 162nd Division HQ at the Kishuf perimeter. He commandeered the jeep of a history department officer stationed at Tasa, picked up Lipkin-Shahak, and tried to find his way to the HQ. At 1630 hours, he was still somewhere on Akavish Road, halted by an endless traffic jam. The entire division was searching for the prodigal son over its radio network. Due to his straying, Yairi had to receive most of the operational briefing, before he reached the HQ at night, via radio, or by phone calls, some of which turned into "broken telephones (Chinese whispers)."

Meanwhile, the brigade intelligence officer, Dror Zoref and its operations officer, Maj. Gil David, tried to gather all relevant intelligence reports. David met in some HQ, to his surprise, another member of his kibbutz, Beit Hashita, Maj. Natan Shunari. Exhausted, Shunari told David all the ordeals his battalions had been through attempting to clear Tirtur, telling him that his brother, Yehiel, had been killed there, together with many others. He asked David, to "tell Uzi not to commence firing before making sure there are no wounded men of mine in the ditches, though I'm sure none is still alive."*

At 2000 hours, a desperate Yairi reported to Tamari, deputy division commander, that he had returned to Tasa after failing to reach him at 162nd Division HQ. Tamari suggested he should ask his brother, Lt.-Col. Shai, Front Command's operation officer, for "the proper means" for reaching the HQ. Eventually, Yairi only reached the HQ by helicopter, late at night, shortly before the bulk of the paratroopers landed, thus, losing several precious hours of operational briefings and studying the assignment.

The 890th Battalion, which followed the Brigade HQ, had to undergo an odyssey as well. The force traveled crammed in buses, all the way from Refidim to Tasa. There, they waited for helicopters to airlift them to the launching point at the 55th kilometer of Akavish Road. Meanwhile, the divisional operation officer, Gil David, briefed the battalion's officers, using a 1:100,000 cm scale map. They received no further briefings during the waiting time. At about 2230 hours, the battalion was transported on board CH-53 helicopters, in three shifts, to the 55th kilometer of Akavish road. Arriving there, the battalion's officers rushed to the Divisional HQ for briefing.

The Knesset, Jerusalem, October 16, 1900 hours:
At 1900 hours Prime Minister Golda Meir addressed the Knesset plenum, in her first wartime speech. She spoke in length, going into many details, yet managed to sneak in one statement

---

*   Segal, p. 78.

which fired up her audience. It was phrased after consulting General Staff members, yet neither the Defense Minister nor the Chief of General Staff. She announced: "Right now, as we speak, Israeli forces are operating on the west bank of the canal as well."* Dayan was infuriated by Golda for not consulting him, and he clearly expressed this when he was back in the GHQ later that night: "Why was it necessary to announce, in a parliamentary address, that we had crossed the canal?!" Then, he added, "This bridge thing enrages me. Now, after announcing our crossing, what happens if we have to retreat?!" and cited his explicit orders not to make the crossing public.

* * *

A few hours earlier, Egyptian President Anwar Sadat had also addressed his nation, in a triumphant and visionary speech. Strangely, he chose to disregard the latest developments in the field.

He exalted the achievements of Egyptian Army officers and men, declaring the political map of the Middle East had already been redrawn, and asserting that the Egyptian people would keep sacrificing their children until all of their war objectives were achieved. Expecting a long and difficult war, he restated its objectives: regaining all territories occupied by Israel in 1967, and restoring the Palestinian people's dignity and legitimate rights. Toward the end of his speech Sadat offered, "out of a sincere wish for peace," a ceasefire, based on UN and Security Council Resolutions, in return for an immediate withdrawal of Israeli forces from all occupied territories. Yet Sadat didn't even

---

*   Medzini, *Golda*, Yediot Aharonot Press, 2008, p.567.

hint of the Israeli forces roaming west of the Suez. *

Indeed, once Golda had revealed, in her parliamentary address, the Israeli forces' operations on the west bank, Sadat ordered Colonel-General Shazly, Chief of Staff of the Egyptian Armed Forces, to get to the front in order to keep Cairo updated and to organize the checking of IDF forces operating at the Bridgehead.** Besides dispatching Col.-Gen. Shazly to the front, Egyptian minister of war, Ahmad Ismail Ali, ordered the 16th infantry Division to attack, on the night of the 16th and 17th of October, within its boundaries, cooperating with the 21st Armored Division. It was an attempt to seal the breach and destroy the Israeli forces which had already crossed the canal.

Yet, at least the international clock seemed to start ticking: surprisingly, Soviet Prime Minister, Alexey Kosigin, rushed to Cairo. The Russians probably realized something the Egyptians didn't.

Post factum, the Egyptian leaders tried to downplay the Israeli crossing, or, as they referred to it, the "battle of the breach." General Gamasi, promoted to Chief of General Staff after Col.-Gen. Shazly's removal, described it as follows:

"Today, the enemy's main effort has been an attack on the right flank of the 2nd Army near Deversoir. Their purpose was to encircle the 2nd Army's right flank with a northward attack,

---

*   Sadat definitely knew about the Israeli foothold on the west bank, yet one cannot say whether he had been informed about the 421st Brigade's raid.

**   See: Sadat, *In search of Identity: An Autobiography*, [in Hebrew] [ff. "Sadat, *Autobiography*"], P.197. Here, he accused Shazly of taking his time to reach the front, thus preventing the containment of the infiltrating forces.

making a breach allowing some of their armored forces to reach the west bank of the canal [....] The forces facing the enemy were the 16th Infantry Division, reinforce by an armored brigade, as well as the 21st Armored Division under Brig.-Gen. Urabi. Yet the enemy managed to break through our division's right flank. During the night between the 15th and 16th of October, under cover of fierce fighting, an Israeli paratrooper and tank force infiltrated the west bank of the canal near Deversoir. They were pursued by a seven to ten tank strong company, yet managed to get out of sight among the dense, tall trees... as a result of our forces' fighting east of the canal, the Israeli crossing force was isolated."

On the morning of October 16th, General Ali attended, with President Sadat, the People's Assembly, where Sadat announced the Egyptian plan for resolving the Middle Eastern crisis. As Ali wrote:

"Shazly and I were in the Armed Forces' Operation Center, when we received an alarming report from 2nd Army HQ of seven enemy tanks emerging near Deversoir. Taysir Al-'Aqd, 2nd Army Commander, assumed that this small enemy tank force had managed to sneak to the west bank under cover of the fierce fighting on the east bank. He believed these tanks would be soon destroyed. Eventually, we found out the enemy had already delivered thirty tanks west of the canal, as well as paratroopers, during that night...The GHQ decided to rapidly surround the enemy in Deversoir and close the breach on the east bank, to cut off enemy forces operating on the west bank. At the same time, enemy forces on the west bank were to be encircled and destroyed."

General Gamasi blamed the failure on the field armies' commanders who under assessed the strength of the Israeli force west of the canal, and, consequently, failed to see that it was a strategic turning point. This resulted in their minor scale and irresolute response. Another mistake of the Egyptian command was focusing the counterattacks on the Bridgehead east of the canal, while disregarding the forces operating on the west bank. Until a very late stage of the campaign, Egyptian GHQ had mistaken the Israeli main effort to be aimed at the Egyptian forces on the east bank. Rather, it was the crossing, evolving into a territorial gain threatening the Egyptian forces on both banks.* Indeed, the Egyptian command spent its best forces on southwardly and northwardly attacks attempting at eliminating the Bridgehead on the east bank. The best Egyptian tank force, the 25th Brigade, equipped with T-62s, the best tanks of the Egyptian army, was deployed from the 3rd Army zone to the scene of the fighting, probably in the afternoon of October 16.

Colonel-General Shazly, the Egyptian Army Commander, claims in his post-war book that the Egyptian Army was not surprised by the reports of a small enemy force's breakthrough, received from 2nd Army HQ on the morning of October 16th.** After all, the gap between the northern, 16th Division, and the southern, 4th, was a classic objective for breaching. According to that report, the 2nd Army was taking the appropriate action to destroy the enemy force, so the initial reports gave no reason for panic, and the 16th and 4th Divisions commanders were properly instructed. Yet Shazly goes on telling that in the afternoon, things looked different: armored forces, "emerging out of the blue," have been raiding Egyptian missile bases,

---

* See: Bar, *Yom Kippur War through Arabs' eyes*, pp.60 ff.

retreating unscathed, just to reappear unexpectedly elsewhere.

* * *

West bank of the canal, 421st Brigade, October 16, 1300 hours:

The Egyptians really had no idea where that armored force, which took them completely by surprise, came from. At 1300 hours, twenty tanks and a force of seven APCs, under Maj. Giora Lev, in the lead, and Col. Haim Erez in the rear, stormed from the Bridgehead deep into the west bank of the canal, searching and destroying missile bases, particularly SAM-6 bases, the missile that, as the saying goes, "bent the wings" of the Israeli Air Force. In his briefing, the brigade commander stressed the keys to success were speed, constant firing, and exploiting successes. Their rapid movement and firepower met confounded, helpless Egyptian forces. As Erez recalled, "MIGs flying overhead waved their wings to greet us, since the Egyptians didn't understand what hit them." The raid yielded four missile bases destroyed. At Makztera perimeter, the force faced a hastily deployed Egyptian patrol. In a short battle, the Egyptians lost nine tanks, 34 APCs, tens of trucks and hundreds of men. "Arik asked me," Erez recalls, "whether I can thrust west. I said: all the way to Cairo. But our command didn't let more tanks cross the canal. If we had poured in substantial forces that day, we could have reached wherever we wanted. But, due to a shortage of ammo, I was ordered back."

Erez was ordered back to the Freshwater Canal bridge. Eventually, he scored an impressive achievement: in a swift 100 kilometer drive, twenty-five kilometers into enemy territory, losing not a single tank or man, his force hit the surface-to-air missile envelope which blocked the western Sinai from the Israeli Air Force. Another effect, of no lesser importance was that it spread confusion among Egyptian forces and shocked their entire command.*

By early evening the force, despite the brigade commander's protests, withdrew to its launching point. A subunit was allocated to secure the concrete bridge east of the Freshwater Canal, and the rest linked up with the 247th Paratroopers Brigade in the crossing zone, securing a defense perimeter. A post factum dispute started on whether the IDF missed a chance of seizing the western ford across the Freshwater Canal by deployment on Havit Road, about ten kilometers west of the canal. This issue proved most significant when two days later the 162nd Brigade had to force its way out, taking heavy casualties, through the passages across the Freshwater Canal, after the Egyptians quickly reinforced them. Yet Erez's forces' strength was not sufficient for such an extensive deployment.

* * *

In the afternoon, after Egyptian Minister of War Ismail Ali came back from the People's Assembly meeting, a decision makers meeting was convened at Operation Center 10, or Egyptian GHQ. Chief of Staff Shazly repeated his October 14th suggestion to recall the 21st and 4th Divisions to the west bank of the canal. "Recalling them would allow us to contain the breakthrough at the crossing point," he asserted. Quite expectedly, Ali

---

*   See, for instance, Sadat's, Shazly and Gamasi's comments on the reports of Israeli tanks emerging "out of the blue".

disapproved, ruling out the recall of any Egyptian forces from the Sinai. In doing so, he definitely reflected the intentions of his Commander in Chief, Sadat. Even the support of other senior officers proved useless, and Shazly's reasonable idea was vetoed by the minister. Sadat joined the meeting in the evening. Shazly gives the following description of Sadat's response to his suggestion: "Suddenly, the President lost his temper: 'Why do you always offer to withdraw our troops from the east bank?!' he shouted. "You deserve to be court-martialed for that. Keep making such offers, and I'll have you court-martialed. I'll have none of it!' I was deeply insulted, trying to reason with Sadat, yet he wouldn't listen. I considered submitting my resignation right away, yet my sense of duty stopped me, so I kept silent."* But that midnight, after the orders had been given, Shazly, in an attempt to salvage something, ordered, at his own discretion, some AT battalions back to the west bank.

Thus, Shazly blames the fate of the war on the politicians' decision not to withdraw forces from the Sinai. Apparently, despite participating in the drawing up of his president's limited strategy, he failed to see its political aspects. Recalling the Egyptian troops from Sinai might have been militarily reasonable, yet politically disastrous.

In his autobiography, Sadat gets even with his defiant Chief of Staff: "On October 16th, I ordered Chief of Staff Shazly to go to Derversoir, in order to deal with the Israeli counter-crossing. Back then, it was easy to deal with the penetrating force, but

---

*   *Shazly*, p.185
**   Sadat suspects his general of tarrying in order to build himself a pow-erbase to counter the Minister of War, probably hinting at what Shazly said about winning senior commanders over to his school.

it was a race against time. It he had just gotten there in time, they could have been destroyed easily."** Eventually, Sadat argues, the Chief of Staff's tarrying lost the campaign. Sadat betrays no details about the discussions in Operation Center 10, only reporting that on October 19th, Shazly came back his nerves shattered, suggesting recalling all forces from the east bank. After the Supreme Council of Armed Forces declined the suggestion, Sadat ordered, on the evening of October 20th, to replace Shazly with General Gamasi as Chief of Staff.

* * *

Yehuda Geller, the 600th Brigade's 410th Battalion commander, knew nothing about the difficulties caused by the Roller Bridge, "except from a film I watched a year and a half ago." Neither did his troops, yet at midday of October 16th, his superior ordered him to commit his battalion to towing the just repaired bridge. At 1200 hours the battalion started off from its position in the Hamdiyah hills toward the 43rd kilometer of Akavish Road, where the bridge with its numerous attendants awaited them. Later on Geller argued, "We tried to follow our own towing technique. The new technique was an improved version of the previous one: twelve tanks were coupled to the bridge: one tank moving ahead of the bridge, followed by another two; two pairs of tanks at each flank of the bridge, and another tank behind the bridge. All tanks were connected to the same radio network and given serial numbers. The column was commanded by the deputy battalion commander, in the front tank, accompanied by Engineering Corps specialists under Menashe Gur and Deputy Division Comander Yaakov Even. They soon found their hasty training to be useless. After remaining coupled to the bridge for hours, they found out that Tirtur Road was blocked, so the battalion had to suspend its task, retreating for the night to Hamdiya.

Sharon's division's situation was rather complex: the troops were still licking their wounds after last night's harsh fighting. Nonetheless, its commander pressed for engaging in more operations. Sharon was furious at the halting of the crossing and for the Front Command increasingly meddling with his division's business. It all started when the Alligators' commanders told him they had been ordered, directly by Front Commander Bar Lev, to stop delivering any more tanks. He called Bar Lev, telling him: "It cannot work this way! We're in the middle of a harsh war, so cut it out! After all, the only safe place out there is around the Alligators, while a hellish war rages on all sides. For the last forty hours, not a single artillery shell has hit near the Alligators. They have been able to move freely, yet have not been allowed to deliver any forces," Sharon muttered.

The night between the 16th and 17th of October was relatively peaceful for the division, the major battles being fought by the neighboring division, about ten kilometers away from Matzmed Yard.

As Sharon confessed, "We were totally unaware of a paratrooper attack taking place on that road. Reshef and I had been planning something, and were terribly tired that night, so we both fell asleep on the tank's hull, unaware of the attack."

* * *

At midnight, after a well-attended conference, Elazar asked the Defense Minister to talk to him privately, "about the ongoing troubles with Arik, who insisted on taking center stage even at the expense of executing the original order of the divisions' operation. He wants to be in charge of the west bank as well, even before finishing securing the Bridgehead. Even Bar Lev finds him difficult to control, and it disrupts the planned campaign." Elazar remarked he did not wish to see any infighting, but he was troubled by the rumors Arik had been spreading, such as those about the hundreds of tanks he wasn't allowed to get across the canal.

Dayan, too, didn't favor changing horses in midstream, and just commented vaguely that "in this sense, we are, indeed, an unlucky people." He expressed his great appreciation of Sharon, mostly for considering nothing to be impossible. This meeting, besides letting off steam, had little effect.[*]

---

[*]   Bartov, *Dado*, p.251.

PART 5:

CLEARING THE WAY.

1. A JOB FOR THE PARATROOPERS.

162nd Division HQ, the night between October 16 and October 17:
"I landed at the 55th kilometer of Akavish Road at about 2230 hours, on the second airlift," Lt.-Col. Yitzchak Mordechai, 890th Battalion Commander would later recall. Upon landing, he met Maj. Avner Hermoni, a member of the brigade's HQ, who told him to report to the division's HQ in Kishuf, for briefing. Mordechai said that when he arrived he saw a bunch of windswept tents. He entered the division commander's tent, where Brigade Commander Yairi was already present.

In his words, "I was given a 1:50000 scale map, and I asked them to briefly repeat the operational commands, since so far, I had only received very general information. They told me there was no time and we must start off at once, but that the situation hadn't changed by then. The divisional operation officer reported the current situation, with an

occasional confirmation by the division commander* [....]
I was briefed about our task for no longer than a couple of
minutes. When I asked about artillery fire support, I was
told that it would take an entire hour to find an artillery
fire support officer, and time is running out, since if the
operation dragged on till daylight, it wouldn't go anywhere.
If you need artillery fire, I was told, ask for it on the
command radio network. It's all been agreed on with the
brigade commander. Don't worry: after all, the Brigade HQ
will follow the battalion."**

The entire operation during the night between the 16th and
17th of October was marked by hastiness. The execution of all
operations was falling behind schedule, and the delay was made
even worse by the late deployment of the 890th Battalion. Uzi
Yairi, with the operations and intelligence officers only managed
to arrive at 162nd Division HQ at 2130 hours, after eight hours
of wandering about and failed attempts to link up. As mentioned
above, Mordechai and his HQ, with the rest of the battalion,
showed up an hour later. As a result, the briefing of the 35th
Brigade's senior commanders, including Yairi and Mordechai's
HQ was slipshod. While the brigade commander was briefed
by the division commander, the battalion commander was
briefed, very quickly, by his deputy division commander and
the operations and intelligence officers.

---

* See Mordechai's story in *The Chinese Farm*, a restricted booklet
published by the 890th Battalion in 1974, and circulated among the
fallen soldiers' families. Adan says he never met Mordechai, so "they"
probably referred to Yairi.
** The most accurate account of the 890th Paratroopers Battalion is in
Maoziah Segal, *Sand-Level Testimonies*, Modan Pubslishers, 2007.

Adan would later write about it: "I briefed Uzi and his staff: his deputy, Amnon Lipkin-Shahak, Operation Officer Gil David, and Intelligence Officer Dror Zoref, providing them with intelligence. The operations officer showed them photocopied maps, showing small forces and AT missiles in the ditches. Judging from a similar experience I had in the 1948 War, I suggested that they should advance between Akavish and Tirtur Roads, clearing the ditches. They should have used a search and destroy tactic, in wide deployment, and upon encountering the enemy, concentrate and attack. They should have just cleared the ditches between the two roads. That was the objective."* Thus, when the forces did take to the field, there were still many loose ends. Uzi Yairi referred to them after the war: "I had no idea where the enemy was exactly. They were all over the place between Akavish-Tirtur Junction and the canal. There were tank hunter teams in the Chinese Farm ditches, and I had to clear the road."

He didn't know it was an enemy defense perimeter, the strength of a reinforced company, entrenched on the southeastern edge of Missouri perimeter. As he later recalled, "considering the intelligence we had received, I think we were somewhat shocked [...] you must allow for a situation in which you don't know what's going on. There's a way to handle it, called battlefield intelligence (only collected by engaging the enemy). We were just ignorant of and inexperienced in it. Well, I had a battalion and was ordered to attack an entire army. Well, the die was cast. I knew there

---

*   Adan, *On Both Banks*, p. 211.

was a defense perimeter, so first of all, I gathered information. If I cannot read the field with aerial photographs and maps, I use an entirely different approach, send some patrols ahead, commence firing at several locations, and draw a plan in the field. But it didn't work this way. Well, I knew they had some troops in the field, but the intelligence was they were tank hunters, and I was to clear them out, moving from A to B. So in such a situation you should advance in a wide deployment formation, to safeguard your force, and keep a reserve of course. In this way you keep moving until you engage. The intelligence was a major issue, since we had been so spoiled with accurate intelligence, and all of a sudden, this thing hit us, so we were shocked. I was ordered, 'At such-and-such hours, before dawn, clear point so-and-so. Just get there quickly and the road will be won.' Now, I kept asking myself whether I had insisted hard enough on receiving sufficient information. It still haunts me, and I cannot say whether Bren knew something he didn't share with me."

Yairi explained this in hindsight, tormented with guilt over the ordeal suffered by his troops at the Chinese Farm. On one hand, as a worthy commander, he assumes responsibility, blaming neither his superiors nor anybody else for the insufficient intelligence, since one must figure out a solution even without accurate intelligence. On the other hand, he hints that had he known what he learned later on, he would have taken an entirely different approach. Nonetheless, he realizes that accurate intelligence was a luxury under those circumstances, and that due to the urgency of the mission one had to make do with what one had.

* * *

So far, the question of the kind of intelligence the 35th Brigade HQ and 890th Battalion officers received before going into battle is still disputed. What exactly Yairi and his staff were told before going to battle is one question, and whether the 162nd Division command provided them with all available intelligence is still another question. According to what the 35th Brigade's Operation Officer Maj. Gil David testified, he and the brigade's intelligence officer, Cap. Dror Zoref, received intelligence from the 143rd Division Operation Center in Tasa, regarding the position of the Egyptian division on the southern edge of Missouri, which threatened Tirtur Road. 890th Battalion commander, Lt.-Col. Yitzchak Mordechai, remarked that he had received no substantial intelligence during the three-hour-long time he waited for his flight to Refidim. During the initial briefing the brigade commander gave his staff in Tasa, before their flight, using a 1:100000 scale map, he only referenced a small portion of the enemy and friendly positions.* He was to receive more detailed information in the 162nd Division's HQ tent, but, as mentioned above, the brigade commander, Yairi, wasted precious time on futile attempts at reaching that HQ, so he had no time to get updated.

Another mystery is what information Natan Shunari, the commander of the 582nd Battalion which was hard beaten on Tirtur Road, revealed to Gil David, the 35th Brigade's operation officer, during their encounter in Tasa. It is to be stressed that

---

*   See, *Chinese Farm: The Battalion's War*, a booklet issued by the 890th Battalion, p.19.

Shunari's force had been pushed back about one kilometer east of Lexicon-Tirtur Junction, while Mordechai was to face the enemy defenses at the 55th kilometer of Tirtur, about three kilometers southeast of that spot. However, that information was not included in the "enemy section" of the briefing in the Division's HQ, and failed to ring the alarm bells in Col. Yairi's mind. Yet no one accuses the 162nd intelligence officers of hiding information they had possessed.

The question to be asked is whether they used this information in order to properly alert the paratroopers force of what they were about to face in the Chinese Farm ditches. The bulk of this information was retrieved from the frontline, both from forces' reports and observations. They had no recent aerial photographs of the area, and therefore failed to detect the trenches of the Egyptian 16th Division defense perimeter at the 42nd kilometer of Tirtur Road, the southernmost tip of the massive Egyptian Missouri defense perimeter. To properly understand what intelligence the division did possess, one must bear in mind a report the Divisional Operation Center had received that morning from a deputy brigade commander of 143rd Division: "The trench south of Amir [Chinese Farm buildings], all the way to the 42nd kilometer of Tirtur, as well as two trenches south of it, are alive with AT missile operating infantry. This also goes for the 41st and 42nd kilometers of east Tirtur." A radio exchange, in which the division commander took part, began with what is meant by "AT missile." It was explained as "infantry with a lot of missiles." Somehow, this information was lost along the chain of reports, or, for some other reason, was not included in the intelligence report. Thus, the briefs failed to stress the threat of AT missile operating infantry, entrenched north of Tirtur Road, even if there was no detailed information regarding this. Instead, they stressed the presence of scattered AT units, called "tank-hunters" on and between the roads. In a later interview, Adan stated: "We saw nothing through observations, and therefore supposed that the Egyptians were in the ditches between the roads. Actually, they were north of Tirtur Road, commanding over it from that location. Thus, the search parties, instead of encountering tank-hunter teams, encountered an orderly entrenched Egyptian infantry force."

Gil David, the 35th Brigade's operation officer, interrupted the briefing that Deputy Division Commander Dov Tamari was giving to the 890th Battalion's officers, reporting that Shunari had told him about the well-organized, strong enemy defensive perimeter on Tirtur road. In fact, the divisional intelligence officer had shown them aerial photographs of numerous trenches. Later on, they were found to have been taken several days before. He interpreted them as tank-hunter positions. When David insisted his report was accurate, Tamari ordered him out of the briefing tent.*

Definitely, the information 162nd HQ gave the paratroopers was inaccurate, misleading, and disastrously affected the outcome of the battle.

After the war, an aerial photograph dated from October 15th, which the force didn't possess back then, was found to have existed. It revealed a five-platoon strong Egyptian infantry defense perimeter, arranged linearly with flank defenses, at the

---

*   A letter of Col. (ret.) Gil David to the author.
** An aerial photograph of the 42nd kilometer of Tirtur Road, dated from October 15.

42nd kilometer of Tirtur Road. Two tanks could be detected at its rear. So the Egyptians probably reinforced the perimeter during that night.**

Doubts were not only raised about the enemy positions, but also about the tactic chosen, considering the terrain the paratroopers were to search and clear. Barring the irrigation canal ditches and some low dunes, the battlefield was an empty, exposed plain, "as flat as a boundless football pitch," in the words of one senior officer. For the entrenched enemy, it was a classical killing zone. For the attackers, the best cover was the night, yet here too, the Egyptians had an edge. Being familiar with the area, they carefully arranged its defenses. On top of that, a full moon shone that night, making the force clearly visible against the white dunes.

After the war, Yairi recalled Bren had told him at the 162nd HQ: "Arik's across the canal, but we are blocked by tank-hunters. So take whomever you have, spread out as wide as possible, move in and kill them." So, in the briefing, the Egyptian front units positioned north of or right on Tirtur Road were described as tank-hunters. This was a rarely used expression, and was not mentioned during radio briefings. Its origin could be traced back to Egyptian Army doctrine, according to which AT missiles must be a part of all tactics. In the words of an Egyptian Army textbook, "Tank-hunting is a decisive combat operation, complementing the effects of other weapons."* Tank-hunter squads, equipped with AT weapons, were to be positioned on the flanks, securing the main forces and disrupting enemy armored forces movement on the roads. Their location at the 42nd kilometer of Tirtur perfectly suited these purposes. As one Southern Command Command intelligence officer explained, "Tank hunters" referred to the "AT elements of a non-orderly force."** The critical question was whether these were just a few squads dispersed in order to disrupt the advancement on the road, which could be easily dealt with by the probing infantry; or, the front line of a large, brigade strong defensive perimeter. Indeed, unfortunately for him, Mordechai, the 890th Battalion commander faced a battalion strong dug-in defensive perimeter reinforced with a variety of weapons.

The 890th Battalion's engagement on Tirtur Road came to be known as the Battle of the Chinese Farm, but this is somewhat of a misnomer. The battle was actually fought near the 42nd kilometer of Tirtur, about two and a half kilometers away from the Farm buildings area, codenamed Amir. At any rate, the entire Farm area was crisscrossed with ditches. Though the operational command specifically referred to the area between the two roads, it occasionally spoke of "the Farm," which is somewhat inaccurate, geographically speaking.

* * *

As we said, it was Bren who suggested the tactic to Uzi Yairi. As Bren explained, "Since the enemy positions are unspecified, I suggest restricting the operation to an area which we should clear in order to allow unobstructed transportation on Tirtur. So you should start clearing an area from the 52nd kilometer of Akavish Road, moving toward Lexicon, clearing all the area between Akavish and Tirtur, plus a few hundred meter wide margin north of Tirtur." Adan suggested using a three company

*   Dani Asher, *Shattering the Concept*, p.221.
**   Col. (ret.) Barkan, in an interview

strong force, wide deployed, just as he did in the 1948 War and in the Battle of Um Kataf, during the 1967 Six-Day War.

Yairi approved it. In his words, "Since we do not know exactly where the enemy positions are, and since we're dealing with tank-hunters, the right way is to spread out as wide as possible, searching for them. It is not a defensive perimeter, but a field contaminated with enemy units."

Neither had Adan suggested, contrary to Front Commander Gonen's "advice," that Yairi's force be supported with tanks or APCs. What Adan had in mind was a neat, quiet infantry operation, so he thought there was no point in throwing noisy armored vehicles into a nighttime attack, where they would be of little use anyway. One must bear in mind that Adan's main concern was the task assigned to him by the High Command, delivering the rafts, by which his division was to cross the canal. Thus, he regarded the paratroopers' road-clearing operation as just a necessary step. His eyes were already set on the other bank of the canal.

Yet, contrary to widespread accusations, the 890th Battalion was not heartlessly sent on a suicide mission. Except for the Defense Minister's comments on the extent of Yairi's force's assignment and the necessity of backing it up, none of the front commanders doubted the Paratroopers success: the force was well-trained and eager to fight, in full strength, and many experienced officers, both regulars and reservists, had joined it. After the war, Yairi commented: "Well, one might wonder why a battalion goes to fight with no artillery fire support officer, or artillery support, or ammo. But let nobody dare say that the Armored Corps officers sent them there to be ground up. I'll have none of it." Yairi had to ward off accusations, already voiced back then, that his battalion taken to the field unprepared, serving as the Armored Corps' cannon fodder. If he had any doubts, they were suppressed by the sense of the pressing necessity to clear the roads. According to the strictest sense of his assignment, he was to advance along the roads, clearing them off enemy units. Judging from the intelligence he had received, the paratroopers battalion should have handled the problem. Nobody mentioned the Egyptian force entrenched at the 42nd kilometer of Tirtur. As Yairi recalls, "Back then, I didn't know exactly what was meant by Chinese Farm and Missouri perimeter. I was ordered to mop up the two roads and seize Amir perimeter. Therefore, I said I'll cross that quagmire when I come to it. First, let's reach Amir, and we'll see."

It should be noted that no evidence was found to corroborate Yairi's statement that he was ordered to seize Amir. Bren repeatedly stressed that one must consider the purpose of the battalion's operation to be the clearing of the roads, in order to let the rafts through, not the seizing of Amir and the expansion of the crossing corridor.* After being briefed by the divisional operations officer, the 890th Battalion commander perceived his task was clearing the area near Tirtur and Akavish roads, and deploying forces north of Tirtur, in order to keep Egyptian squads from targeting Israeli forces advancing on the roads. His battalion was to assume positions two and a half kilometers—A Sagger AT missile's range, north of Tirtur, to guarantee that no missiles could hit the tanks and other vehicles traveling on the road.

---

* The numerous inquiries into this battle include several testimonies, yet Adan categorically denies he had ever mentioned the seizing of Amir in the briefing, calling it a slip of the tongue or a misunderstanding on the part of the 35th Brigade commander. So says the 890th Battalion commander, as well.

Though the orders didn't specify seizing the Farm, they did mention deployment north of Tirtur. Anyway, anyone walking, unobstructed, between the two roads, would necessarily reach the Farm canals, about two kilometers south of the Farm buildings.

2. A BEAUTIFUL MOONLIT NIGHT.

At midnight, between the 16th and the 17th of October, the 890th Battalion started marching, in two columns, from the 55th kilometer, heading for Tirtur-Akavish Junction, five kilometers away. Its commander, Yitzchak Mordechai, marched in the lead. Hundreds of soldiers watched them from the road, some with the bizarre empathy of those watching a procession to the gallows. One regular army private was jeered by two reservists: "You suckers, you have no idea where you're going to! Shunari's Paras (paratroopers) have already gone there and were butchered!", and similar phrases.*Yet the paratroopers realized that the fate of the crossing campaign rested on their shoulders.

They were suddenly surprised with a burst of bullets, which hit nobody, and was fired from the position of the 630th Raft carrying battalion, parked on Akavish road. Nobody had informed them that a friendly force was about to move through. Lt. Zisi Barkan, recognizing it was the 890th Battalion, started crying out to his brother, Pini. But they only met days later, on the Tel Aviv beach, when Zisi was on leave and Pini was recovering from an injury.**

---

*   Segal, p.92.
**   ibid., p.91.

Once the force reached the junction where the two roads started paralleling each other, it spread out, starting to search for the enemy, in the pure white sandy plain. As one of the officers recalls, "It was all white sands, with a full moon shining. With such a beautiful moonlit night, where the hell were we going!? Why war?!"*

They were reminded why after passing by an abandoned half-track, with bodies of paratroopers still in it. Yet the silence hadn't been broken for about two hours. At 0240 hours Yairi, who had followed the force on foot, with his HQ, radioed he was moving on and "so far, it's all quiet."

But then, even before this communications' echo had faded away, once the force reached the 42nd kilometer of Tirtur, seven kilometers away from launching point, two burst were heard, and the force stood still. While wandering about the source of firing, the vanguard platoon faced hellfire. At 0245 hours, the point company, under Captain "Yaki" Levi, reported an encounter with an entrenched Egyptian force, having no idea about its strength or formation.

After the war, when visiting the battlefield shortly after the battle, Mordechai commented: "The Egyptians assumed positions on the west bank of a canal between the two roads, north of Tirtur. There were enemy compounds all over the place. Yesterday, I counted between eight and ten Guryonov machinegun emplacements. Here, there was a tank platoon, some Sagger missile positions, and many RPG-launchers positions; with infantry positions in the

---

*   ibid, p.93.

rear; here, in the flank, yet another defense perimeter, about the same strength, with 20mm-calibert canons, two tank platoons behind, and, behind it, a line of defensive perimeters 100 to 200 meters from each other. The major problem was we saw no flanks of it. Short-range small arms fire kept us lying low, while long-range mortars hit us. It was a gigantic compound, and it looked as if one could never finish it off."

The engagement was reported back, and at 0310, a concerned Adan asked Yairi how far he had reached. Yairi replied, "The 42nd kilometer of Tirtur," and added right away, "I can push no further. I'm halted by a canal going all the way to Amir." He also asked for artillery fire support. His force took on broad frontal fire, including some Saggers, which instantly hit some of the brigade commander's team. Maj. Avner Hermoni sustained a severe injury, while Capt. Nehemiah Tamari, a hand injury. The rest jumped into a nearby ditch, where they tried to figure out what was hitting the battalion. With the battle being practically conducted by the battalion commander, Yitzchak Mordechai, the brigade commander had little to do. Hardly any artillery fire support had been provided during the early hours of fighting, mostly because no radio network was dedicated to it, and because no artillery fire support officer was assigned to the battalion. Thus, the entire burden rested on the brigade commander. By the first engagement, the medics had their hands full. At 0330 hours Yairi reported to the Division HQ in a grave tone:

Yairi: I want Adan, right away. We got a situation. We're engaging, and took on very intensive fire in the front, from both sides. That is, we are taking on intense fire between the roads*. We are hearing heavies [= tanks] on the road. Are they ours?

Adan: Our forces are not moving on Tirtur.

Yairi: The trouble is the intense firing between the roads, probably of tanks. I'm taking a hell of a shelling once in a while. I see things are not going very smoothly here. Let's see how it turns out. Meanwhile, I am not able to advance at all. I must withdraw some forces about fifty meters back. They are in a terribly exposed plain. I see there are no friendly tanks on Tirtur.

Adan: Right.

Yairi: So it's an enemy tank that is driving through there**.

Adan realized the situation: the force had failed to accomplish its mission, and it was necessary to evacuate the increasing numbers of wounded. But it's uncertain whether he realized how grave it was at that point.

Raft Battalion, Akavish Road, October 17, 0230 hours:

Major General Adan was seriously preoccupied with the task of delivering the rafts to the canal, which the High Command assigned to him that morning, and which he, in turn, assigned to his deputy, Dov Tamari. Meanwhile, thirteen were lying at the 55th kilometer of Akavish Road, waiting for Yairi to clear the roads. Yairi's and Mordechai's entanglement in the Farm had unexpectedly burdened the division. One must also remember that at that stage of the campaign, the Front Command regarded that assignment as what might win or lose the entire

---

*   One cannot figure out what Yairi meant, since the clash took place north of Tirtur road, and the firing was not between the roads, but between the irrigation canal ditches.

**   162nd Division's radio network, at 0330 hours.

crossing. This sense of urgency affected the set of priorities of all forces on the night between the 16th and 17th of October. The long delay in the initiation of the operation on the part of the paratroopers' threatened the success of the entire campaign. The rafts were stalled at the 53rd kilometer of Akavish Road after the October 16th failed attempt to advance them. Once the bulldozer tanks in the lead were hit, it was clear that the same fate awaited the cumbersome Unifloat rafts. For Avi Zohar, the Raft-Carrying Battalion's commander, it didn't matter what division would deliver his force to the canal, either Sharon's 143rd, as initially planned, or Adan's 162nd, as decided that morning. In his words, "I asked Dov Tamari for instructions, so he told me to start off at 1900 hours." Yet the hours went by, while the rafts stood still.

Nobody wanted to delay and risk movement by daylight. As Adan writes in his book: "I saw that it wasn't going anywhere. Time was running out, and there was a threat of the road remaining blocked. It was already 0130 AM, an hour before H-hour, when one should decide whether or not the rafts could be delivered. Then an idea crossed my mind. I ordered Gabi Amir [460th Brigade commander], to deploy 'Bamba' Goren's reconnaissance company along the road, all the way to Lexicon, to check its drivability. It was a risk, but an inevitable and a calculated one. Meanwhile, I ordered Dovik [Tamari] to get the rafts ready to move in a column on my order."*

Originally, "Bamba's" reconnaissance company was subordinate to the 162nd Brigade's reconnaissance battalion, yet

---

*   Adan, *On Both Banks*, p.211

it was detached from its tanks and deployed, until October 15th, as mechanized infantry during various engagements in central and northern Sinai. On October 15th it was placed under the command of Capt. Shlomo Goren, of the 460th Brigade.

At 0135 hours, Adan radioed instructions to his deputy, Tamari, telling him that after "Bamba's" company checks the road, he should deliver the rafts to their destination, on Akavish Road, by 0300 hours.

The reconnaissance force took to the road at 0215 hours, moving without suffering hostilities, but its commander witnessed the intensifying fighting of the 890th Battalion a few hundred meters up north. It advanced fast, and at 0255 hours the commander reported to Adan they were on Akavish, near the 42nd kilometer of Tirtur, and that everything was OK. By the roadside, he found a wounded paratrooper who told him that he had been lying in the field for forty-eight hours. He also saw a burnt out tank nearby, the remains of the last failed crossing attempt by the raft column. When he started withdrawing, Adan ordered Tamari to get bulldozers, and advance with the rafts.

The column started off from the 54th kilometer of Akavish, led by the deputy division commander's jeep and three of Bamba's APCs, followed by the half-track of the Raft Carriers battalion commander, Avi Zohar, followed by a front-end loader, followed by a raft carriers company half-track, and right next to it, the twelve tank drawn rafts. Two bulldozers were driving along the side of the road. This gigantic slow moving column could only pray that it would remain unnoticed by the Egyptians. Tank obstacles and other vehicles were cleared away, and pits in the road were filled in. While moving, the column was targeted by small arms fire directed from Tirtur Road, as well as what was described as ineffective artillery firing. All the while, the raft carriers kept hearing in the background, the sounds of the terrible battle raging at the 42nd kilometer of Tirtur.

At 0315 hours, Adan reported to Sharon, who had been at Matzmed, that he had undertaken the delivering and securing of the rafts, urging him to take charge of "receiving" the rafts and clearing the road. By daybreak, at about 0520 hours, its lead units had reached Lakekan Junction. It impressed Tamari as being a "terrible traffic jam," so the 162nd Division HQ asked the neighboring division's HQ to make way for the rafts. About thirty minutes later, at 0555 hours, Tamari reported to Uri Ben Ari that he had delivered all the rafts to Lakekan and had handed them over to "fatso," i.e. Sharon.

At 0630 hours, Tamari reported to his superior that he had just left the beach and that things were messy, since "it's terribly crowded down there." Yet he also broke the good news that "we'll have the first raft launched within thirty minutes, and all the delays are due to over crowdedness and jams." Now, for some reason, Uri Ben Ari insisted on him staying there "to see the job through".

When Tamari argued he would be "a fifth wheel," and that the place was overcrowded already, Ben Ari ordered: "So some cars need five wheels. Stay there!" Tamari instantly contacted Adan, arguing that staying there would be pointless, since the entire 143rd Division HQ was there already. Yet Adan informed Tamari he should stay near the beach "even if he was doing nothing," just to supervise the operation. This hesitation provoked Sharon, so Tamari left hastily.

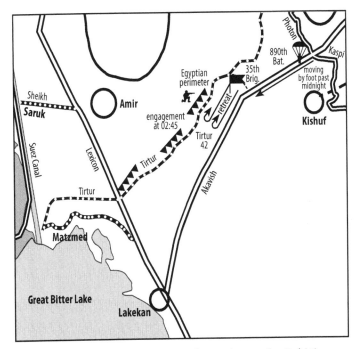

The fighting of the 35th Brigade's 890th Battalion at the 42nd kilometer of Tirtur Road, the night between the 16th and the 17th of October

890th Battalion, Tirtur Road, October 17, 0400 hours:

It was only at 0400 hours, about an hour and a half after the 890th Battalion's first engagement that the 162nd Division realized that the operation had deteriorated. Now it wasn't about accomplishing the mission, but rescuing the battalion's survivors from the killing zone. However, the extent and significance of this complication had not been realized. So, at 0400 hours, Adan ordered Gabi Amir, the 460th Tank Brigade commander, to standby to support the battalion.

At that point, the 890th Battalion was in complete disarray; its attempts to outflank the Egyptian perimeter having resulted in many men killed and wounded, including two company commanders, Captain "Yaki" Levy and Lt. Aharon Margal. Nighttime made it even harder to control the troops and read the battle. Battalion commander, Yitzchak Mordechai, with his HQ, was conducting the fight from a nearby trench. Near them was the HQ of Brigade Commander Yairi, practically with no effects on the fighting, except for its reports, occasionally unclear, to Division HQ. Most of the paratroopers were desperately seeking cover on the exposed sandy plain. The increasingly loud cries of the wounded rose from everywhere, while medics rushed among the scores of injured men, trying to reassure them and dress their wounds. Some of them were retrieved to a small dune out of range of Egyptian fire, which came to be known as Casualties Hill.

At about 0400 hours, the battalion commander ordered Maj. Yehuda Duvdevani, who had replaced Margal as 3rd Company commander, to retreat. Duvdevani, whose father was killed during the retreat from the Battle of Latrun in the 1948 War, found it hard to accept the order, but he had no choice. In his words, "The word retreat was foreign to me. I grabbed some hand grenades, planning to storm the Egyptians on my own…yet the battalion commander ordered a retreat. I ran to the nearest canal, reaching it exhausted."

This is also what one combatant recalls: "Duvdevani ordered everyone who could, to run for the canal. So we all stoop up, and, running like hell, with bullets all around, got into the canal. What we saw there was like a horrible scene out of a bad war movie: the entire paras battalion, defeated, licking their wounds…I was shocked, and started to weep."*

---

* Segal, p.145

Not all of the men retreated to safety, some were lying in the field, in small groups, unable to move. One such group, led by Lt. Hezi Dahbash, took cover in a shell crater a few meters from the enemy.

At 0420 hours, 35th Brigade HQ ordered Bamba's reconnaissance force of APCs to go to Tirtur Road and help evacuate the injured from front medevac positions. Reaching the Akavish-Tirtur Junction, the force spotted an area fully lit by illumination charges, at the scene of the paratroopers' engagement. Three APCs moved into the killing zone, starting the evacuation to the battalion aid station. They managed to run two rounds before daybreak.

A few minutes earlier, Adan ordered the tanks to standby for rescuing the paras. At any rate, for the rescuing force, it was anything but simple to link up with the force, so at 0500 Adan ordered Col. Amir, 460th Brigade commander, to take charge of the entire rescue operation. At the same time, the 100th Battalion, under Lt.-Col. Ehud Brog (later Barak), started off.

The 460th Brigade commander, trying to reassure Yairi, said he had sent Barak with the tanks. Yairi, being well acquainted with his ex-subordinate from his special forces days, considered it a major morale booster.

* * *

The outbreak of war found Ehud (Barak), who had resigned a year earlier, in command of IDF's special forces, in the middle of a Stanford University school year, so he rushed back to Israel. Arriving on October 7th, he looked for a job, using his GHQ contacts. On October 9th he was approached by the Chief of

General Staff: "Ehud, you're to command a tank battalion on the Southern Command. So talk to Brig.-Gen. Tzipori, [Chief of Armored Corps], and form a battalion." In the time since Barak had been reassigned to the Armored Corps, this was the first time he was to command a battalion. Barak comprised the battalion, numbering 100, of Armored Corps men returning, just like him, from abroad, to join the war. One of them was Lieutenant (later Major General) Moshe Sukenik, whom he made a company commander. The newly-formed battalion's men had to scrap for tanks and other means from wherever possible. They lacked elementary equipment, mostly machineguns. Yet eventually, Barak managed to raise a two-company strong battalion, with 20 tanks, and a mechanized infantry company. On October 14th it was attached to the 460th Brigade under Gabi Amir, and, on October 17th, went on its first mission.

From the 35th Brigades radio network, Barak received fragmented reports by the 890th Battalion commander, that about seventy paratroopers, some wounded, were scattered without ammo at the scene, and in close range to the enemy.

As Barak recalled, "I only received intermittent reports, with alarmed requests to sweep the scene quickly. We failed to recognize friendly positions even after being 800 meters away from the 42nd kilometer of Tirtur. At about 0530 hours, I tried to explain to the 35th Brigade commander that the support of tanks is useless, as long as it was too dark for effective tank fire. Meanwhile, we detected a smoke signal from a friendly force, about 300 meters from the referred to location. From his position in a trench, 600 meters to the left, the 35th Brigade commander told me that the time of attack was at my discretion. Hearing the desperate calls for help of the 890th

Battalion commander, whom I knew to be a ruthless fellow, made me realize the gravity of the situation."

The 100th Battalion moved on, arriving at the scene of battle at about 0530, yet at that point, darkness had rendered any intervention impossible. Barak addressed the paratroopers' battalion commander without coded words, saying: "Hello, Yitzik, we came to help you out." At that darkest hour, even that was a silver lining. Yet, the dawning day did not brighten the horizon of those forces that were still exposed and pinned down less than a hundred meters from Egyptian positions. The morning of October 17th dawned on a group of paratroopers struggling to survive, their division engaged in rescuing them, a Front Command struggling to read the situation, and an Engineering Corps battalion eagerly beginning construction of a bridge.

PART 6:

HOLD ON UZI!

1. YAIRI REQUESTS AN EXCAVATION OF THE WOUNDED.

42nd Kilometer of Tirtur Road, October 17, 0600 hours:
On October 17th, at 0545 hours, Major General Gonen, over breakfast with some Front Command officers in Dvelah HQ, took to task 143rd Division Commander Sharon, whose acts he called "acts of treachery." "For the first time of my life," he complained, "I finally realized Arik's war maneuvers were mostly driven by political considerations."

Sharon saw it from another point of view. He held that all the chances of a decisive victory, created by his division on the 16th and 17th of October had been missed. As he saw it, there had been a chance of securing a substantial bridgehead on the banks of the canal, to be used for delivering more vehicles to the west bank—if only the decision-makers in the rear HQ had let him do his job. After all, it was he, not they, who was in the field. Consequently, they had failed to read the emerging situation correctly.

Meanwhile, only several kilometers away, the 890th Battalion was fighting for its survival.

* * *

The force was pinned down at the 42nd kilometer of Tirtur Road, and the rescuing force, the 100th Battalion under Lt.-Col. Brog, had only linked up with it just before dawn. Brog, leading two tank companies and an armored infantry company, stopped 800 meters short of the 42nd kilometer, hesitating about his next move. He failed to locate the pinned down paratroopers, so their commander, Lt.-Col. Yitzchak Mordechai, risked igniting a smoke grenade. The Egyptians, in response, opened fire.

Brog sighted bands of paratroopers, fifteen to twenty men each, deployed on the front slope of a low dune, takingres. The Egyptians were fifty meters away from the farthest band, several hundreds of them, by Brog's assessment. They were deployed in very small teams, entrenched up to their heads, armed with AK-47s and RPG launchers with night vision systems. Judging from the fire they had been launching, they had no shortage of ammo.

As Brog recalled, "We took intensive artillery shelling which directly hit the vehicle of 2nd Company's Lt. Bari Mart, killing the platoon commander. I left a covering force in our positions, and led an attack of 2nd Company on the right of the objective, which was free of friendly forces. Reaching the objective, we faced intensive small arms firing, so we tried to take on the infantry. Passing the crest line, while storming on westward, we took tank fire from the front, yet the close range small arms firing was by far more lethal. Our battalion had hardly any tank commander machineguns, so we used our individual small arms, throwing grenades and trying to run over them driving forward and backwards. The Egyptians had deep trenches, and some of them kept firing at point blank range, after our tanks drove over their trenches."

While the armored infantry under Brog was rescuing other men, its own commander and three men were hit with heavy small arms fire, clanging on the turrets, at a few meters range. Brog asked Mordechai to lend him his uninjured men for clearing the trenches, but was told they were short of ammo. From the farthest right, about 200 meters north, Sagger missiles started flying, clearly visible for fifteen to twenty seconds. Brog tried to keep the forces' radio networks free, to alert the vehicles about incoming missiles, so they could take cover on time. It didn't always work: within three or four seconds the missiles had hit four tanks, including that of Company Commander Lt. Sukenik.

Being launched from the flank, the missiles could hit the unfortunate company from both sides of the crest line. "It dawned on me that in a few minutes none of our vehicles would escape a missile hit, so I ordered them to back off about 700 meters down, and to assume defensive positions," said Barack later accounting for his withdrawal.

The 100th Battalion's assault on an unknown objective, and its withdrawal, had made matters worse, due to the increasing numbers of casualties as well as the Israeli forces' realization that the Egyptian perimeter was deeper than expected, and the resulting paratroopers' entanglement. Col. Yairi was the first to realize the futility of holding the area between the 51st kilometer of Akavish Road and the 42nd kilometer of Tirtur Road. Therefore, by 0600 hours he requested from Adan permission to withdraw. In response, Adan ordered Col. Amir, who was in charge of the rescue, to closely assess the situation.

Gonen, too, started hearing reports from Yairi about his situation, from 0600 hours on, but the severity of it had probably yet to dawn on him. "Can you hold on and secure

Akavish Road?" he asked. "Only the segment where I am, all the way to its 51ˢᵗ kilometer," Yairi replied.

At 0730, a few minutes after talking to Gonen, Adan told Yairi: "Stay where you are, and we'll evacuate your wounded as soon as possible. The rest should guard Akavish Road against attacks coming from Tirtur. I see you are between the 51ˢᵗ and the 42ⁿᵈ kilometer. I can spot you on the map, but cannot see you."* Thus, the permission to withdraw was being discussed between all levels of command for many hours, too many for the 890ᵗʰ Battalion's troopers.

Yet there was some inevitable facing of reality. While Adan and Gonen were persuading Yairi he should hold on, the battalion's men started rescuing themselves from the killing field, most of them just running to the rear. This is how an armored infantry man, who came to the rescue, described the scene: "I imagined the desert was the snow covered Russian steppes, and the paras as Napoleon's defeated troops. I saw paratroopers with their webbing unbuckled, and a trooper with his weapon dragging behind him. I called to him to get on my APC, but he didn't hear me. It felt as if we we're going to lose the war."**

Battalion Commander Mordechai ordered all officers and men to jump into the trench from which he had been conducting the battle, standing by the nearest trench and directing his men in. Yairi, too, was in that trench. His spirits were low, his force had failed in its mission, taking many casualties, narrowly escaping, and his request to withdraw had been declined. He

---

*   162ⁿᵈ Division/14ᵗʰ Brigade's radio network, at 0740 hours (from 14ᵗʰ Brigade's website).

**   Segal, p.192.

watched his hard-beaten troops crawling into the ditches. As one of them later explained, "It was an unforgettable moment. We lit a cigarette, and started talking about how it feels to die." As another soldier recalled, "The entire battalion was depressed. The men started spreading rumors about the number of dead, speaking about forty or fifty killed. We lost half of the force."*

By about 0930, even Adan realized it was pointless to keep the force where it was, so he asked the front commander to authorize the withdrawal of Mordechai's HQ and entire force. He was surprised to meet with Gonen's fierce disapproval, who argued that Yairi's men had kept Egyptian infantry from crawling through the ditches to Akavish Road.

About thirty minutes later, Adan had the following conversation with Gonen:

Adan: Can we pull Uzi out?

Gonen: No, he should secure the road.

Adan: Who's going to support them?

Gonen: Lend him some tanks, and later on, we shall set up an HQ, under Jacky Even [143rd Div. deputy commander] to handle it. Let Uzi secure the area all the way to the 50th kilometer of Akavish, keeping the enemy from crawling back to their old positions. His job is to keep Akavish cleared, east of its 50th kilometer. I want a report on Uzi's condition.

A few minutes later, Adan reported: "He's with all his boys in the ditches, with nearly no ammo. They have many casualties, and are practically making no difference in the field. I'd like to give him a few hours rest, let him replenish ammo, so by evening he and his squad leaders could have a fresh start.

---

*   Segal, p.171.

Gonen: So who's to secure the area till evening?

Adan: But his men are just lying in the ditches, doing nothing.

Gonen: Negative. We must hold Akavish Road, at all cost, and I don't care who pays the price. We must keep their infantry from crawling to the road. We have another infantry force in Refidim, which we can fly in right away to the 55th kilometer of Akavish, and deliver them from there to Uzi. Uzi must hold on, even for several days."*

Gonen told his operations officer to find more infantry companies which could be flown to the 55th kilometer of Akavish. As Adan later wrote:

"I had a long argument with him, telling him it was pointless. But Gonen was just looking at maps, away from the field, struggling to read the battle. Gonen's orders hardly made any sense: my tanks had already been deployed, and the rafts had already been delivered, so at that stage, holding the road by Uzi's paras had no tactical point when we already had four tank battalions of the 460th, 217th and 600th brigades. Yet Gonen stood his ground."**

Between 1000 hours and 1030 hours, the minister of defense, as well as Front Commander Bar Lev, arrived at 162nd Division HQ. The minister suggested to Gonen that if the 35th Brigade is of no immediate use, it should be allowed to disengage. The front commander shared this opinion, and Bar Lev's intercession

---

*   14th Brigade's radio network
**   Adan, *On Both Banks*, p.216

forced Gonen to concede, allowing the battalion out of the battlefield. At about 1100 hours, the APCs of "Bamba" force and of 100th Battalion started retrieving the paras from the ditches. The last to get evacuated were Brigade Commander Yairi, his deputy, Amnon Lipkin-Shahak, and 890th Battalion Commander Yitzchak Mordechai. The force was driven to the 55th kilometer of Akavish Road, and from there, marched to Tasa, where Brigade HQ started regrouping its remnants.

* * *

Yet not all troopers were evacuated. Lt. Hezi Dahbash's team, alongside an officer of the 100th Battalion and some tank crewmen and other combatants, lay, at midday, in a pit, a few meters away from the Egyptian lines. Some were injured yet alive while others had expired during the hours they waited for their rescue. All the forces in the area had been engaged for many hours rescuing them, yet they felt deserted. Many bodies were left in the field, only found the day after.

The commanders in the field, as well as individual troopers, initiated private operations to search for and evacuate injured men left in the field. These operations also involved checking the Egyptians' attempts of crawling toward Tirtur and re-blocking Akavish Road. Egyptian tanks, advancing from the Farm eastward, were blocked by 600th Brigade tanks supported by the 100th Battalion. At noon, a single APC of the 460th Brigade's reconnaissance platoon took to the field. It was commanded by Lt. Yaki Haimovitch-Hetz, who made himself a name in the Battle of Ammunition Hill, during the 1967 Six-Day War. Running amuck, zigzagging through the killing zone, Yaki and his men managed to rescue wounded men left

260 | AMIRAM EZOV

deep in the field. And all the while, Dahbash was crying to be rescued.

At 1300 hours, the 460th Brigade's operation officer gave the following report to his counterpart, of the 162nd Division: "I talked to Uzi about the 35th Brigade. He probably had eight men left behind, and another two who cannot be moved. There's an enemy vehicle above their position."* Dahbash, with seven of his men, were crammed in a shell crater, unable to move. The Egyptians, thirty meters away, above them, left them alone, to take their lunch break.

Toward 1500 hours, under cover of tanks and artillery barrage, two APCs took to the field, rescuing Dahbash and his men, the last group to have survived the twelve-hour long battle.**

* * *

The painful postwar debate over the refusal to evacuate the battalion, even after it had been proven unable to carry out its mission, helped to build up the myth of its deliberate abandonment, from the planning of the attack to the rescue operation. It was used to support the accusation levelled at the decision-makers, of being indifferent to and ignorant of what

---

*   14th Brigade's radio network

**   See a detailed discussion on the attempts of rescuing Dahbash's men in *Global website*, particularly Uzi ben Zvi's article. See also Barack's testimony during the inquiry of the 100th Battalion's fighting, as well as Segal, p.198. ff. All but one injured man were rescued from the killing zone and Casualties Hill. He was found the day after, by an element of the 600th Brigade (see below)). Tens of injured men were left on the Hill, to be evacuated a day later.

happened on the dunes. Indeed, there are some arguments supporting it: to begin with, the 890th Battalion, as it was then stated, was useless, especially since around it, three tank battalions were engaged in keeping in check the enemy forces as well as clearing the road. Secondly, the objective it was fighting for—letting the rafts through, had already been achieved. Thirdly, Gonen had demonstrated indifference to the force's distress, and, what is worse, had failed to read the situation properly. On top of that, the frontline force's men felt as if they were abandoned. The forces' radio communications reflected that sense of helplessness. For example: at 1300 hours, on the 14th Brigade's network: "Arad [35th Brigade] calling. 42: believe me, I haven't forgotten. Cannot respond right now; wait."

However, a close examination of the alleged abandonment calls for looking at the battle's time frame. On the one hand, had the battalion withdrawn later that night, it most probably would have had fewer casualties. On the other hand, during the night nobody considered the fighting useless or that the battalion should be withdrawn. No one asked for it, either. Even by the beginning of the next morning the Southern Command commanders still believed they could, with tank support, evacuate the wounded, as well as close the breach and defend Akavish Road. In practice, Gonen's stubborn objection later that morning made no difference: by that time, the battalion had already started withdrawing to the irrigation ditches, and were evacuating the troops from the field. That afternoon, when Gonen finally authorized the evacuation, the battalion was not engaging the enemy any longer. Only the brigade's and battalion's HQ remained in a rear ditch, licking their wounds. Though one cannot argue it with feeling, the abandonment allegation still seems far-fetched, considering the time frame presented here.

262 | AMIRAM EZOV

After the war, Uzi Yairi explained: "Could we have done it differently—for instance, to keep assaulting? I say no. I cannot think of anything we could have done differently, considering the information I had."*

* * *

During the afternoon, the 890th Battalion was being shuffled to Tasa, where it was quickly regrouping. The regrouping involved a painful accounting for those present and those missing, among the decimated ranks of the survivors. Platoon Commander Roni Bar Nir wrote down, on a piece of cardboard, the names of the living, slightly injured, those left at a known location, the missing in action and those killed.** The results were appalling: in the 2nd Company, out of 82 men who went into battle, only 27 able-bodied men survived; in the 3rd Company, of the 92 men, 60 able-bodied men survived; in the 5th Company, 20 out of 50 combatants survived; the 4th Company had 16 casualties, and battalion's and brigade's HQ had their share of casualties as well.*** The battalion lost nearly all its regular commanders, who were replaced with officers of various units, attached to the battalion. In total, it had 40 men killed and another 120 injured. The 100th Battalion had nine men killed, one missing and 20 injured, seven tanks hit, three of which were abandoned, and two APCs hit. It was the baptism by fire of both the 100th

---

*   Ronen Bergman, *Real Time,* p. 259.
**   Segal, p.235.
***   See *The Battalion's War: the Chinese Farm,* a booklet published by the 890th Battalion, 1975, p. 32.

Battalion, which was an ad hoc force, as well as the 890th Battalion, and it had cost them dearly. Yet despite the woeful atmosphere, the battalion got ready to fight on that very night.

* * *

On the morning of October 18th, 24 hours after the evacuation had been concluded, a company of the 600th Brigade's 410th Battalion, while securing the area near the 55th kilometer of Akavish Road, noticed that Tirtur Road had been empty. Noticing that the road, which had taken such a terrible toll, was now free of any enemy presence, the force advanced to the 42nd kilometer of Tirtur. Then, the leading tank stopped, when a pile of corpses was spotted at some distance. Suddenly a figure arose from it. The tank commander, suspecting it to be an Egyptian, was about to open fire, but something held him back. Approaching, the troopers found that it was an Armored Corps lieutenant of the 100th Battalion. He said he had been lying there since the morning of October 17th, for the entire night and the next day, waiting for dawn, to see the exact position of the sunrise in order to know where to retreat. He lay between two torched tanks of his battalion, wearing a tank crew suit. Approaching him, the troopers were shocked to find that the corpses were of the 890th Battalion men, numbering about thirty. They were probably mowed down by the very first volleys, before any of them had been able to reach a trench. They were lying in perfect rows, right on the banks of the trenches, their weapons alongside them, as if about to advance. They died in formation, by squads, probably cut down by fire from their flank. No traces of mutilation were detected. There was evidence that this was the unit's aid station: many of the killed were wearing bandages, and one body belonged to a doctor killed while bending over another man. Though the company was ordered to clear the bodies, only three officers eventually cleared all thirty bodies, the rest of the men disobeying. Many men stepped 100 meters to the side, overwhelmed, while some were traumatized. The company remained unfit to fight for the next twenty-four hours.

After the war, Adan remarked: "Let me tell you something about the paras' fighting. Though they took terrible casualties during this battle, I must credit them with the fact that on that same morning, because of their fighting, though I don't know for sure how it affected the enemy, our rafts were delivered by this road undisturbed by enemy missiles." Battalion Commander Mordechai, too, frequently stressed this causal link. In one of his many comments on the battle, he stated: "IDF forces were able to just drive the rafts down that road, as safely as if they were on parade, not suffering a shot. It was the ultimate absurdity, since, in the midst of that terrible carnage I realized that we were actually doing the job of clearing the roads, while the Command kept radioing us to not give an inch."

Some do not believe this cause-and-effect link between the battle over the 42nd kilometer and the smooth delivery of the rafts. They argue that Akavish Road had been free of Egyptian forces even before the 890th Battalion had been deployed, a fact supported by the unobstructed advance of "Bamba" Force during that night. The Egyptians' not firing at the rafts is accounted for by the Egyptians' inaction, rather than the actions of the 890th Battalion, and the entire fighting of the battalion is perceived as merely an engagement and a rescue operation.

Noone dispute that the paras failed to achieve their assigned objectives and failed to handle the Egyptian forces they engaged, since Tirtur Road was only cleared the following day.

Egyptian General Gamasi offers a different point of view, in his written account of the battle: "It ended with heavy losses of the Israeli paratroopers. But, the fighting distracted the attention of the 2nd Army Command, while fighting took place on its right flank, in their 16th Infantry Division's sector. Meanwhile, General Adan managed to deliver the rafts to the waterfront, where the Israelis built a ford on October 17th."

So one must conclude that the paratroopers' fighting, despite failing to achieve its objectives, distracted the Egyptians from the traffic on Akavish Road, thus enabling the undisturbed advancement of "Bamba" Force, followed by the raft-carriers. The question of whether the rafts could have been delivered even without the engagement at the 42nd kilometer of Tirtur cannot be answered irrefutably. One must also bear in mind that since the early morning of October 17th, armored detachments of three divisions had been fighting to eliminate the threat on Akavish Road, and it wasn't until 1100 hours that 460th Division Commander was able to report that the road was absolutely enemy-free. So the 890th Battalion attack was just one element of the general accumulating pressure on the 16th Division's southern perimeter. It proved fruitful the next day, when an element of the 14th Brigade, storming the perimeter, met with practically no Egyptian resistance in the Farm proper. One may also attribute the Egyptians withdrawing from the 42nd kilometer of Tirtur to their fear of being cut off as elements of Sharon's division advanced on the west bank of the canal.

2. KISHUF SUMMIT.

162nd Division HQ, morning of October 17:

Since the morning of October 17th, the 162nd Division HQ, situated in Kishuf, had been serving as a mini-scale war room for the entire front. One by one, all the decision-makers of the war arrived there: Defense Minister Moshe Dayan; Front Commander Haim Bar Lev; Chief of General Staff David Elazar, and his advisor, Maj.-Gen. (res.) Rehavam Zeevi. The issue in question, after the paras had been withdrawn from Tirtur, was when the 162nd Division could cross the canal. All agreed that it must be crossed as soon as possible, but so far, the division was no longer prepared to cross, with its divisions being scattered all over and engaging the enemy one way or another.

Thus, the brigades of Natan Nir and Gabi Amir supported the rescuing of the paras near the Artillery and Akavish roads junction, and also watched for any enemy attempts to block this only route west. At dawn, they detected the advancement of the Egyptian 25th Elite Armored Brigade from near the abandoned Fort Bozter, south of the Bridgehead, in an attempt to cut off the Matzmed foothold. The 162nd Division was to block the Egyptian advance, so by late morning, it started preparing for a massive operation.

When asked by the Defense Minister whether the 143rd Division could hold on to Lexicon-Tirtur Junction, Bar Lev replied sarcastically that the 143rd Commander does not carry out his assignments anyway. The Minister accepted that once the three requirements of Bar Lev were met—the raft bridge was built, Akavish Road was secured and the battle with Egypt's 25th Armored Brigade was over, elements of the 162nd Division would be forded, starting from 1600 hours, and an approximate time frame for the entire division's crossing was set.*

The attendees decided to use the ad hoc meeting to discuss the next stage of the campaign, so Dayan summoned the 143rd Division Commander, Sharon, who arrived at 1230, from Matzmed, grim-faced.

* * *

On the morning of October 17th, Major General Ariel Sharon settled in Matzmed Yard, assuming command of the Raft Battalion and conducting the crossing from that post. He felt as if a great chance had been missed, believing that "those on the ground" could see what "those up there," meaning Dvela HQ and Front Command leaders, could not. Sharon poured out his fury over the halting of the crossing both at the time that it occurred as well as post factum. Anyway, for thirty-six hours after he had received the Front Command's orders to stop crossing, no substantial Israeli force crossed the canal.

On the morning of October 17th, the 143rd had jobs to be completed: receiving the twelve rafts; assembling them into a bridge; securing the eastern part of the Bridgehead; and in addition, the 14th and 600th Brigades were assigned with expanding the bridgehead on the west bank. The 35th Paratroopers Division, under Danni Matt and the 421st Division, under Haim Erez, were to secure it.

The division was deployed over tens of kilometers, on both

---

*   Bar On, *Dayan*, p.195.

banks of the canal, as if performing a split, engaged in numerous tasks. Tuvia Raviv's reduced 600th Brigade, forty tank strong, was positioned in Hamdyyah, without significantly contributing to the war effort. Later on, it sent a battalion to help tow the roller bridge, while another battalion was deployed to support the paratroopers securing the east side of Akavish Road. The 14th Brigade, under Amnon Reshef, fifty-two tank strong, was still licking its wounds, trying to find some respite after the ordeal it had gone through the previous thirty-six hours. Likewise, the 421st Brigade, under Haim Erez, operating west of the canal, had been split up, with Ami Morag's battalion struggling to rejoin its original formation on the west bank. Danni Matt's paratroopers division was engaged in securing the west of the Bridgehead. Nearby, Egyptian forces rushed to surround it. Logistical difficulties were no less a problem. Without a bridge for delivering supplies, the troops on the west bank were short of fuel, ammunition and even food.

* * *

The twelve rafts which the 630th Battalion was towing, commanded by Avi Zohar and led by 162nd Division Deputy Commander Dov Tamari, reached the launching Yard at 0630 hours, twenty-four hours behind schedule. Near the entrance to the perimeter, a raft sustained a direct artillery hit, which killed all of the seven man carrier's crew, under Lt. Yehuda Monheit. It caught fire, blocking the road. A tank, coupled to it in order to pull it aside, failed to uncouple, so another tank's crew fired a shell at the tow shaft, freeing the tank. All the other rafts were successfully launched, nearly undisturbed by the Egyptians.

Practically, the division's main task was building the bridge.

It started at 0930 hours, yet the connecting of the rafts together took many hours, much longer than had been planned and expected according to practice. At 1100 hours, Deputy Division Commander Col. Yaakov "Jacky" Even arrived at the Yard, and from then on, supervised all operations directly affecting the crossing from the east of the bridgehead, as explained below. By 1130 hours, after a long, painstaking effort, nine rafts had been launched.

This particular compound, constructed when Ariel Sharon served as Southern Command Commander, was originally designed to accommodate the various units the main task of which was to secure unobstructed transportation across the canal. The personnel subordinate to Jacky were assigned with supervising the bridge construction, as well as clearing and maintaining the approach routes, regulating transportation across the bridge, securing the overall area, which had become an extremely vulnerable target, and operating a medevac system for the numerous casualties.

Little by little, the Yard was filled with all kinds of dedicated units. During the night between the 15th and 16th of October, the Yard was secured by an ad hoc force of the 247th Brigade, under Paratroopers Col. Yossi Friedkin. AA elements, frogmen teams and others, mostly medical teams, joined later on.

Between the 16th and the 17th of October the Yard remained relatively peaceful, in complete contrast with the raging inferno around it, sometimes only a few hundred meters away. It wasn't until October 17th, due to the arrival of the rafts, that the Yard turned into the Egyptian artillery's target of choice. The Egyptians too, realized that the Crossing Point was the Achilles heel of the entire campaign, and its cutting off could threaten the precarious Israeli foothold on the west bank. As early as 0810 hours, on October 17th, Egyptian artillery started pounding the launching zone, hitting three rafts. As mentioned above, one of those, commanded by Lt. Monheit, was incapacitated. This routine went on for the duration of the war. From now on, the everyday life of the Yard's men turned into a struggle for individual survival.

Watching the west bank of the canal from his position in the Yard, Sharon became furious: the other front commanders were not sharing in almost any of his ideas, their mutual distrust growing worse. At 0630 hours, probably responding to rumors, Gonen ordered Sharon: "Don't deliver any 'heavies" [i.e. tanks] without permission." "Only a small number have crossed. I stopped it," Sharon replied. "No 'heavies' crossing without permission, from now on," Gonen concluded.

At 0740 hours, Gonen radioed Sharon: "Some tank force [probably the Egyptian 25th Brigade], advancing south, heading for the bridge on the east bank. Bren's dealing with them. I assigned the 600th Brigade to Bren for his current task, [rescuing the 890th Battalion]. You carry on with your assignment, while Bren finishes off those heading for you."

Thus, Gonen reported to Sharon that the 600th Brigade, originally a part of Sharon's division, had been assigned to Bren's division, to help it rescue the paras. Sharon was very bitter about this decision.

At 0900 hours, 143rd Division HQ, positioned at Matzmed, was surprised by a couple of Egyptian tanks which happened to infiltrate the Yard. Sharon radioed the 14th Brigade commander, Amnon Reshef: "There are enemy vehicles in the area where you've deployed today. Some Egyptian tank is pounding at us opposite Tirtur junction." When Reshef replied that he would deal with it, Sharon said, "I believe it's most urgent. I think some enemy vehicle infiltrated there, and now it's battering our position in Nahala."

Sharon would later recall: "The Yard, where we stayed, was very heavily shelled. I ordered the HQ to assume position at the entrance of the perimeter, and suddenly we realized that we were being shelled not by artillery only, but by tanks as well. I found it strange. I thought we had misunderstood (what was happening), so we drove, once again, toward Nahala-Lexicon Junction, where we saw an Egyptian tank battalion advancing from the Farm, attacking the Nahala-Lexicon Junction. We were greatly surprised. The HQ assumed their positions right away, opening fire. We rushed there, seizing the spot. Then I called the 14th Brigade, who arrived in a few minutes, knocking off some enemy tanks." Sharon might have slightly exaggerated. As Maj.-Gen. Reshef commented, "It was not a tank battalion attack: only a few tanks penetrated. I, myself, destroyed the infiltrating tank."*

That incident also bred one of the war's symbols. An Egyptian projectile hit right behind Sharon's APC, causing it to fall into the shell crater. As a result, the division commander's head hit the heavy machinegun affixed to the vehicle's wall, and was covered with blood. Though it was just a superficial wound, the white bandage crowning Sharon's forehead became an icon. Rumors were spread over radio networks about the division commander being seriously injured.

Sharon, reporting to Gonen about the incident, complained about the loopholes opened in the defense lines due to poor coordination between divisions. He believed somebody had poorly

---

organized the relief of the 600th detached from Sharon's forces, and consequently, as Sharon blamed Gonen at the time, "the enemy directly threatens Nahala road and Matzmed, and therefore, the entire crossing force. An enemy force, advancing from Amir to Tirtur junction, has blocked the approach to the road." Sharon also complained his forces were too widely deployed to allow him a main effort in the center, and that he found the Front Command's interference of reassigning forces and boundaries, troublesome.

Gonen responded by offering to support Sharon with the 162nd Division. Sharon took it as an insult:

"I can fend for myself. But let me tell you that I consider what we're doing a top priority. As I already told you, we must push the Egyptians to advance this way. I need no support of the 162nd. I need to be able to use my own forces, and their support does me no good. I repeat: just let me manage things here."

Gonen: It's up to you, of course. I can give you the 162nd for support, but, if you don't wish it, I won't. But, in case you fail, just let me know and I'll assign the task to them. If you don't need them for the time being, I'll tell them to stay away.

Sharon: I don't want their interference. All I want them to do is secure the road from Fort Lakekan, southward.

Gonen: Okay. But if you cannot clear the Nahala-Lexicon Junction, let me know.

Sharon: I already cleared it.

Thirty minutes later they talked again. This time, it got loud, and they alluded to possible post-war vendettas:

Gonen: We are reassessing the situation, allocating assignments. So try harder.

Sharon: Excuse me, don't you tell me to try harder. I try at least as hard as any of you!

Gonen: We'll talk about it in good time, as well as other matters.

Sharon: And whatever we discuss, it is going to be very unpleasant, you can bet on it!

Gonen: Certainly.

Sharon: All I want is for you to just not restrain me as hard as you can!*

Gonen, turning to his Chief of Staff, Brig.-Gen, Asher Levy, remarked: "Arik's being himself again, playing his old tricks." His deputy, Uri Ben Ari remarked "He's out of his mind."

* * *

In such a mood, Sharon arrived at the conference Dayan convened at Dvela HQ, with a two APC motorcade, his forehead wrapped with a white bandage. In addition to his usual entourage members, such as Brig.-Gen. Avraham "Abrasha" Tamir, he also brought his favorite journalist Uri Dan.

Major General Adan would later recall:

"I was amazed to see how crowded Sharon's APC was. I recognized there at least one journalist [referring to Uri Dan] and some of his close friends. Handing over my microphone to the operations officer, I took a 1:5000 scale map, stepped about fifty meters away from the HQ, and we all knelt on the sand, around the map. I also asked the journalist and Sharon's acquaintances to move away."**

---

*   Bergman, *Real Time,* p.263.
**   Adan, *On Both Banks,* p.219.
**   Their friendship served as the inspiration for *The Two of Us,* a popular Israeli mourning song.

As mentioned above, Sharon arrived rather gloomy. On his way to the conference, he had heard about the serious injury of his closest friend and tactical HQ member, Maj. Zeev Sluzky. He had not yet been informed of his death. ** Sluzky had been Sharon's companion since they served in the 101ˢᵗ Unit which made its name during the 1950s reprisals. He was frequently at Sharon's house and had been a permanent member of his staff since the 1967 Six-Day War. His death was one of the hardest blows Sharon had taken in that war.

Though the gathering at Kishuf was accidental, to a great extent it had resulted from a pressing need to sort out with Sharon, face to face, two major problems: an operational one—what was to be done regarding the plodding campaign; and a personal one—the need to look Sharon straight in the face, and to make him see things eye to eye with the decision-makers. In other words, to demand that Sharon align himself with the plans and orders of the Front Command. This was also the reason for the cold shoulder Sharon had received upon his arrival.

That was the first senior decision-makers' conference since the night of October 14ᵗʰ. Although it had been merely two and a half days since then, under the circumstances of the crossing campaign, it had amounted to ages. Present at the meeting were the Defense Minister, the Chief of General Staff and his assistant, Major General Zeevi, who only showed up at 1300 hours, as well as the front commander and the two field divisions' commanders—an unusual war council under the circumstances.

Since early morning, the front commander had been thoroughly examining the strategic challenges threatening the orderly course and success of the crossing campaign. They were aware of the jammed roads; that it would take a long time for the raft bridge to be fully constructed and launched; that the Roller Bridge was still some distance from its destination, and that the Alligators were on the verge of destruction. They were aware of the intensive grinding of 143rd Division forces; that the plan's execution was falling behind schedule, and they feared an Egyptian response on both the east as well as west banks. They expressed their concern about the insufficient width of the corridor and the precarious state of the foothold on the west bank. Nonetheless, they were resolved to carry on the offensive there. During the entire discussion, of about an hour and half, the various war rooms of the Command had been monitoring the advance of the 25th Egyptian Brigade and the preparations of the 162nd Division's 217th Brigade, to face it on the 57th kilometer of Kaspi Road. Major General Adan was edgy, looking forward to the imminent clash.

Sharon, with his entourage, approached the HQ members at a quick pace. Front Commander Haim Bar Lev, with a cigar in his mouth, looked at him. As Sharon wrote in his autobiography:

"I was met with general silence. No one breathed a word, except Dayan, who greeted me with just a 'hello'…Then, Bar Lev said, speaking extremely slowly and quietly: 'Arik, there's a gulf between what you promised and what you delivered.' At that point I felt dead tired, after all our bloody battles and losses…I looked around, seeing them all smartly dressed, neat and tidy. I felt that there was just one thing I must do: slap Bar Lev's face."*

---

*   Sharon, *Warrior*, [in English] p. 326.

This extremely emotional quotation expresses both the aggravating personal antipathy as well as the profound operational disagreements between Sharon and the Front Command. Yet Sharon restrained himself, stopping his hand in midair, and the conference, despite the high tension and profound disagreements, was conducted quietly and relatively calmly.

Bar Lev started, stating with his typically slow speech, that the bulk of the forces must not be delivered across the canal as long as there was no solid bridgehead. The 162nd Division commander, as well, argued that the foothold on the west bank hardly deserved the name of "bridgehead," since the corridor was still being occasionally infiltrated. So, he concluded, as long as the bridgehead is not secured, we must not deploy any substantial forces across the canal, as Adan would later write, "I suggested sticking to the original plan, by which I was to thrust from the bridgehead westward and southward."[*]

Sharon seized the opportunity to reveal his own and his division's ordeal during the two previous days. The gulf between the "men in the field" and "the staff" never struck him as deep as now. He disputed every point Bar Lev presented, particularly his preconditions for the crossing.

He argued that there were indications of the enemy forces on the west bank starting to break down. Though his division had its tanks in the Yard, he was ordered not to let them across the canal, for some reason he failed to see. The time to do it, he

---

[*] Adan, *On Both Banks*, p.219. One must bear in mind that by the original plan of Operation Valiant, the securing of the bridgehead was to be followed by a two-division strong offensive southward, aimed at encircling the 3Rd Army.

argued, was now: the road was clear, his forces had secured the junction, and enemy pressure seemed to have ended. Within three hours, the rafts could be fully connected, and there were other rafts [he meant the Alligators] which could deliver tanks. There was also a road prepared for the Roller Bridge, so now was the time to get up and go.

Bar Lev didn't accept Sharon's optimistic outline. He had been fed up with promises, so he just disbelieved Sharon's words. He insisted that a sufficiently wide corridor is a precondition for the second phase of the crossing campaign. Since, as he argued, Akavish lacks "margins" up north, it needs a further clearing that night.

At that moment, at about 1300 hours, the Chief of General Staff arrived, and Bar Lev made the surprising suggestion of splitting the forces and their command between the two banks. Sharon and Adan would command the forces on the west bank, while their deputies, would command those left on the east bank. Neither Adan nor Sharon were thrilled by the suggestion, Sharon repeatedly urging the Chief of General Staff for an instant crossing of the canal, in an attempt to expand the Bridgehead northward, with four armored brigades. "Let's just dash, and they'll all collapse." "Well, you've been telling me about their collapse for the last week, but that hardly has anything to do with reality," Bar Lev remarked. Sharon retorted: "It worked exactly to plan. It wasn't my fault that the Roller Bridge broke down. I suspect that eventually you'll decide that I didn't fight in this war at all."*

The Chief of General Staff said he didn't see the point of splitting up divisions.

---

*   Bar On, *Moshe Dayan,* p.196.

Bar Lev: What's there not to see? So far, the plan hasn't worked.

Elazar: Let bygones be bygones.

Elazar didn't need much explanation as to what this suggestion meant. He saw that Bar Lev, too, was conceding to Sharon's ambition to play a more active role in the fighting on the west bank. Elazar would later comment about that compromise, which gave both divisions the right to cross first, at the cost of splitting their forces between the two banks: "This is my only argument against Bar Lev's decisions in that war. I perfectly understood the pressures he had been under, that everybody wanted to get to Africa [the west bank of the canal], and he had other considerations as well. But, at that meeting, I told Bar Lev: No! I only have one consideration, making sure the war is conducted in an orderly manner."[*]

Elazar shared Sharon's view that the more Israeli forces that were across the canal while the Egyptian divisions were not prepared, the better. On all other points, he accepted Bar Lev's view. He held that one must only run calculated risks, so substantial forces were not to ford before the bridgehead and the corridor were secured. It would be disastrous to deliver four brigades across the canal, and then lose the bridgehead, so it was better to be safe than sorry. His conclusions were: the bridgehead is too narrow, and must be expanded, and Egyptian counterattacks are still possible. Therefore, Sharon's division should hold the bridgehead. "We've got a foothold on the other shore, so let

---

[*]   Bar Tov, *Dado*, p.257.
[**]   Adan, On Both Banks, p.219.

162nd Division cross," he told Sharon. "You, finish the job you were given, and then, you can cross too."

Adan would later comment on Elazar's decision: "The relief I felt then defies description. Since the very beginning of that campaign, I'd been waiting impatiently for the moment I could cross the canal, and I suddenly felt as if my participation was questioned. Bar Lev's suggestion came as a surprise to me."** The Defense Minister didn't see fit to speak his mind, and just kept silent for the entire ninety minute long conference, which ended at 1415 hours.

After the conference, Elazar and Bar Lev started off to Dvelah HQ. Their major preoccupation, on top of all the strategic dilemmas, was the growing distrust between them and Sharon.

* * *

Major General Adan was glad to see that the original plan was being followed, which left the crossing and the charge southward to his own 162nd Division. It had a full agenda that day, mainly facing the Egyptian 25th Brigade southeast of the Chinese Farm (Grafit and Yahfan perimeters), and then, crossing the canal. So far, it wasn't clear whether the division could get out of the mess on Akavish Road, on the edge of Missouri perimeter, and, if it could, could it meet the planned schedule. Adan, considering that his division needed to replenish its fuel and ammunition supply before the crossing, and that the bridge was planned to be completed no earlier than 1600 hours, disbelieved that his forces could cross by the scheduled time.

Sharon left the conference infuriated and frustrated, both due to the attitude of the decision-makers, as well as their rejection of his ideas, and hurried back to the Yard. There, he was surprised by Minister Dayan who wanted to join him in watching the completion of the bridge.* Sharon agreed. Dayan was also the only one who asked about his wound.

On their way, they drove by a group of Egyptian POWS being led eastwards. One of them, an Egyptian officer, recognizing Dayan's face, asked that they be fed. Dayan, cynically remarking that as far as he knew it was Ramadan, still ordered that the POWs be fed and given medical attention.

Dayan and Sharon arrived at the Yard at about 1445 hours, and watched Engineering Corps men toiling to fit the last rafts onto the bridge.** At 1500 hours, Dayan reported to Uri Ben Ari at Dvela HQ, that the raft bridge would be crossable within an hour. Right afterward, Sharon offered Dayan a treat: crossing the canal on board an Alligator, to have a first-hand view of reaching the west bank. Sharon's court journalist didn't fail to photograph that event, and the visit boosted the morale of the paratroopers deployed along the embankments and in the trenches west of the canal. Bar On, Dayan's adjutant, recalls that "we heard explosions all around, yet our spirits were high. The minister was impressed by the Egyptian tank positions on the west bank, or Africa, as it came to be called from then on. Sharon tried to get him meet with the field commanders, but some of them were too busy with their assignments.

Sharon and Col. Haim Erez, the Armored Brigade commander who had initially crossed the canal with the Alligators, at that time had the following conversation:

---

*   Bar On, *Dayan,* p.197.
**   Dayan, *Story of My Life*, p. 649; see also Uri Dan, *Sharon's Bridgehead*, p.211.

Sharon: I visited your sector, with a fellow who is short of a certain body part. He wanted to shake your hand, and really liked what he saw.

Erez: I know what part he is short of.

Sharon: well, that part he happens to have...huh-huh. The part he is short of is an upper one. We had fun, anyway.

By the time Dayan was back in Matzmed, the bridge had already been completed*. Then, after a short visit at Dvela HQ, he went back to Tel Aviv, to report the good news that the tide of war was turning.

3. FIRE IN THE YARD.

Matzmed Yard, the morning of October 17:

Since the morning of October 17th, tens, or even hundreds of Egyptian artillery pieces had been targeting the bridgehead, directed by observers positioned in nearby groves. All that artillery bombarded the small compound, taking a heavy toll on Israeli forces. On top of that, there were occasional air attacks by Egyptian aircrafts and helicopters, targeting the bridge and the perimeter with bombs and napalm. The numerous casualties won the perimeter the nickname "Death Yard." It also became the medevac point for wounded personnel from all over the west bank, who were delivered there on board rubber boats and Alligators.

The off-duty Alligators' battalion men served as stretcher bearers, alongside the ad hoc force of paratroopers under Yossi Friedkin. The improvised aid station had very few medical

---

*   Dayan, *Story of My Life*, p. 650.

supplies left after the truck delivering the supplies was hit and torched on its way to the Yard. Dr. Uzi Barak, the Alligators' battalion medical officer (a pediatrician in his civilian occupation), and his team had their hands full. He was assisted by a young, newly graduated doctor, assigned to the paratroopers in the Yard. They worked around the clock, with not a moment's respite, treating scores of injured men suffering from all forms of trauma. The number of injured was mounting, but with no means for evacuating them, they were piling up within the compound. One medic would later recall: "During a five day long constant heavy shelling, the seven of us worked day and night, treating over 200 injured men." The increasing number of those killed, were just left on the ground by the aid station since there were no stretchers to carry them away. At one point they numbered as many as fifty. That place came to be known as the "Hill of the Killed," in the "Death Yard." Though an earthwork embankment was erected around the aid station, there was a constant threat that the station or its surroundings might be hit. Therefore, to minimize the risk to those casualties being evacuated from the waterfront, they were transported in a front-end loader bucket. The aid station presented terrible scenes of the injured and wounded, with severed limbs, men crying, and medevac helicopters not able to land because of the sporadic fire. Neither were there any medevac vehicles in the Yard, and no vehicle was able to drive into or out of it. It wasn't until two days later that ambulance tanks managed to drive into the Yard and commenced evacuation of the most seriously wounded.*

---

*   As attested by Amikam Doron.
**   Col. (ret.) Yossi Fridkin, in an interview.

Once the raft bridge had been completed, at 1600 hours, the men in the Yard began to prepare for the crossing of the 162nd Division. It commenced no sooner than 2200 hours, as described below. As Lt.-Col Yossi Friedkin, commander of the Yard's paratroopers explained it: "Once the bridge was drivable, there was no authority regulating the jammed traffic of forces. I, with four men, did my best. The only thing the division sent there was Jacky Even's APC. That was the only authority regulating that traffic. We had neither communication equipment nor personnel, and the outcome was incredible traffic jams, columns hit, and ammunitions trucks blowing up. Danni Matt, in an attempt to handle the mess, sent us during the night, Nahman Sirkin's bunch. Then, once the order of movement had been set, the road was cleared within two hours."**

Paratroopers 1st Sgt. Yoram Shubek-Ronen remembers the first casualties were predominantly paratroopers operating west of the canal: "We used to carry the wounded men, evacuated from the waterfront on board rubber boats, on our shoulders, climbing the unprotected embankment, and then descending to the Yard. Hence, we took up the practice of looking under the dead men's blankets, checking who wore the paras' red boots. Except for a small bunker which had survived from the abandoned fort, we had no shelter from the constant shelling. During one shelling, I took cover under the bucket of a bulldozer tank which happened to be parked nearby. When the shelling was over, I looked up, seeing a pair of eyes staring at me with amazement. They belonged to a tank driver who was a member of my kibbutz."

For his relentless effort, from his first day in the Yard until the ceasefire, Ronen was awarded the Exemplary Deed Decoration.

* * *

On the night between the 18th and the 19th of October, an Egyptian commando unit unsuccessfully tried to attack the raft bridge; on October 19th, eight MIGs targeted it, killing one man and injuring another ten servicemen including officers. Until the ceasefire was announced, hundreds of men were hit in the Yard, including two senior Engineering Corps officers: 143rd Division's chief engineer officer, Lt.-Col. Baruch De Leon, and 605th Battalion Deputy Commander Maj. Yehuda Hudeda. However, from October 18th, Matzmed started to follow an orderly routine. The general command and control was assigned to three officers subordinate to Division Deputy Commander Even; the paratroopers, engineers, AA units, frogmen and general command of the engineers, to Col. Menasheh Gur.

* * *

The artillery shelling of the Yard put nearly all of the Alligators out of action. As 634th Battalion Deputy Commander Maj. Amikam Doron, recalls: "I and some officers boarded an Alligator loaded with two tanks. It took a direct hit while in the water, capsizing. I found myself in the water, burdened with a bulletproof vest and a helmet, with no life jacket, which nearly caused me to drown. Somehow, with my last strength, I managed to swim to the farther bank, where I hid. But all of the tank crews drowned, since their hatches were closed. From among us, nearly none were injured, barring one company leader. On the night of October 17th, a heavy shelling hit nearly all the Alligators, so by October

18th we only had one usable two-way raft."[*]

By the 21st of October, out of sixteen Alligators delivered to the canal, one was hit on land, nine sank, and only six were returned to land safely. Of those, only four drove from the Yard toward the assembly point in Fort Lakekan (after the war, thirty-four Alligators were repaired). This, practically, ended the Alligators contribution to the crossing. Yet, though marginalized before the war, they proved to be an essential asset during it, rescuing, on October 17th, the crossing campaign from its quagmire. As one Alligator battalion officer explained: "After we had already learned that all other fording machinery had run into troubles, Sharon comes and tells us that the entire crossing campaign depends on us Alligators, and that the only ones capable to deliver tanks across the canal at that stage are us. We had already felt these vehicles were useful, and everybody knew we were to be the first to reach the canal."[**]

Most probably, if it hadn't been for that reduced, sixteen-Alligator strong battalion, which managed to reach the canal by dawn of October 16th, the fate of the crossing campaign would have been very different. Thanks to the Alligators, more than 120 tanks, artillery pieces, and hundreds of armored vehicles were delivered west of the Suez, with no men killed and relatively few wounded.

---

[*]   Doron, "Alligators Battalion, from Marginalization to Glory," an article in *Engineering Corps Bulletin*, no date; Col. Doron, in an interview.
[**] A part of a series of radio interviews by Journalist Arieh Arad.

* * *

Finally, at 1610 hours, the raft bridge was ready. As Avi Zohar told it later: "If even one more raft had been hit, we wouldn't have completed the bridge. Earlier on, our commanders told us we were to cross the canal when 'not a bird shall sing', that is, when there's no enemy fire. Well, when we did, not a bird sang, since the Egyptian artillery and aircrafts were doing a hell of a job. I believe it was a great day for all, and for us, who feared it, it was an unforgettable event. Yet we were aware that were that bridge not erected on that very day, on that very night the men would have boarded their boats, retreating, Dunkirk-style."

Unexpectedly, the first to cross the bridge, at 1845 hours, weren't the 162nd Division's tanks, but those of 143rd Division, of 421st Brigade and remnants of the 247th. Nevertheless, with these exceptions, the bridge remained unused until 2200 hours, when the 162nd Division started crossing. As Brig.-Gen. "Jacky" Even recalls: "On October 17th, in the afternoon, the Defense Minister crossed the canal on board a Gillois, and it was an idyllically peaceful scene. The bridge was completed by 1600 hours, but nobody had reached it. So I told Adan: Look, we've got a bridge so you can cross. Today, thinking of it, I can tell you that between 1600 and 1830 hours we could have delivered forces easily, with no exceptional difficulties. Yet nobody crossed. Then, at 1900 or 2000 hours, the Egyptian started shelling the bridge, when they finally realized what was on. That shelling injured the bridging battalion commander, Avi Zohar, who was replaced by his deputy, Capt. Yishay Dotan. Back then, the Gillois were still intact. They only started taking hits later on."

Although there was only one bridge erected across the canal, while the plan required a minimum of two bridges, the Unifloat bridge served as the essential means for deploying the divisions westward. From the night of October 17-18th to October 19th, most of the divisions' armored vehicles, including those of the 252nd, had crossed the Unifloat bridge.

4. KADMONI'S SHOW

247th Brigade, West Bank of the Canal, October 17th, 0900 hours:

The bridgehead on both banks, had been taking incessant Egyptian artillery since 0630 hours. When the shelling intensified, Ariel Sharon with the 143rd Division, ordered 247th Division commander, Danni Matt, to search the agricultural barrier to the north for artillery observers and firing sources, in order to force the Egyptian artillery away from the bridgehead.

The Egyptian artillery had been targeting the bridgehead from two opposite directions, on both banks of the canal, at various ranges of up to twenty-seven kilometers. In other words, to force enemy artillery out of range of Matzmed, 143rd Division elements had to expand the area under their control much beyond what was their reach at that moment. Another way to neutralize Egyptian gun batteries was by "blinding" them, by spotting the Egyptian observers that were scattered and concealed all over the place—on treetops, behind walls, and in trenches, and taking them out.

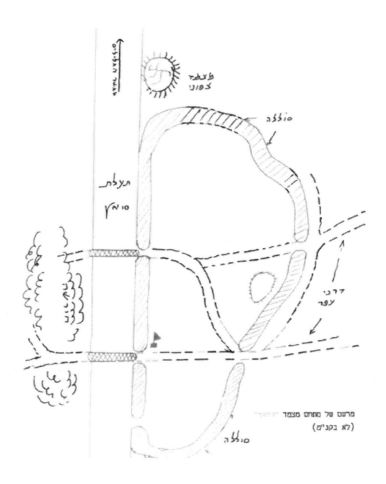

A sketch of Matzmed Yard (courtesy of Yaakov "Jacky" Even)

Danni Matt and his paratroopers were eager for action after two long days of stressful inaction. On October 17th, at 0900, Matt ordered the 565th Battalion commander, Dan Ziv, to lead a company strong force northward, mounted on half-tracks and two tanks, mopping up all the way to the 29th kilometer of Masecha Road (Freshwater Canal and railroad), north of

Vardit Road, and the village of Serafaum*, east of the Orha perimeter.**

Due to earlier reports of Haim Erez, whose force had searched the area for AA missile batteries, and had met little resistance, Ziv got the impression the section was relatively empty.

Lt.-Col. Dan Ziv was a battle-hardened Paratroopers officer, a Medal of Valor (Israel's highest military decoration) recipient for rescuing wounded men during the 1956 Sinai War Battle of Mitla Pass. He ordered a company commander to lead a force of about eighty men, on board six half-tracks, along the railroad running along the canal, on the west bank. The battalion commander mounted the front vehicle, while his deputy, the rear one. As mentioned above, the force was also reinforced with two tanks.

It advanced for about one hour along the Freshwater Canal and the railroad, with no exceptional obstructions. Shortly afterwards, it reached what it supposed to be the 31st kilometer of Masecha Road, about three kilometers southeast of the Orha perimeter, and seven kilometers away from Deversoir. Here things started getting messy. Ziv struggled to identify his location, a difficulty that became critical later on. He was surprised to see, a kilometer away, the Serafeum railway station, surrounded with many Egyptian troops.

---

*   Not to be confused with Serafeum Coast Guard Station, Serafeum railroad, and other places of the similar name.

**   As was typical of the 247th Brigade in that war, on October 17th, the 565th Battalion was widely dispersed: its 1st Company was still east of the canal, while its 3rd Company was on the Freshwater Canal, serving as the support fire element of the 416th Battalion, under Lt.-Col. Zviki Nur. Thus, the only force available to the battalion commander was the 2nd Company, under Capt. Reinitz.

As he recalled: "We hesitated over what to do next. I wasn't positive about our location, and had a feeling my reports were inaccurate…I assumed the Egyptian force was rather small. While we were observing the Egyptians near the station, I started my tank, and made up my mind to go on attack. I had been standing idle for forty-five minutes, and had to decide. All the while, I'd been reporting to the brigade commander and all friendly forces that I was at the 31st kilometer of Masecha, while I was actually elsewhere, so, throughout the fighting I couldn't coordinate an artillery support fire… My battle plan was simple: a single file attack along the railroad, destroying the disarrayed force, and then regrouping, in anticipation of whatever may come… but we were in for a complete surprise. We found out that the compound was held by a substantial force, I could not tell how strong. My intelligence officer said they had two battalions there…After our tank had been knocked off, I thought I could withdraw to the other end of the village, for regrouping, but was surprised to find another enemy perimeter there." (Among the men of the rescuing force was war reporter Ron Ben Yishai, who also took photos of the fighting).

When the force attacked, at about 1230 hours, it engaged a superior Egyptian force. The assaulting column took on heavy fire, first from small arms and then RPGs and AT weapons. One of their tanks got hit, while the other suffered a damaged tread. The battalion commander's team, riding in the lead half-track, was effectively isolated from the rest of the force and split up. The commander himself, his staff and another fourteen men, were surrounded in the village, near the Serafeum railway station, north of Vardit Road.*

The paratroopers dismounted their half-track, each team running for cover in some house. The battalion commander and his team assumed position in a mud hut, where they were pinned down for the rest of the battle. From then on, everyone was fighting for his own and his team's survival and rescue. The lead group, under Captain Asa Kadmoni, held a yard situated between two huts.

Soon, after all his comrades had been injured, Kadmoni was surrounded by hundreds of Egyptians, and gave an incredible, four-hour long one-man show of fighting. Like a hunted, unvanquished beast, he kept shooting, throwing grenades, launching missiles, jumping sideways, recovering magazines from wounded comrades, destroying two truckloads of Egyptians and single-handedly holding off the Egyptian advance until the rescuing force arrived. By then, he had only a few bullets left.

He would later be awarded with the Medal of Valor for his fighting. It was possibly this ordeal that drove him to lead the post-war protest, and into the mental breakdown which haunted him for the rest of his short life.

The brigade HQ had been informed about the encirclement as early as 1240 hours, and at 1330 hours its commander, Danni Matt, reported to Sharon that, "things

---

* Brigade HQ was informed about the situation of Ziv' force at 1240 hours. That Battle was intensively discussed. See, for instance: Baruch Nevo & Nurit Ashkenazi, *Back from Serafeum*, Maariv Pres, 2006, , pp. 165 ff., and Blum Halevi, *Consecration: Yom Kippur War Memoirs*, Mitam Publishers, 1999, p. 397 ff.

** *Nevo & Ashkenazi, Back from Serafeum.*

are getting messy down there, and it will take an entire detachment to handle. We must go for a major rescuing operation, according to his [Dan Ziv's] own reports. Well, you known him. I guess he's hard pressed." When Sharon wondered why artillery support wasn't being used, Matt replied, hopelessly, that "we've been targeting them for the last hour, with all kinds of corrections, and so far, we've been only hitting friendlies." It was because Ziv had given them an incorrect location.

For some reason, it took the rescuing force a long time to reach the scene. Meanwhile, for nearly five hours, Ziv's dispersed and surrounded forces had been fighting off the Egyptians, running low on strength and ammo. Ziv's desperate calls for help finally drove elements of his brigade to rescue his force. At 1430 hours the leading rescuing force reached the team of deputy battalion commander, Uzi Eilat, who were encircled in a section of the railway station east of the railroad. Then, another force, under Deputy Brigade Commander Yehuda Bar, started off from brigade HQ, successfully accomplishing the rescue mission at the very last moment. The battle had a grim outcome, with twelve reservist paratroopers and two tank crew men killed and another twenty-two injured during the battle and rescue mission.

The course and cost of this engagement bred bitter vendettas that survived for years afterward. Ziv's staff harshly criticized him for his performance, while Kadmoni, who demanded an inquiry into the battalion commander's conduct during the battle, was dismissed while the war was still raging on. The Serafeum perimeter, codenamed Orha, was captured by Israeli forces two days later, in a set piece attack by the 14th Brigade and paratrooper detachments.

* * *

On October 17th, before dawn, 599th Battalion, under Ami Morag, joined the 421st Brigade on the west bank of the Suez. The day before, it had been kept on the east bank to support the 14th Brigade. The eight tanks Morag had brought, significantly boosted the morale of brigade commander, Haim Erez, since by dawn, his brigade had started fighting for the Freshwater Canal's bridges.

At daybreak, the Egyptians started targeting, with tank guns and small arms, from Uri perimeter, the reduced armored forces of Giora Lev and Ami Morag, which was holding the Freshwater Canal against the build-up Egyptian forces west of the canal. The theater west of the canal was nothing like the open desert east of it. Irrigation canals, drawing from the Nile to the area known as Farming Barrier, formed a fifteen kilometer long and five kilometer wide perimeter crisscrossed with canals and spotted with groves, vegetation mud huts and small army bases, teeming with infantry forces of varying strength reinforced with Egyptian armored forces sent from Uri perimeter. Armored Brigade Commander Haim Erez conducted the battle, constantly moving between the bridgehead, Deversoir Airbase, and the clash points.

At about 0800 hours, at Uri Junction, the 264th Battalion engaged an Egyptian tank and infantry force, destroying ten tanks. Of those, five were concealed among the trees, while another five were dug in at the junction. Such skirmishes marked that entire day, and the night following it wasn't peaceful either.

As part of the battle, Israeli forces fired at the village's huts and at enemy forces positioned or sheltered in the fields and thickets along the road.* Throughout that day and night, the 599th Battalion struggled over a Bailey bridge across a canal in the south, and when the night was over, it still held the bridge.** The successful raiding by the 421st Brigade, the day before, of Egyptian AA missile bases, drove the Egyptians to reinforce their positions in Uri and Tzah perimeters.

By the night of October 17th, the 143rd Division had managed to maintain its foothold on the west bank. It was about three kilometers wide, bounded by the Freshwater Canal, and about seven kilometers long, bounded by the village of Serafeum.

5. SITTING DUCKS

Egyptian 25th Brigade, East Bank of the Canal, October 17th:
East of the Suez, October 17th was marked by Egyptians attacking the bridgehead that had been established under their very noses. Early in the morning, the 198th Battalion, under Amir Yaffeh, was alerted about a possible attack, of an about sixty tank strong force, on its northern flank, in the area of the Chinese Farm. That battalion was reassigned to Sharon's division, to secure Shiekh Road to the north, and it was the force planned to contain the attack. The battalion waited for the attack, at its battle stations. The Egyptians didn't stand a

---

*   See: Kedar, *The History of Mahatz Battalion*, pp. 84 ff.

** The battalion and paratroopers platoon took some casualties during that day's fighting. That night, Morag deployed most of his forces to secure the bridge. There were no Israeli casualties during the night's fighting and the morning after, tens of dead Egyptians were counted near the force's positions. Morag himself returned late that night to the bridgehead, to brief 217th Brigade Commander Col. Natan "Natkeh" Nir.

chance. During that battle, which lasted from 0900 hours till midday, the battalion claimed to have destroyed about forty enemy tanks.* That was one of the most successful tank hunting battles that occurred. After the Egyptian threat to the north of the bridgehead had been checked, the 198th Battalion looked forward to rejoining its original formation, the 460th Brigade.

The Egyptian 25th Brigade's plan to attack to the south of the bridgehead didn't stand a chance either. It was an elite brigade, under Brig.-Gen. Ahmad Hilmi, equipped with T-62 tanks, the Egyptian Army's latest model tanks, and commanded by its best officers. Its three battalions crossed the canal, one after the other, between the 7th and 9th of October, and it joined, as an independent detachment, with the 3rd Army, subordinate to the 7th Division. It secured a perimeter between Fort Bozter in the north and the 94th kilometer of Lexicon Road. Its west flank was bounded by the small Bitter Lake, and its eastern one, by the 401st Brigade under Dan Shomron, who kept a close watch on it.

The deployment of the 25th Brigade on October 17th had been bitterly disputed between Egyptian Chief of Staff, Colonel-General Shazly, and War Minister Ismail Ali, who disagreed on the best way to handle the Israeli bridgehead. They both agreed that the 21st Division, positioned at Missouri perimeter, should thrust south toward the bridgehead, yet Ali insisted on the 25th Brigade's participation in the attack, leaving its positions and thrust to the north. As Shazly would later write, "That plan was reckless and irresponsible. I explained the threat to the brigade

---

*   Wexler, *198th Battalion*, p.98.

to Ali, over and over again, if it was to advance forty kilometers with its left flank covered by the canal, while its right flank was exposed to the enemy, yet he couldn't comprehend it." Shazly immediately shared his views with the 3ʳᵈ Army commander and the 25ᵗʰ Brigade commander, both of whom agreed with him. Yet War Minister Ali, reluctant to listen to any alternative view, had forced him to accept his plan. As Shazly wrote in his memoirs, "On October 17ᵗʰ, at 0300 hours, I was awakened by the officer in charge, to answer a phone call from General Wassel. He told me that the 25ᵗʰ Brigade would not be able to go on an attack at dawn, due to technical problems. Despite what I felt, I told him that the attack had been coordinated with others, so it could not be called off or postponed. When I insisted, he muttered in desperation, 'We are all powerless against Allah!', telling me he would follow orders. Yet he remarked that he knew for sure that the brigade was about to be doomed the next day. I hung up, heavy hearted, but I was obliged to follow the order."*

Indeed, one can hardly see the reason for this order: the way the brigade had to go to reach the bridgehead was long and challenging, full of obstacles and pitfalls, all known in advance. This time, the IDF knew how to seize the opportunity.

Southern Command's intelligence had intercepted the brigade's standby order as early as the evening of October 16ᵗʰ. From that moment, both the Front Command as well as its divisions started monitoring the Egyptian brigade's advance. Sharon's division was ordered to block its advance from the south, at Fort Lakekan, while Adan's division was ordered to prepare to destroy the brigade.

---

* Shazly, *The Crossing of The Suez*, p. 185.

Though Israeli forces were thinly deployed to the south of the bridgehead, between Forts Botzer and Lakeran, yet a line of observation points overlooking Lexicon Road would offer them sufficient alert about any potential advance of the Egyptian brigade northward or eastward. The main Israeli force was situated at the Hurva stronghold, opposite the central Bitter Lakes, where a tank platoon could detect any suspected movement.

The Egyptian brigade's route, from Fort Botzer, along Lexicon Road, was commanded by low hilltops such as the 120 meter (394 feet) high Idra, west of Artillery Road, six kilometers away from Great Bitter Lake; hilltops codenamed Grafit and Yahfan, of about twenty-meters (sixty-six feet) altitude, and by Lexicon Road, situated about two kilometers away. Two large wetlands, on the 269th and 275th kilometers of Lexicon Road, impassible by tanks, channeled the force's advancement into one northbound road. And the battlefield offered one more advantage to any force ambushing the brigade: the planned killing zone was absolutely flat, stretching alongside the banks of the canal and Bitter Lakes.

The Front Command and the 162nd Division command saw the opportunity to crush the Egyptian brigade between Lakekan and Botzher in the very first operational assessment. It was soon found out that the enemy brigade was advancing in a column, along Lexicon Road, with nothing to secure its flank.

Naturally, Front Command assigned the main effort of facing the 25th Brigade to the 162nd Division, under Adan, who was fortunate enough to have the available forces to outflank it. He assigned the first stage of the attack to the 217th Brigade, who was available near Idra.

* * *

On October 17th, at 0805 hours, Col. Tuvia Raviv, 600th Brigade commander, radioed 162nd Division commander, Major General Adan: "I have troops in Hurva, down south. I spot a large enemy force advancing from the 285th or 283rd kilometer of Lexicon, north-northwest, four kilometers away from Hurva."* This was the first alert that the 162nd Division received regarding the Egyptian force's northbound advance. Adan responded promptly, ordering the 217th Brigade to head for Grafit.** The massive ambush plan started to materialize. The core of the plan, suggested by Adan, was a brigade strong force emerging from an ambush near Yahfan and Grafit hilltops, hitting the enemy division's flank at a range of 1500 to 1000 meters. Making the ambush most effective required placing a strong, stationary blocking near Fort Lakekan, and a mobile force at the rear of the enemy. The northern blocking was assigned to the 14th Brigade under Amnon Reshef, subordinate to the neighboring 143rd Division. It was to serve as the anvil for the blows the 217th Brigade, under Natan Nir, was to deal to the Egyptian column's flank.

From that moment, the battle with the 25th Brigade was the 217th Brigade's main task. Its commander, Natan Nir, rapidly

---

*   162nd Division's radio network. A few minutes earlier on, 14th Brigade commander was reported to by his 79th Battalion, which was securing Grafit area, about a considerable enemy force advancing north.

**   162nd Division's radio network, 0508 hours. Actually, a few minutes earlier the 14th Brigade element positioned in Grafit reported to the commander about "a cloud of dust moving north." That was the very first alert, but it failed to reach 162nd Division.

**   Adan, *On Both Banks*, p.215.

led his battalions to Irda hilltop, east of the 58th kilometer of Kaspi Road. He saw it as a chance to get even for all the blows he had taken from the Egyptians since October 8th. (Actually, his brigade only deployed two battalions, the 126th and the 113th. Another battalion, the 142nd, was left near the Chinese Farm). At that stage, the division commander was in Kishuf HQ, with one eye watching over Akavish Road and Missouri perimeter, and his other eye, watching south, over Idra hill and Lexicon Road.

Meanwhile, the entire theater came alive, with all levels intensively reporting about the hordes of tanks swarming north. Nir carefully remarked in his reports that "we'll have a lot of booty."

Adan considered it critical to start the attack from Idra toward Grafit at the right time, in order not to prematurely betray the plan of attack to the Egyptians. Therefore he ordered Nir to camouflage and conceal his tanks as best as possible, in Idra, only assuming firing positions when the enemy gets in the killing zone at the foot of Grafit.** But the targeted brigade advanced nerve-rackingly slowly.

At 0845 hours, 14th Brigade commander, Amnon Reshef, had the following conversation with Adan:

Reshef: Are you advancing toward the enemy force moving north?

Adan: We are getting ready.

Reshef: I have a subunit at Grafit.

Adan: Tell them we have forces in Irda, and to get ready to act under them in case of a battle.

The trap was being closed: at 0859 hours, Adan briefed and updated the 217th Brigade commander, Nir:

Adan: Report your position.

Nir: I'm at a high altitude position near Idra, detecting a gigantic enemy column moving on Lexicon Road. Soon we'll be in position. I suggest we use aircraft. This will be like the Six-Day War.

Adan: I agree.

(Eventually, aircraft were not deployed in this battle).

Nir: It's a great opportunity. I plan to array in zones 166 and 100. I am commencing deployment now.

Adan: Send out reconnaissance. Contact Grafit. You must give them an unprecedented ambush!

Nir: This is what I'm trying to do. I have gathered together all of my officers, and instructed them to act quietly and wisely. Right now, I'm on Idra hilltop. I'll get their flank.

Adan: I think you should move to Yahfan, and get them between the 269th and the 176th kilometers of Lexicon Road, in a killing zone between the marsh and Fort Lakekan.

Nir: There are friendly forces at Grafit. I can see them clearly.

Adan: Those are Amnon's. Contact them and tell them to get connected to your radio network and to prepare to act under you. It would be better if you get to Yahfan.

At 0903 hours, the Southern Command Commander subordinated the Front's reserve brigade, the 500th under Aryeh Keren, to Bren's division, to serve as the anvil for the emerging ambush. Meanwhile, the advancing Egyptian brigade initiated a series of alerts along its course*: the Israeli company stationed in Hurva detected it at 0900 hours, when the force's deputy commander detected about forty tanks at Havakuk (three kilometers east of Fort Bozter), and later on, near Botzer and the 275th kilometer of Lexicon.

Yet the Egyptians took their time, halting at the 273rd kilometer of Lexicon for about three hours. Some Egyptian tanks starting to advance from Botzer to Havakuk, met, at 1030 hours, with long-range firing from Jurvah, three and a half kilometers away, and withdrew west. From then on, the Egyptian brigade would stop without making observations and advance without securing its flank. It wasn't until 1200 hours that it resumed its advance north.

Meanwhile, at 1025 hours, Col. Nir reported to Adan that the Egyptian vanguard had covered another kilometer, but that he was still holding his fire, waiting for the enemy to enter his killing zone. Then he "will sweep down the hills, pushing them into the sea."

At 1050 hours, Adan sent the first alert to the 500th Brigade, under Col. Aryeh Keren, who was stationed at the 73rd kilometer of the north-south Mavdil Road. From that moment,

---

*   Zeev Eitan argues that at 0900 hours, a battalion of the 164th Brigade under the 252nd Division started firing from Chronika position on elements of the 25th Brigade near the 289th kilometer of Lexicon, destroying some tanks. He also argues that four tanks of the company stationed in Hurva started firing at 1030 hours, also destroying some tanks. Though the force positioned in Hurva did start long-range firing at that time, it only had a deterring effect. According to the 410th Platoon leader who was stationed in Hurva, he only started the fighting at 1430 hours. Likewise, the 14th Brigade commander was reported to by the 79th Battalion, positioned in Grafit, about the Egyptian brigade's advance. See *14th Brigade History,* pp.191-192, 233.

this brigade's troops started racing to the planned battlefield, to attack the enemy's rear. By 1230 hours, its battalions had covered about twenty kilometers, along Pazum Road. "You command the field from Yahfan, all along the enemy column," Adan's operations officer ordered Keren.

The Egyptian brigade was first engaged about two kilometers south of Lakekan, by the 1st Company of the 79th Battalion, under Major Ehud Gross, a 407th Battalion survivor. It had just four tanks. The force, on its way from Shiekh Road, for regrouping on Artillery Road, was suddenly redeployed to secure the 14th Brigade's flank south of Lakekan, on the 263rd of 265th kilometer of Lexicon Road. At 1200 hours, the commander spotted several Egyptians heading toward his force.* They were either the vanguard or a reconnaissance unit. He ordered to commence firing at 2500 meters range, hitting, so he claimed, all twelve tanks opposite his force.** For many minutes, nothing but these four tanks checked the Egyptian vanguard.

Captain Ehud Gross reported to the 14th Brigade commander, Col. Amnon Reshef, who happened to be near Lakekan, that he was engaging the enemy with fire. Rushing to the scene, with just his own tank, Reshef joined the fighting at about 1300 hours. Later, his deputy, Lt.-Col. Arieli, joined the battle-line.

As Gross recalled, " My tanks halted the enemy tanks, and

---

*   As Adan puts it, "It would be an exaggeration to refer to the 14th Brigade's tanks as the 'anvil.' They were there for regrouping and securing. Spotting the dust of the 25th Brigade, they excitedly started crying for help, and we had to calm them down."
**   For the exact number of destroyed enemy vehicles, see below.
*** Natan Nir, *Natkeh,* pp.179.ff.

scored the first knocking out of enemy tanks, even before the southern division (the 162nd) did its job, wiping them out. Toward midday, we ran out of ammo, so I asked the 8th Company of the 87th Reconnaissance Battalion to relieve us. By that time, the brigade commander had arrived at the scene, to participate in the battle. Then his deputy arrived, joining 1st Company at the defensive stage. After we got replenished, we reassumed our battle stations and resumed firing, until all enemy vehicles in sight, either standing or moving, were destroyed."

Meanwhile, the two battalions of the 217th Brigade stationed in Yahfan and Grafit continued preparing and waiting for their chance. Between 1300 hours and 1400 hours, Col. Nir ordered his battalions to move out quietly, following his own reconnaissance jeeps, to their firing positions. That feat required cold-blooded patience. Through his binoculars, spotting many enemy tanks heading north, he feared that the handful of tanks south of Lakekan would not be able to stop them.*** During the initial formation, at about 1345 hours, the positions assumed proved ineffective: in order to effectively damage T62 tanks, his force had to fire at a maximum range of 1500 meters, so he ordered the battalions to get closer.

As Col. Nir recalled it, "I urged the two battalions engaged, the 126th in the south and the 113th in the north, to get closer to the targeted brigade. It started getting dangerous, since the observing units reported to me about twenty-five enemy tanks near Fort Lakekan, and I felt it was my duty to keep them at bay. If they broke through and seized the bridges, it would have been the end of the world. So I decided to close in on them and commence firing. But the two battalion commanders were reluctant to advance. Being too careful about watching their flanks, they were afraid to go downhill, into what looked

304 | AMIRAM EZOV

like a terribly flat area. But it had plenty of potential as firing positions. After some arguments on the radio, I told them, 'So what do you suggest?! Should we just stand idle four kilometers away, while this brigade drives on?! If so, nobody will be able to hold it!' Only then did they get the message, and they closed in on the enemy completely. After a great delay, their performance was perfect and in time."

* * *

Meanwhile, Major General Adan was on his way from Kishuf HQ to the battlefield, about twenty minutes fast drive on board an armored vehicle. In his words: "I took a hasty leave from the attendees at the conference in Kishuf,* mounted my command APC, ordered the driver to move straight ahead, fast, and Gilad Aviram, to navigate to the 59th kilometer of Kaspi Road. I was experiencing a sense of elation, eager to fight…"

By 1400 hours, everything seemed to be turning out fine. Adan had reached the 59th kilometer of Kaspi Road and was observing the operation.** It looked glorious. At about 1420 hours, approaching the enemy as close as within a distance of 1500 meters, Nir's battalions commenced firing at the Egyptian column's flank, which passed by like a row of sitting ducks.

---

*   The conference ended at about 1345 hours. According to Oren, Adan left for the battlefield at about 1400 hours, which means he arrived there at about 1430 hours or earlier. Adan was heard reporting to Ben Ari, on the 162nd Division's radio network, at 1422 hours that he was on his way to Nir's forces. Nonetheless, Adan remembers arriving at the scene before the firing started.

**   Adan, *On Both Banks*, p.219.

"How many of them have you torched," Adan asked Nir curiously. "Too many to count," the 217th Brigade commander replied. "Numerous enemy tanks in the sector are torched. Their attack is crushed. The bad news is that their rear vehicles are escaping toward Botzer, where the 500th, under Keren is. So I asked him to take them on." Adan expressed his concern that Nir had initiated the operation prematurely, when the trap hadn't been fully closed yet, since the 500th Brigade still wasn't in battle positions.

Adan: Too bad you initiated too early, not waiting for Keren to get into it.

Nir: That would've been very risky.

Adan: You are saying that it went perfectly, and I agree. Soon we'll throw in Keren's 500th.*

At 1445 hours, Nir radioed to Adan, with great excitement: "We're in the midst of engagement, torching them, while they are running around like rabbits. Currently, they're gathering at the 265th kilometer, among the undergrowth. I believe we can wipe out that brigade within thirty minutes. I suggest you should join me."

Adan: I'd like to join you with Keren's force, in clearing the road. I can see you guys. Keep hitting them. I'm on my way.**

That battle didn't last long, and the bulk of the massacre was carried out by the 217th Brigades two battalions. As early as 1500 hours, Nir reported to Adan that "we see so many fires they are countless."*** A handful of Egyptian tanks, risking an assault on the 217th Brigade's positions, were instantly wiped out. Most

---

enemy tanks acted confusedly and incompetently: some, while trying to escape toward the Bitter Lake, hit a minefield. The 126th Battalion, under Lt.-Col. Giora Koppel, faced between twenty and twenty-five tanks, while the 113th, under Lt.-Col. Zeev Ram, dealt with a similar number. Though most enemy tanks were destroyed, some tried to escape south. Toward the end of the battle, Natan Nir managed to throw in the brigade's third battalion, the 142nd, which also hit some targets.

At 1530 hours, the 500th Brigade, under Keren, arrived at the battle theater. Adan urged him to deploy one battalion in positions south of Yahfan hill, while deploying another one in a wide outflanking maneuver. In his words, "I set the small marsh in front of Yahfan as the boundary between the two brigade's field of fire, using my jeep company to guide the tanks to their positions and for coordinating the brigade's operations." The Egyptians, travelling in a single unsecured column, were caught in the worst possible killing zone: between the Israeli tanks, the Bitter Lake and minefields.

The 500th Brigade as well, joined in the happy hunt, taking on the APCs and unarmored vehicles on the misfortunate Egyptian brigade's rear.

By 1600 hours, the two battalions making up the Egyptian 25th Brigade had been removed from the battle. At 1600 hours, the 217th Brigade commander, Nir, radioed:

Nir: We have taken partial revenge. You can delete this brigade's name off the records as well.

Adan: Will do so, but just delete as much of it as you can, since we need to use this road.

Nir: Roger, OK. That's what we're doing, torching more of them.

Adan: What are you torching, just tanks, or other stuff too?

Nir: We also torched BTRs (Soviet-made APCs used by the Egyptians).

Adan, too was pleased about it, so he quickly broke the news to Gonen:

Adan: Shmulik, do you have a clue about what's going on?

Gonen: I'm listening to the radio, but better tell me yourself, since seeing is believing. What about that (Egyptian) tank battle?

Adan: It's the greatest one ever fought.

Gonen: Come on, tell me more.

Adan: We're busting them all, from Fort Bozter, all the way to Fort Lakekan. We're in advantageous positions. They are using no artillery, and neither are we. We're just dashing on and knocking off the 25th Brigade.

Gonen: How many tanks did they have in the first place?

Adan: Over 100. This is what Natke said, when he was still scared of them.

Indeed, Adan had reasons for boasting, and the Southern Command Command had a joyous moment. Thus, for instance, when talking to Northern Sinai commander, Brig.-Gen. Yitzhak Sasson, Gonen couldn't help bragging:

Gonen: Did I tell you about the 100 smashed tanks yet?

Sasson: You did.

Gonen: How many times?

Sasson: Twice.

Gonen: Well, it's still the same. Bye.

Toward the end of the battle, more forces preyed on the corpse: the 252nd artillery supported the 433rd Battalion of the 500th Brigade, and 410th Battalion's company positioned in Hurva joined the fighting alongside the 217th Brigade's forces. Nearly 110 tanks of the Southern Command Command were engaged throughout this battle.

At 1620 hours, eight Egyptian MIGs strafed the 252nd Division tanks, which were deployed in an open space, causing some casualties. One MIG was downed, and, as usual, both the 500th and the 217th brigades claimed credit. By twilight, the battlefield looked like a tank slaughterhouse, with scores of Egyptian tanks burning, blackening the sky with smoke. Just about ten managed to retreat to their stronghold near Botzer. Some tanks might have escaped to the 3rd Army sector. In the 113th Battalion's battle theater, several enemy tanks managed to hide themselves, and were found, intact yet abandoned, after the battle.*

Comparing aerial photographs from October 17th, to those taken on October 18th, one can recognize between fifty and fifty-five egyptian tanks destroyed. Armored vehicles, artillery

---

* The dispute over the exact number of tanks destroyed is undecidable. Col. Zeev Eitan, analyzing aerial photographs, detected sixty-four enemy tanks engaged. During the post-war inquiries, when each of the participants claimed tens of tanks destroyed, they sounded more skeptical already. Thus, for instance, Tuvia Raviv, commenting on the fighting of the force positioned in Hurva, said: "The company leader claims to have destroyed twenty-five tanks. Of this amount, we must reduce some 'natural exaggeration percent.' Another one said he had destroyed ten tanks. I don't want to get into that."

pieces and trucks were destroyed as well.**

The Egyptian brigade's captured operations officer told how only ten of the brigade had survived, which corroborates the aforementioned calculation, provided that only two of its battalions were deployed to the north.

All in all, in this battle, the IDF used its forces masterfully, even if the operational coordination between the divisions was not flawless. The removal of that brigade from the Egyptian Army's order of battle significantly altered the balance of power east of the canal, freeing up considerable Israeli forces from the necessity to secure the southern flank of the corridor, and

---

**   Adan, *On Both Banks,* p.223.

***   The following forces were engaged in this battle, to one extent or another:
1. Main forces: 162nd Division's 217th Armored Brigade, about 50-tank strong:
   a. 126th Battalion, under Lt.-Col. Giora Kopel,
   b. 113th Battalion, under Lt.-Col. Zeev Ram.
2. The 142nd Battalion, under Lt.-Col. Natan Piram, 20-tank strong, arrived at the field too late to actively participate in the fighting.
3. The 500th Southern Command Command's reserve brigade, two-battalion strong, subordinated to the 162nd Division.
4. Reduced companies of the 79th Battalion, reassigned from the 407th Battalion and 87th Reconnaissance Battalion, 10-tank strong, directly subordinated to the 14th Brigade's commander, deployed as a blocking force south of Lakekan.
5. A four tank strong company of the 600th Brigade, under a deputy company commander, positioned at the Hurva stronghold and at the 61st kilometer of Kaspi, later on joined the artillery firing of the 162nd and of the 252nd Division's artillery elements.
6. The 217th and 50th brigades' mechanized Infantry and reconnaissance companies, who were assigned with securing positions, guiding tanks, and observation.

significantly reducing the actual threat to the entire southern flank. These forces, particularly the 252nd Division elements, joined the decisive campaign on the west bank later on.

6. IF YOU DON'T CROSS, ARIK WILL.

162nd Division, Matzmed Yard, 16th and 17th of October:
By 1600 hours, the raft bridge had been laid between the two banks of the canal, yet nobody was crossing the canal westward. Adan's division was delayed due to many reasons: he had a heavy agenda, such as disengaging the 460th Brigade from the battle at the 51st kilometer of Akavish Road, deploying it to secure the roads, and relieving it by the 600th Brigade; replenishing fuel and ammo spent during the afternoon battle with the 25th Brigade, and arranging his forces' by order of movement.*

To the accusations leveled at him, mostly by Sharon, of delaying his crossing and failing to use his available assets, Adan answered, "Two of my brigades were engaged in a tank battle with the Egyptian 25th Brigade, and a third one, the 460th under Gabi Amir, was supposed to be relieved by his (Sharon's) 600th Brigade, which was still engaged. That's what I have to say."

Adan accused Sharon of failing to keep his word about brigade-swapping, and this is what had delayed his preparations for the crossing. At one point, all of the senior commanders, including the General Chief of Staff, started taking sides, some pressuring Sharon to get on with the relief, while others urging Adan to rush to the bridge.

And there were other reasons for pressuring 162nd Division

---

*   Adan, On Both Banks, p.224.

commander Adan. Initially, he wasn't aware of them, yet they were hinted to in a talk he had with Gonen at 1745 hours:

Gonen: I repeat, let your 1 [Nir's brigade] cross. Leave those engaged alone. If you don't cross, my 2 [Sharon's forces] will be ordered to cross. So you cross right away. Do you understand?

Adan: I do, but I'm out of supplies. I have an idea: I have one half-battalion almost fully replenished. Let it cross first.

Gonen: So cross with that half-battalion. Let Nir's force cross as it is, unreplenished. Am I clear?

Then Adan discovered the reason for the pressure on him: "At a certain point Gonen threatened that if my forces don't move, no matter their conditions: half-replenished, or with half a brigade's strength, that task would be reassigned to Sharon. That attitude pained my heart....they would have done better to have pressed Sharon to relieve Gabi Amir on time."[*] These pressures and counter-pressures went on until 2230 hours, when the 162nd HQ finally crossed the canal.

Meanwhile, Adan, Gonen and Sharon were engaged in a tripartite negotiation over the reassigning of the 198th Battalion to the 460th Brigade. It wasn't until October 18th, at 0420 hours, that the battalion was freed from the 143rd Division. By then, it was too late for it to reach its brigade, which had already dashed across the canal.

At about 1900 hours, Adan found time to have a nostalgic chat with Gonen over the last several days and the next day's event.

Adan: Look, Shmulik, it doesn't feel nice to be pressed in all the wrong places.

---

[*]   Adan, *On Both Banks*, p.224.

Gonen: Bren, you are wrong, and I don't wish to discuss it now, because there are a lot of people with me. We really appreciate your work today, and I speak for everybody. For, Dado who is here, too.

Adan: But can't you see, we are starting to get messy!?

Gonen: You'll manage, and you saved the bridgehead today.

Adan: Oh, let me tell you—it was a really legendary tank battle.

Gonen: Tell us about it. Dado hasn't heard it yet.

Adan: It was just fabulous.

Gonen: So now start crossing.

The delay racked the decision-makers' nerves, so at 1940 hours the following edgy dialogue took place between Gonen and Adan:

Gonen: So what's new on the bridge?

Bren: We're still not there. I'll be there in person in fifteen minutes.

Gonen: That's not good, Bren!

Bren: Well, that is how it works here.

Gonen: It's no good! Get moving unsupplied, and unprepared, but get on the bridge!

Bren: Look, it doesn't work that way.

Gonen: Bren, I'm not kidding! I can't discuss it over the radio, but there's a reason for it. Get resupplied and move on as you are!

That "reason" was not an operational one. The first to cross the Unifloat Bridge was Adan's command APC. At 2200 hours, he happily radioed, "Finally, we've crossed," and shortly later he reported to Ben Ari: I'm down in Egypt Land already. I'm fine though slightly smelly. My forces are following me." That was followed by another moment of elation. As Bren would write later, "Suddenly, the view had changed. The nearly full moon revealed to me the Suez Canal, with its ripples shining. In the middle of it, a massive bridge stood. No enemy shells fell. It was silent everywhere. Excited, I radioed my troops: the bridge is a magnificent sight, and it is impatiently waiting for you...The spirit in my APC was high. We reported to the Front Command that we were in Africa, and that my forces are crossing."* Adan's faithful APC driver uncorked a bottle of whisky, and Adan drank to the drive into Africa.

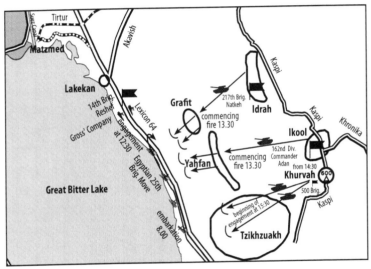

The Battle with 25th Egyptian Brigade,
October 17, 1220 hours to 1620 hours

It wasn't until about 2200 hours that the 460th Brigade's commander, Col. Gabi Amir, reported to Adan, "We started

---

*   Adan, *On Both Banks*, p.224

off this very moment. We managed to replenish, partially but sufficiently." His brigade advanced slowly probing its way in the dark, guided by its reconnaissance company under Maj. Mark Yams, later killed on the west bank of the canal. It was followed by the brigade's armored battalions: the 19th, under Maj. Eli Zeira, the 196th, under Lt. Col. Lapidot, and the 100th, under Ehud Brog.

It reached the bridge at 2240, and somebody calculated that it took Adan's vanguard brigade six hours to set foot on it, from that moment. The brigade commander complained about nobody guiding them, since "we're practically blind over here." Adan quickly reassured him, saying that somebody had been sent to guide them.

It was the finest hour of the Yard's men:

Adan asked Col. Jackie Even, who commanded the Yard, to arrange a guidance team. He received a surprising reply: "I myself am serving as a traffic cop, standing there and begging them to drive slowly and carefully." Thus, a commissioned deputy division commander stood in the dark, with a small team, personally directing, with a flashlight, one tank after another, toward the bridge. Occasionally, an artillery shell hit the water, so the tank crews got nervous, closing their hatches and crossing the bridge as quickly as possible. At about midnight, after three tanks had crossed it, the bridge broke apart.

As Col. Amir recalled, "Divisional HQ had already crossed the canal, and finally, some Engineer Corps fellow came to guide us. Zeira's 19th Brigade started mounting the bridge, and after two or three tanks had crossed, the Bridge broke. Then a blame-game started all over the radio networks, we being accused for driving either too slowly or too fast. We were sent to another raft [Alligator], but after one round, a tank capsized and it was unusable. Then we were sent yet another raft".

The breaking of the bridge quickened the pulses of all senior commanders who blamed it on a direct hit of an artillery shell. Yet the cause was much less dramatic: the stress and unskillful driving of some tank driver. But once again, luck, or perhaps adherence to procedures, came to the rescue: among the vehicles which had crossed was an armored vehicle-launched bridge, so the commanders quickly deployed it to bridge the gap.

Even would later comment: "In that vehicle, was Engineers Corps Major Bruchi, holding chains, which seemed awkward to me. When I asked him what was it for, he told me he's making sure the Bridge stays firm in place. In other words, an entire division had to cross the Canal, relying on Bruchi's hands. Yet it worked. We saw we must direct the tanks from ground level, one by one, otherwise nobody could cross. I took up the job of standing on the bridge, directing every tank driving on it".

Adan quickly redirected his forces to the Alligators, and Even asked Adan: "tell our men to drive carefully, with their hatches opened. We're doing our best over here, but don't let your guys break this thing down. There's a full moonlight."

All the while, the 460th Brigade's tanks kept crossing the Canal in board Alligators, under artillery fire, one slipping off the raft and nearly drowning. One unloaded Alligator was hit and sank. However, the bridge was quickly repaired, and at 0135 hours the tank-launched bridge was already unfolded, so the Bridge was drivable once again.

At 0315 hours 217th Brigade started crossing the Canal, and two hours later, the two-brigade strong 162nd Division, with about 140 tanks and an artillery battalion, occupied its assembly zone west of the Canal. It was nighttime, so Adan radioed operational orders: the brigades should thrust eight kilometers west of the Canal, into perimeters codenamed Arel and Tzah. In the next stage, the entire Division was to turn south, heading for Suez.

At 0550 hours, Adan reported Gonen: attack initiated. The 217th thrusts into Arel perimeter, and later on, to Makztera perimeter. The 460th should occupy Uri perimeter, and later on, Tzach"*. This was the beginning of the decisive campaign stage of Operation Valiant.

7. ARIK CAN'T REMEMBER.

Dvelah HQ, October 17th, 2020 hours:
At 1930 hours, front commanders met the Chief of General Staff to draw that night's and the next day's plans. Though the 143rd Division expected a night's rest, Front Commander Gonen reassigned tasks to its 247th Brigade under Dani Matt: raiding the Freshwater Canal bridge and sabotaging the water supply pipes recently laid over it. This task wasn't carried out, and the following talk between Col. Oded Messer, 143rd Liaison Officer to Front Command and Sharon, at 2020 hours that day, explains why:

Oded: You were given some Wingate-style job. Do you happen to know about it?

Sharon: No.

Oded: Well, you were asked to do some Wingate-style job. Shmulik [Gonen] alluded to you about one of the jobs yesterday.

---

*   Southern Command Command Operations Log

Sharon: I cannot remember any details. Can't tell you what it was about. Listen, Danni Matt's men have been fighting all day, untill late night, and so have my forces. We didn't do that job, because I hadn't time to prepare, and now it's too late. It's one of those things....

Oded: So, you're not willing to do that. Let me refresh your memory. He talked to you about what Anthony Quinn did in Burma, Wingate-style.

Sharon: I really cannot see the point. To be honest, I didn't really know what he wanted of me.

Oded: Can't you remember? A wooden construction, a line of troopers....

Sharon: I can't.

Oded: Well, if you cannot do it, regardless of the target, I'll have to report to him about it.

Sharon: Listen, we all have been fighting very hard all day, so I cannot force men out of their trenches in the dead of night. Such orders are to be given in the morning, not by night. Yesterday, too, they woke me up at 2300 hours, asking me whether I happened to remember what Anthony Quinn did in some movie. I didn't. Let me tell you this: if you have any ideas, suggest them in the morning. I can't do it now.

Oded: Okay. And they also gave you another job through normal channels. Does your previous reply also go for the latter, rather easy job as well? It deals with facilitating friendly transportation and disturbing the other guys' transportation.

Sharon: I can't remember anything.

Oded: But there is no practical reason not to do it, if you manage to do it quickly. All they want is for you to deploy a couple of "heavies" about five kilometers north of your positions, and do a 1950s reprisal-style job.

Sharon: Well some things need to be asked in the morning. I received no messages, so we made no preparations, period. I cannot deploy the men in the dead of night.

Oded: Well, Arik, as the liaison officer, I'll have to report about it.

Sharon: Just tell them this: all day long I haven't received any message. Oded, let me tell you as a friend: we, down here, not just me, by the way, but most of the men in the field, feel that you generals, treat everything we're doing here like...

Though this conversation may sound amusing, the Front Command thought otherwise.

The Command assigned the 143rd Division with many tasks on the morning of October 18th: on the east bank, Tirtur Road was yet to be cleared thoroughly, which was to be carried out by the 600th Brigade; 410th Battalion prepared to resume the towing of the Roller Bridge, waiting for the OK to deliver it to the waterfront; and 14th Brigade was assigned with incessantly pressing the enemy forces in Amir perimeter, the objective being the seizing of the Chinese Farm buildings. The Yard was found to be the weakest link of the crossing campaign positions; the deputy division commander was assigned with handling the administrative and logistic problems of the crossing. The insufficient width of the crossing corridor still worried the Front Command, and this tactical problem would keep preoccupying the forces in the field as well as fueling the mistrust between the Front Command and Sharon.

421st and 247th Brigades, stationed west of the canal, were assigned with strengthening the foothold, thrusting north, and making a two-pronged threat on the Egyptian Second Army.

GHQ and Dvelah HQ had started discussing the decisive

strategic objectives once the crossing was accomplished. They were based on the original Operation Valiant plan, with the city of Suez being the major territorial gain, and the encirclement of Egyptian 3rd Army the final strategic objective. So the main effort was reassigned to the 162nd Division.

EPILOGUE

Early on the morning of October 18th, 162nd Division commander, Major General Avraham Adan, ordered his 460th and 217th Divisions to thrust west and south, out of the bridgehead, heading for Genifa Plains and the City of Suez. On that misty morning, at 0600 hours, the 460th started off from the shores of the Great Bitter Lake, heading westward, on Sakranut Road, to carry out its job.

On October 19th, at 0130 hour, the 410th Engineer Battalion, under Maj. Yehuda Geller, finally launched the Roller, about one kilometer north of the Unifloat bridge. The column carrying it was led by Lt. Col. Aharon "Johnny" Tenne, Chief of Southern Command Command's Engineering Corps. Approaching the canal, he was killed when fighting an Egyptian squad, so the bridge was named after him. The Roller Bridge, the object of so much expectation, was the last fording technology launched in the canal.

A third bridge, named after Lt. Col. Baruch De Leon, nicknamed "Austerity Bridge," was built a day later. These three bridges kept serving IDF vehicles for the duration of the war, and another two were built after the war ended.

These were the last stages of the crossing campaign and the beginning of the decisive campaign waged west of the canal.

* * *

The crossing campaign was launched on October 15th, at 1700 hours, and was waged for sixty hours. This campaign indisputably turned the tide if the war, but it was very costly. The question of whether its cost could have been minimized is being disputed until this very day, and no researcher could claim to have an impartial answer to it.

In the area known as the Chinese Farm, IDF's Armored Corps, Combat Engineering Corps, Paratroopers and other elements lost hundreds of men, on the night between the 15th and the 16th of October. During just one night, the 14th Armored Brigade under Amnon Reshef sustained about 120 dead and sixty-two injured—an unprecedented number of casualties for a single battle, in all of Israeli military history. It also lost about fifty tanks in that battle. (Some of the men killed belonged to the 407th Battalion, originally subordinated to the 600th Brigade, and others to the 582nd Battalion, attached to the brigade ad hoc for that night only. By comparison, on the 17th of October, the brigade had only one man killed. In total, it lost 303 men during that war.*

In a postwar lecture, Major General Sharon estimated his division's losses on the night of the crossing to be about 200 men, out of a total 1,480 killed and about 1,200 injured lost on the Southern Command during the entire war. Of those, about one fourth, 450 men, were killed in four days, between the 15th and the 19th of October (it is to be noted that there are contradicting data from different stages of the war. More

---

*   14th Brigade's website

than half of Israeli losses, including killed and POWs, occurred between the 6th and the 10th of October).

The Israeli Engineering Corps, throughout the war, had seventy-four men killed, two missing, three POWs and 305 injured. Of those, twenty killed (twenty-seven percent of all the Corps death toll), and eighty-seven injured, belonged to the battalions participating in the crossing. Among the killed officers were Lt. Col. Tenne; 143rd Division's Chief of the Engineering Corps, Lt. Col. Baruch de Leon; 605th Deputy Battalion Commander Maj. Yehuda Hudeda (killed during the very last minutes of the war); a battalion commander and several company leaders. The battalions engaged in the crossing made up fifteen percent of the entire Engineering Corps' order of battle on the Southern Command.

Israeli forces also suffered massive material losses. Thus, for example, during the night between the 15th and the 16th of October, the 14th Brigade lost fifty-six tanks and many other armored vehicles.

* * *

It took the IDF sixty hours of fighting to secure the crossing corridor to the canal and to establish a bridgehead on the opposite bank. That fighting was marked by major chaos, and terrible human and material losses. Israeli forces went to this battle hastily, yet the IDF's doctrine stood up to the challenge: all of the planned objectives of Operation Valiant were achieved, including the strategic one—forcing Egypt to cry for a ceasefire.

At any rate, it wasn't doctrine that won the crossing campaign. Rather, it was the spirit and determination of the combatants and logistics men. Even when facing obstacles which occasionally seemed unsurmountable, when taking losses of an extent unexpected by any of the decision-makers, even when entire formations disintegrated, Israeli forces kept rolling west, on and on, until a ceasefire was declared. This unremitting advance cannot be accounted for by a successful plan, but mostly by the fighting spirit. It is evidenced by about sixty citations of all kinds, including the Decoration of Bravery, awarded to commanders and men who had fought in the crossing zone between the 15th and the 18th of October.

In hindsight, Southern Command Commander Major General Shmuel Gonen would remark: "It was only the vrossing that turned the tides of war, regaining the initiative for the IDF. If it wasn't for the ceasefire Israel was forced to accept, due to global political considerations, we could've exploited our successes more effectively, and maybe even decisively won the war."

Within another week of heavy fighting, the IDF had assumed positions 101 kilometers from Cairo, while surrounding the Egyptian 3rd Army, as well as the city of Suez. It took the Israelis a breach of the ceasefire, planned to start on October 22nd, to achieve all of the planned objectives of Operation Valiant. As mentioned above, its planners had given it no more than thirty-six hours.

The crossing of the Suez threw the Egyptian Army off balance, taking its command by surprise. It misread Israeli maneuvers, taking its time to respond. Starting from October 17th, one could see some indication of a collapse of Egyptian forces east of the canal, those positioned at Missouri compound: many Egyptian solders were seen swimming for their lives across the canal. Yet it would be an exaggeration to conclude that the entire Egyptian Army ceased to be an effective fighting force. The grip of the 2nd Army, west of the canal, north of Shiekh road, remained firm, even after the crossing, and the attempt by the IDF's 600th Armored Brigade to expand the corridor, at 2nd Army's expense, proved costly.

When Egyptian President Anwar Sadat accepted a ceasefire, the Egyptian Army was still standing, but under serious threat. As the Egyptian Chief of Staff Saad el-Shazly wrote after the war: "On October 24th, our military was in a shambles: the 3rd Army was absolutely cut off, the enemy starting a massive aerial grinding. Our situation was desperate."* The neutralization of the 3rd Army spelled a crushing defeat for the Egyptian Army, and if it wasn't for American diplomatic intervention, Israel could have achieved a decisive victory on the Southern Command.

Sadat looked at it differently. In his words, "I chose peace. I was all for peace, and following this principle, I decided for the peaceful elimination of the Deversoir enclave." In this spirit, he accepted the agreement on disengagement that the US offered both sides about a year after the war. As he and his successors saw it, the October 1973 War ended with an Egyptian victory, since Egypt had managed to set foot in the Sinai on October 6th.

---

*   Shazly, *Crossing,* p.196

* * *

The controversies within Israel, including the so-called "generals' wars" concerning the crossing, which raged during the battle, grew even more intense after it ended. They were motivated by different, occasionally contradictory views on how the war should have been conducted. Personal antipathies and accumulated years of bad blood, also contributed to it. Apparently, Israeli generals, just like their counterparts in other armies, attempt to write the history of war in the heat of battle.

Major General Ariel Sharon definitely made his mark on the entire crossing campaign, through his example and leadership, being the driving force and invigorator of his entire division, from its senior commanders down to privates. This leadership was demonstrated in his decision-making capability during critical moments of the night of the crossing, especially when dealing with the breakdown, both technical and operational, of the fording equipment being delivered to the canal.

On the other hand, one must acknowledge that Sharon's 143rd Division failed to achieve its planned objectives by October 16th, as Sharon's superiors saw it: securing a bridgehead allowing for a massive deployment of forces west of the canal. Yet at the end of the day, despite all the failures, such as falling behind schedule, blocked roads, heavy losses and disrupted execution, Sharon successfully carried out the essential parts of his plan: partially securing a crossing corridor; delivering the fording machinery to the waterfront; establishing a foothold on the west bank; delivering armored elements west of the canal, to strengthen and expand the bridgehead; a successful raid by the 421st Brigade on a missile base within range of the bridgehead. He was also capable of correctly responding to the quickly changing battlefield, for instance, regarding the columns bearing the fording equipment which lost their way on that horrible night. As a result, his division never stooped rolling on west, not for a single moment.

Yet many of Sharon's tactical ideas conflicted with his superiors' strategic thinking. Southern Command declined many of Sharon's suggestions, all aimed at making his division the spearhead of the post-crossing decisive battles; as well as many suggestions for operations on the west bank before the corridor had been secured. They were declined because the Front Command had its own way of reading the battle and conducting the war, a way not without logic. These differences bred mutual distrust impairing cooperation between the forces. At least partially, they were the inevitable effects of battle plans disrupted, and probably are a part of any war.

Due to the ambiguous outcome of the Yom Kippur War on the Southern Command and the inner conflicts within the IDF that remained, it kept haunting the Israeli public and military establishment even after the war had ended.

The failures that occurred at the beginning of the war as well as the fiasco of its last stage, the attack on Suez, caused the controversies and protests from within the military establishment to spread to the general public, putting the war's decision-makers on trial. The 1974 Committee of Inquiry, headed by Judge Shimon Agranat, sealed the fate of some, while others were judged by the people. Sharon was acquitted by both: driving home back from the Sinai, his division's vehicles were decorated with banners praising him; Sharon came to be the war's greatest hero for his reservist troopers as well as for the general public, in part because he had a better public relations machine than his fellow commanders. He successfully leveraged it to start his long, turbulent postwar political career.

His Southern Command superiors were bruised, more or less: Effective Front Commander Bar Lev was stigmatized for the collapse of the defense line named after him; Front Commander Gonen was barred by the Committee from any military command, and his meteoric military career was for all purposes, ended. Afterward, he wandered far away, to Africa, forever bearing a grudge over his discharge from the military. 162nd Division Commander Major General Avraham Adan, who was responsible for two major fiascos in the war—the failed October 8th counterattack and the failed attack on the town of Suez on the last day of the war, but also for the major successes of the attack on the west bank and the surrounding of the Egyptian 3rd Army, sailed through being battered with both criticism and praise. For a short while, he served as Southern Command Commander, and then, Israel Defense and Armed Forces Attaché to the United States, where he ended his glorious military career. Col. Amnon Reshef, the epitome of an Israeli Armored Corps officer, kept serving in the Corps. In 1974, he was promoted to 162nd Division Commander, and in 1979, to major-general in the IDF's Armored Corps. Col. Haim Erez, whose tanks were the first to cross the canal on board Alligators, thrived in the Armored Corps. Four years after the war, he was promoted to 162nd Division commander, and in 1982, to Southern Command Commander. In this job he came full circle, when conducting the final stages of Israeli withdrawal from the Sinai under the 1979 Israeli-Egyptian Treaty.

Yaakov "Jacky" Even was promoted to brigadier-general while the war was still raging, and in 1974, was made commander of the 143rd Division, where he served as deputy commander during the war. In 1980 he was promoted to major-general and appointed Israeli Military Academy Commander, where he tried to teach new officers the lessons of the Yom Kippur War. Until this very day, he regards that war in general, and the crossing campaign in particular, as the defining moments of his life.

That war profoundly affected the life courses of them all, both commanders and servicemen.

* * *

I would like to assert, and not simply as a gesture of academic modesty, that in spite all the effort spent on the present work, it must be regarded as a mere initial study, and that many major issues related to the Southern Command in particular and the Yom Kippur War in general are far from being fully revealed and exhaustively examined. Many questions are yet to be answered, while others are waiting to be further discussed in future studies.

The illustrious military historian Basil Henry Liddell Hart wrote, decades ago, in *Why Don't We Learn from History?*, about the fear of the truth: "Always, the tendency continues to be shocked by natural comment and to hold certain things too 'sacred' to think about [....] This camouflaged history not only conceals faults and deficiencies that could otherwise be remedied, but engenders false confidence—and false confidence underlies most of the failures that military history records." *

Therefore I hope, with no false presumptions and while being aware of all the challenges the writing of contemporary history pose, that this work showed no fear of truth.

---

*   http://infohost.nmt.edu/~shipman/reading/liddell/c01.html#c1-6

MAPS:

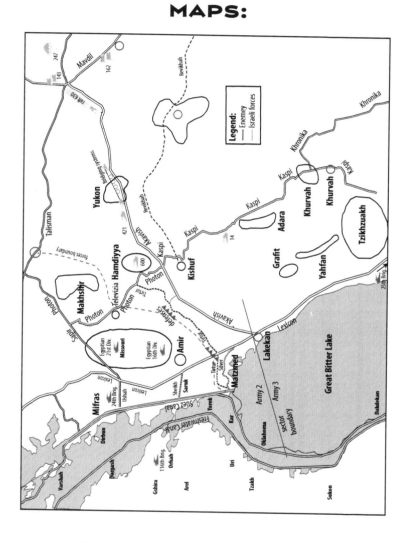

Forces' positions on October 15, 1973, at 1700 hours

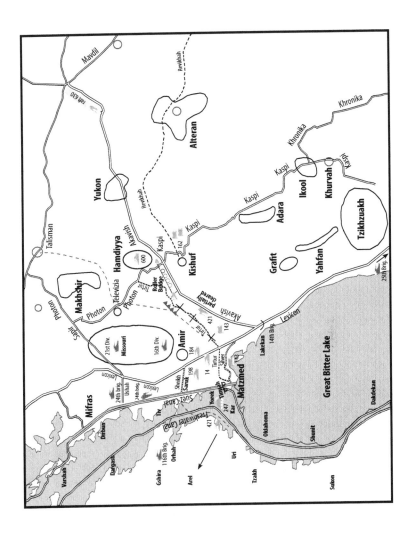

Forces' positions on October 16, 1973, at midday

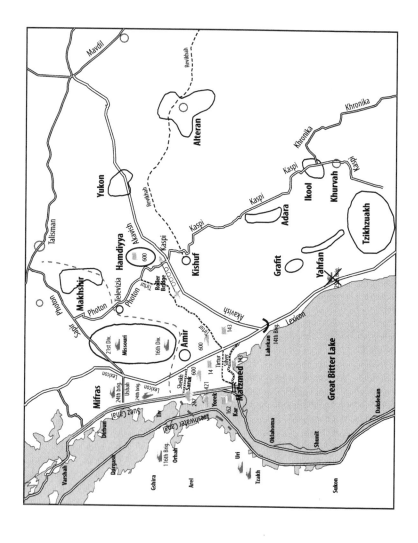

The forces' positions on the morning of October 18

TIMELINE OF THE YOM KIPPUR WAR ON THE SOUTHERN COMMAND

DATE	TIME	EVENT	OUTCOME
October 6 1973	1403 hours	Egyptian shelling of Israeli defenses along the canal.	IDF initiates Dove Nest defensive plan.
	1425 hours	Five Egyptian divisions cross the canal across the entire Bar Lev Line.	Israeli 252nd Division engages Egyptian forces.
October 7	Morning	Most of the Egyptian forces cross the canal eastward.	Israeli forces in critical situation: 252nd division has only 100 tanks left out of its original strength of 300.
	Daytime	162nd and 143rd Israeli reservist divisions arrive at the frontline.	Southern Command Command divides the canal zone into three operational sectors.
	Evening	Egyptian forces secure a line along the canal, delivering 400 tanks to the east bank.	Most Bar Lev Line forts are either taken or surrounded.

DATE	TIME	EVENT	OUTCOME
October 8	0800 hours	162nd Division initiates a counterattack; later on, 143rd division is sent on a useless maneuver southwards.	
	1600 hours	Counterattack fails.	IDF establishes a defense line near Artillery Road, about 10 to 12 kilometers east of the canal.
October 9	Morning	Israeli Southern Command Command prepares for a defensive campaign. Failed attack by 143rd in the center.	IDF secures a defense line.
October 10	Morning	Bar Lev assumes the effective command of the Southern Command.	
	Midday	162nd Division repels Egyptian attacks in the north of Central Sector, codenamed Havragah.	
From the 10th to 13th of October		IDF wages a defensive campaign.	

DATE	TIME	EVENT	OUTCOME
October 13	Midday	252nd Division Commander, Maj.-Gen. Albert Mandler is killed in action, and replaced by Maj.-Gen. Kalman Magen.	
	Midday	Fort Mezah, the last of the Bar Lev Line Forts along the canal, surrenders.	Fort Budapest is the only Fort of Bar Lev line to survive the Egyptian offensive.
October 14	Morning	Egyptian general offensive all over the defense line.	Offensive repelled, the Egyptian losing about 200 tanks, compared to 15 Israeli tanks lost. Now, the Egyptians have 770 tanks all over Sinai, 140 of which are near Deversoir (the planned crossing zone).
	2300 hours	Operational details for Operation Valiant are drawn at Dvela HQ.	
	Midnight	Israeli Government authorizes the plan.	

DATE	TIME	EVENT	OUTCOME
October 15	0500 hours	Egyptian commando attack on Fort Budapest.	Attacking force repelled with heavy casualties.
	0600 hours	Israeli 274th Brigade (with modified T62 tanks) repels an Egyptian attack in Havragah.	
	0700 hours	Operational briefing for the Crossing by 143rd division.	
	Midday	All roads going to the canal are jammed.	Just half of the planned number of rafts advance beyond Tasa.
	1220 hours	Southern Command Command authorizes 143rd battle plans.	
	1500	Bar Lev authorizes the initiation of 143rd Division advance.	
	1700	A deceptive attack of 600th Brigade at Missouri.	
	1800	14th Brigade starts off from the 56th km of Artillery Road.	About two hours later, it gets on Lexicon Road, heading north, starting to carry out its tasks.

DATE	TIME	EVENT	OUTCOME
October 15	2100 hours	14th Brigade engages an enemy force at Lexicon-Tirtur Junction.	Two battalions and the HQ of the Brigade are on Usha road, which is jammed till next morning. Tirtur Road is blocked, while Akavish is partly cleared.
October 16	During the night	Five failed attempts by 14th at clearing the road, with heavy casualties.	
	2300	The beginning of the troublesome delivery of the Roller Bridge to the canal.	The Unifloat Rafts are bogged, but the Alligators manage to advance.
	0125	"Acapulco"-247th Paratroopers Brigade crosses the Canal, securing a foothold west of the canal.	
	0500 hours	The Alligators reach the waterfront alongside Giora Lev's tank Battalion.	
	0605 hours	The Roller Bridge breaks down.	
	0630	The first Alligator is launched into the canal.	Israeli tanks start crossing the canal westward.

DATE	TIME	EVENT	OUTCOME
October 16	0840 hours	A detachment of 14th Brigade, led by brigade commander, clears the Lexicon-Tirtur Junction.	Tirtur Road is still blocked.
	1100 hours	Southern Command Command orders 143rd Division to stop delivering any tanks west of the canal.	
	1200 hours	162nd Division is reassigned to the forces attempting to clear the roads.	At 1600 hours, 162nd Division's attempts at clearing Tirtur fail.
	1300 hours	A detachment of 143rd Division, led by 421st Brigade commander raids and destroys Anti-aircraft missile bases deep in the enemy territory on the west bank.	
	Afternoon	Addressing the People's Assembly, Egyptian President announces the Egyptian victory.	

DATE	TIME	EVENT	OUTCOME
October 16	1900 hours	Addressing the Knesset Israeli Prime Minister Golda Meir reveals the operation of Israeli forces west of the canal.	
	2200 hours	35th Brigades HQ and 890th Paras. Battalion are flown to the 55th kilometer of Akavish Road, for searching the roads.	

TIMELINE OF THE YOM KIPPUR WAR ON THE SOUTHERN COMMAND

DATE	TIME	EVENT	OUTCOME
October 6	1405 hours	Egyptian shelling of the Israeli defenses along the canal.	IDF initiates Dove Nest defensive plan.
	1425 hours	5 Egyptian divisions cross the Suez eastward, across the entire canal	252nd Division engages the Egyptian forces.
October 7	Morning	Most Egyptian forces cross the canal eastward.	252nd Division is critically low on tanks, with only 100 left out of its original strength of 300.
	During daytime	Israeli reservist 162nd and 143rd divisions arrive at the front.	Israeli Southern Command Commands splits the canal theater into 3 operational sectors.
	By the evening	Egyptian forces secure a defense line along the canal, delivering 400 tanks to the east bank.	Most of Bar Lev Line Forts are either taken or surrounded by Egyptian forces.

DATE	TIME	EVENT	OUTCOME
October 8	0800 hours	162nd Division launches a counter attack. Later on, 143rd Division is launched on a useless maneuver south.	
	1600 hours	Counterattack fails.	Israeli forces secure a defense line near Artillery Road, about 10 to 12 kilometers east of the canal.
October 9	Morning	Israeli Southern Command Command prepares for a defensive campaign; 143rd Division launches a failed counter attack in the center.	Israeli forces establish a defense line.
October 10	Morning	Bar Lev assumes the effective command of the Southern Command.	
	Midday	162nd Division repels Egyptian attacks in the north of the central sector, codenamed Havragah.	

DATE	TIME	EVENT	OUTCOME
October 10 to October 13	Midday	Maj.-Gen. Albert Mandler is killed in action, and replaced by Maj.-Gen. Kalman Magen.	
	Midday	The Pier Fort, the last Israeli position along the canal, surrenders.	Fort Budapest is the only Bar Lev Line Fort to survive the Egyptian offensive.
October 14	Morning	An all-out Egyptian offensive, across the entire defense line.	Egyptian offensive repelled, with the Egyptians losing about 200 tanks compared to just 15 lost by Israeli forces. After the attack, out of total 770 tanks the Egyptian forces had in Sinai, about 140 were positioned near Deversoir, the planned Israeli crossing zone.
	2300 hours	The operational briefing for Operation Valiant is held in Dvela HQ.	Southern Command Command draws the operational details of the crossing campaign.
	Midnight	Israeli cabinet authorizes the crossing campaign.	

DATE	TIME	EVENT	OUTCOME
October 15	0500 hours	An Egyptian commando attack on Fort Budapest, in the north of the canal.	Attacking force repelled with heavy casualties.
	0600 hours	Israeli 147th Brigade, consisting of modified T62 tanks, repels an Egyptian attack in Havraga perimeter.	
	Midday	All roads going to the canal are jammed.	Just half of the rafts are delivered beyond Tasa.
	12:20	Southern Command Command approves of 143rd Division's operational plan.	
	1500 hours	Bar Lev approves the request of 143rd Division commander's request to advance.	
	1700 hours	600th Brigade makes a deceptive attack on Missouri.	
	1800 hours	14th Brigade advances from the 56th kilometer of Artillery Road.	About two hours, reaching Lexicon Road, it advances north, starting to carry out its tasks.

DATE	TIME	EVENT	OUTCOME
October 15	2120 hours	14th Brigade engages enemy forces on Lexicon-Tirtur Junction.	Two of its battalions and its HQ occupy Ushah Road. The junction is jammed until next morning; Tirtur Road is blocked, yet Akavish Road is partly cleared.
	Throughout the night	Five failed attempts by 14th Brigade at clearing the junction, with heavy casualties.	
	2300 hours	The beginning of the Roller Bridge's odyssey to the waterfront.	The Raft-Carriers are halted but the Alligators' advance.
October 16	0125 hours	"Acapulco"- 247th Paratroopers brigade crosses the canal, securing a foothold on the west bank.	
	0500 hour	264th Tank Battalion of the 421st Brigade, under Lt.-Col. Giora Lev, deliver the Alligators to the canal.	
	0605 hours	The Roller Bridge breaks down.	
	0630 hours	The first Alligator takes to the water.	Israeli tanks start crossing the Suez westward.

DATE	TIME	EVENT	OUTCOME
October 16	0840 hours	A detachment of the 14th brigade, led by the brigade commander, clears Tirtur-Lexicon Junction.	Tirtur Road is still blocked.
	1100 hours	Southern Command Command orders the 143rd Division commander to stop delivering tanks across the canal.	
	1200 hours	The 162nd Division is reassigned to the force attempting to clear the roads.	By 1600 hours, all attempts by the 162nd Division to clear Turtur Road have failed.
	1300 hours	A detachment of the 143rd Division led by the 421st Brigade commander raids and destroys anti-aircraft missile batteries deep in enemy territory on the west bank.	
	Afternoon	Addressing the People's assembly, Egyptian President Sadat announces an Egyptian victory.	

DATE	TIME	EVENT	OUTCOME
October 16	1900 hours	Addressing the Knesset, Israeli Prime Minister Golda Meir reveals the Israeli forces' operation west of the canal.	
	2200 hours	35th Paratroopers Brigade HQ and its 890th Battalion are flown to the 55th kilometer of Akavish Road, for mopping-up operations.	
October 17	0245 hours	890th Battalion faces an Egyptian defense perimeter near the 42nd kilometer of Tirtur Road, near the Chinese Farm.	Defeated, the battalion starts retreating.
	0400 hours	The Unifloat rafts are delivered through Akavish Road safely.	
	0430 hours	100th Tank battalion comes to the rescue of 890th Battalion.	890th Battalion is rescued and retreats.
	0715 hours	The first rafts are launched into the canal.	
	1000 hours	Egyptian 25th Brigade starts advancing north.	162nd prepares to ambush it neat Grafit hill.

DATE	TIME	EVENT	OUTCOME
October 17	1200 hours	Senior commanders meeting, attended by the Chief of General Staff and the Defense Minister, is convened in Kishuf HQ.	The attendants decide to let the 162nd Division cross the canal first, as soon as its fighting with 25th Brigade is over.
	1230 hours	A small detachment of the 14th Brigade meets the vanguard of the Egyptian 25th Brigade at the 264th kilometer of Lexicon Road.	
	1320	The 217th Brigade, ambushes the 25th Brigade, and commences firing on the Egyptian Brigade's main force, destroying it.	The battle ends at 1700 hours, with 55 Egyptian tanks destroyed.
	1330	An Israeli paratroopers detachment is engaged in Serafeum, west of the canal.	The paratroopers anage to withdraw after fierce fighting.
	1500 hours	The last men of the 890th Paratroopers Battalion remaining in the killing zone of the 42nd kilometer of Tirtur Road, are rescued.	
	1600 hours	The first Israeli bridge across the Suez is completed.	

DATE	TIME	EVENT	OUTCOME
October 17	1830 hours	600th Brigade relieves 162nd Division of the road-clearing tasks in the east bank	
	2200 hours	162nd Division HQ crosses the Suez west.	
	Midnight	460th Brigade starts crossing the canal.	
	Midnight	The bridge breaks.	A bridge-laying tank repairs it 90 minutes later.
October 18	Before dawn	217th Brigade crosses the canal.	160 Israeli tanks are delivered to the west bank.
	0600 hours	162nd Division starts thrusting westward and southward.	
	0700 hours	600th Brigade clears Tirtur Road.	Clearing is completed at 1100 hours.
		14th Brigade seizes Amir perimeter.	
October 19	0100 hours	The Roller Bridge is launched into the canal, 95.5 kilometers from the north end of the canal.	

DATE	TIME	EVENT	OUTCOME
Between the 20th and the 25th of October		Most of the fighting takes place west of the canal.	162nd advances and makes territorial gains, on its way to the city of Suez; 143rd Division advances north, as far as the outskirts of Ismailia; 252nd Division joins the main effort on the west bank.
October 21	1515 hours	600th Brigade attempts to expand the bridgehead towards Missouri perimeter.	Little territorial gains.
October 22	1900 hours	First ceasefire is announced.	
October 23		All Southern Command forces advance in an attempt to surround Egyptian 3rd Army.	
October 24	Morning	Israeli attempt at occupying the city of Suez.	
	Nighttime	Israeli tanks reach Adabia, south of Suez.	Egyptian 3rd Army is completely surrounded.
October 25	By evening	General ceasefire is announced.	

SENIOR COMMANDERS ON THE SOUTHERN COMMAND, AND THEIR POSITIONS ON OCTOBER 15ᵀᴴ, 1973

Southern Command Command:
Actual Front Commander: Lt.-Gen. Haim Bar Lev
Formal Front Commander: Maj.-Gen Shmuel Gonen
Deputy Front Commander: Brig.-Gen. Uri Ben Ari
Front Command's Chief of Staff: Brig.-Gen. Asher Levi

143ʳᵈ Division
Division Commander: Major General Ariel Sharon
Deputy Division Commander: Col. Yaakov Even
Divisional Chief of Staff: Col. Gideon Altshuller
Brigades Commanders:
    14ᵗʰ (armored)-Col. Amnon Reshef
    421ˢᵗ (armored)-Col. Haim Erez
    600ᵗʰ (armored)-Col. Tuvia Raviv
    247ᵗʰ (paratroopers)-Col. Danni Matt

162ⁿᵈ Division:
Division Commander: Major General Avraham "Bren" Adan
Deputy Division Commander: Brig.-Gen. Dov Tamari
Chief of Staff: Col. Ami Radian
Brigades Commanders:
    217ᵗʰ (armored)-Col. Natan "Natke" Nir
    460ᵗʰ (armored)-Col. Gabi Amir
    500ᵗʰ (armored)-Col. Arieh Keren
    35ᵗʰ (paratroopers)-Col. Uzi Yairi

252ⁿᵈ Division

Division Commander: Major General Kalman Magen
Deputy Division Commander: Brig.-Gen. Baruch "Pinko" Harel
Divisional Chief of Staff: Lt.-Col. Gideon Avidor
Brigades Commanders:
    875ᵗʰ (armored)-Col. Arieh "Biro" Dayan
    164ᵗʰ (armored)-Col. Avraham Baram
    401ˢᵗ (armored)-Col. Dan Shomron

Tiger Force (ad hoc division-strong armored force)

Commander: Brig.-Gen. Sasson Yitzchaki
Deputy Commander: Col. Shmuel Albek
Brigades Commanders:
    11ᵗʰ (armored)-Col. Aharon "Pedale" Peled
    204ᵗʰ (armored)-Col. Zvi Ram
    274ᵗʰ (armored)-Col. Yoel Gonen
    275ᵗʰ (logistics)-Col. Pinchas "Alush" Noy.

FREQUENTLY USED PLACE NAMES AND CODENAMES

Acapulco: the code word used on Front Command's networks for reporting that the first Israeli forces managed to land on the west bank of the Suez Canal.

Africa (also called Goshen): the Israeli-occupied territory west of the Suez Canal.

Agricultural Barrier: a farming area between the Freshwater Canal and the Suez Canal, near the city of Qantara.

Amir: the codename for the buildings of the Chinese Farm (see below) in Sirius Map (Southern Command Command's operational map).

Ashur: operational briefing.

Battering Ram: a tactical exercise without troops, held by the Southern Command Command in August 1972, simulating a war scenario.

Budapest: the northernmost Bar Lev Line Fort, and the only one to survive all Egyptian attacks.

Chinese Farm: a popular name for an agricultural experiments area in a plain east of the Suez Canal. At its center, there was a group of pump-houses and buildings codenamed Amir. Until its occupation by Israeli forces, during the 1967 Six-Day War, the Egyptians had dug irrigation ditches with a total length of 140 kilometers within the perimeter. The Israeli troops who first arrived there, mistook the Japanese inscriptions on the buildings for Chinese, which won the place its popular name.

Dvela: the HQ of Southern Command Command during the war, situated on the Um Hashiba hilltop.

Freshwater Canal: a canal going from the easternmost branch of the Nile to the Ismailia region, where it splits into a north branch, going to Port Said, and a south branch, going to the city of Suez.

Green Light: a planned IDF amphibious operation, designed to deliver forces from the Southern Sinai to the Egyptian shore of the Gulf of Suez. In the end, it was not carried out.

Hamutal: the codename of a ridge west of Tasa, near Artillery Road.

Hurvah: an Israeli strongpoint in the south of the Front.

Kishuf: an Israeli strongpoint in the center of the Front.

Televizia: an Israeli strongpoint in the center of the Front.

Tiger Force: an ad hoc, division-strong armored force, first commanded by Major Ganeral Kalman Magen, and then, by Brig.-Gen. Sasson Yitzchaki.

White Bear: an Israeli armored force armed with captured Soviet-made armored vehicles.

CROSSING ZONE-MAJOR ROUTES EMPLOYED

Akavish (east bank, center): going from Tasa Junction to Fort Lakekan.

Arabesk (east bank, center): going from Wadi Um Hashiba to the Mavdil north-south road.

Kartisan (east bank, north): a north-south road going from Baluza to Tasa Junction.

Khronika (east bank, center): an extension of Artillery Road, going from Porat-Keren Junction to the 39th kilometer of Kaspi Road.

Lexicon: (east bank, north): a road running along the canal, from the 72th kilometer of Aleket road all the way to Port Tawfiq.

Nahala (east bank, center): going from the 259th kilometer to Fort Matzmed.

Photon (east bank, center): an extension of Artillery Road, going from Hamutal (29th kilometer of Talisman Road), to Akavish-Kaspi Road.

Pundak (east bank, center): going from Refidim to Tasa Junction.

Revikha (east bank, center): going from the 71st kilometer of Mavdil to Kishuf strongpoint.

Talisman(east bank, center): going from Tasa Junction west, all the way to Ismailia.

Tirtur (east bank, center): going from the 37th kilometer of Photomn Road to Fort Matzmed, near the Chinese Farm.

BIBLIOGRAPHY

Note: all sources are in Hebrew

Books:

247th Brigade's publication: *Operation Valiant: 247th Brigade in Yom Kippur War,* 1975; (247th Brigade's Press);

890th Battalion's publication: *Chinese Farm, the 890th Battalion in the Last War,* 1975 (890th Battalion's Press);

Adan, Avraham, *on Both Banks of the Suez,* Idanim publishers, 1979;

El-Shazly, Lt.-Gen. Saad Al-Din, *the Crossing of the Suez* [in Hebrew], Israeli Ministry of Defense Press, 1987;

Argaman, Yosef, *The Night was Faintly Lighted,* Yediot Aharonot Publishing House, 2002;

Asher, Dani, *Breaking the Concept,* Maarachot [IDF Press], 2003;

Bar, Shmuel, *Yom Kippur War through Arab Eyes,* Maarachot Press, 1986;

Bar On, Aryeh, *Moshe Dayan in the Yom Kippur War,* Idanim & Yediot Aharonot Press, 1992;

Bartov, Hanoch, *Dado: 48 Years and Another 20 Days,* Maariv Publishing House, 1978;

Benziman, Uzi, *Sharon: stopping at Nothing,* Adam Press, 1985;

Bergman, Ronen: *Yom Kippur War-Real Time,* Miskal &Yediot Aharonot Publishing House, 2003;

Dayan, Moshe, *Story of My Life,* Idanim Publishing House, 1976;

Gai, Karmit, *Bar Lev,* Am Oved Publishers, 1998;

Harel, Israel (Ed.), *Operation Valiant: the Paratroopers Brigade's part in the Crossing of the Suez and the taking of the West Bank of the Canal,* a Paratroopers' Brigade publication.

Hefetz, Nir & Blum, Gadi, *The Shepherd: Sharon's Biography,* Yediot Aharonot Publishing House, 2005;

Kedar, Binyamin Zeev, *October 1973: The Story of 605th Engineers Battalion,* Tamuz Press, 1975;

Medzini, Miron, *Golda,* Yediot Aharonot Publishing House, 2008;

Michaelson, Ehud, *Operation Valiant: The Story of 184th Battalion,* Israeli Ministry of Defense Press, 2003;

Nir, Natan, *Natke,* Yediot Aharonot Publishing House, 2010;

Ohayon, Berti, *We're Still There,* Kineret & Zmora-Bitan Publishers, 2008;

Priel, Yaakov, *a Diary from Dvela,* IDF Archive, 1975;

Sadat, Anwar, *In Search of Identity: An Autobiography* [in Hebrew], Idanim Pres, 1978;

Segal, Maozyah, *Sand-Level Testimonies: the Paratroopers Fighting in the Chinese Farm,* Modan Publishers, 2007;

Shimshi, Elyashiv, *Storm in October,* Israeli Ministry of Defense Press, 1987.

Articles

Eytan, Zeev, "The Battle by the Bitter Lakes", *Maarachot,* issues 247-248, December 1975, p.14.

Radio networks' transcripts released on official websites:

143rd Division radio network.

162nd Division radio network.

14th Brigade's radio network.

421st Brigade's radio network.

356 | AMIRAM EZOV

Interviews (names and ranks of interviewees at the time of interview):

Major-General (res.) Avraham "Bren" Adan, 162nd Division Commander (several interviews);

Major-General (res.) Amnon Reshef, 14th Brigade Commander (several interviews);

Major General (res.) Haim Erez, 421st Brigade Commander

Major-General (res.) Yaakov "Jacky" Even, 143rd Division Deputy Commander (several interviews);

Col. (res.) Aharon Tal, 143rd Division Operations Officer (several interviews);

Col. (res.) Ami Radian, 162nd Division's Chief of Staff;

Col. (res.) Amikam Doron, of the Engineering Corps/Alligators Battalion (several interviews);

Col. (res.) Dan Katznelson, of 87th Reconnaissance Battalion;

Col. (res.) Fredo Raz, Engineering Corps;

Col. (res.) Menashe "Georgie" Gur, of the Engineering Corps (several interviews);

Col. (res.) Yaakov Yerushalmi, of the Engineering Corps;

Col. (res.) Yehuda Geller, 600th Brigade/410th Battalion Commander;

Col. (res.) Yoram Karmeli, 162nd Division's Intelligence Officer;

Col. (res.) Yossi Barkan, of Southern Command Command Intelligence;

Brig.-Gen. (res.) Amazia "Patzi" Chen, Patzi Force Commander;

Brig.-Gen. (res.) Avi Zohar, 630th (raft-carriers) Battalion Commander (several interviews);

Brig.-Gen. (res.) Ehud Gross, 407th Battalion/ 1st Company Commander;

Brig.-Gen. (res.) Giora Lev, of 421st Brigade;

Brig.-Gen. (res.) Natan Nir, 217th Brigade Commander;

Brig.-Gen. (res.) Yaakov Vaknin, of 143rd Division Artillery Support Section;

Brig.-Gen. (res.) Yehuda Bar, 247th Brigade Deputy Commander;

Brig.-Gen. (res.) Yoel "Gorodish" Gonen, 274th Brigade Commander;

Lt.-Col. (ret.) Dani Kariaf, of 407th Battalion;

Lt.-Col. (ret.) Ehud Sadan, of 14th Brigade;

Lt.-Col. (ret.) Imri Ron, of Shunari Force;

Lt.-Col. (ret.) Oko Ilan, of 143rd Division Deputy Commander's HQ;

Lt.-Col. (ret.) Shmuel Baruchi, of the Engineering Corps;

Lt.-Col. (ret.) Yossi Fridkin, 247th Brigade/28th Battalion Commander;

Maj. (ret.) Elon Naveh, of the Engineering Corps/ Rubber Boats Company;

Maj. (ret.) Haim Miller, of the Engineering Corps;

Maj. (ret.) Shlomo Goren, Bamba Force Commander;

Maj. (ret.) Yaakov Giron, Rubber Boats Company Commander (interviewed by phone);

Prof. Dan Zaslavski.

ACKNOWLEDGMENTS

This work is the fruit of many people who selflessly opened their hearts to me, sharing their personal stories. Therefore, I wish to thank, first and foremost, those scores of interviewees who confided in me, freely spending their time talking with me—some for just an hour, and others for many hours.

I wish to express my special thanks to Major Generals (res.) Amnon Reshef, Yaakov Even and Avraham Adan, for spending many hours with me, revealing the thinking behind their military maneuvers of the war. They did it willingly, sparing no necessary criticism.

I wish to thank Col. (res.) Yehuda Wegmann, for helping me, with his enormous military erudition, clarifying several key issues.

I wish to thank my editor, Rami Rotholtz, for masterfully guiding me in my writing, and Shmuel Rosner, the head of the Nonfiction Department of Kinneret-Zmora-Bitan Publishers, for warmly adopting me into the publishing house's family.

I wish to thank my wife, Bella, and all my family, for encouraging my writing and for supporting me through those periods of tormenting hesitations that it involved.

I also wish to express my appreciation to the translator of this book into English, Zvi Chazanov, for plowing through the IDF's wartime jargon, conveying both touches of humor as well as the moments of horror that make up this epic event.

And finally I wish to thank the real authors of this book, those officers and servicemen who fought one of the bloodiest and most complex campaigns in Israeli military history.

Made in the USA
Middletown, DE
20 May 2017